BOOSTERS
AND
BUSINESSMEN

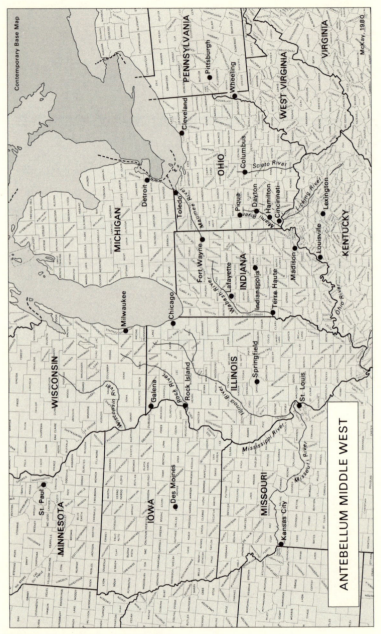

MAP 1   The Antebellum Middle West

BOOSTERS AND BUSINESSMEN

POPULAR ECONOMIC THOUGHT AND URBAN GROWTH IN THE ANTEBELLUM MIDDLE WEST

Carl Abbott

Contributions in American Studies, Number 53

Greenwood Press
Westport, Connecticut • London, England

Library of Congress Cataloging in Publication Data

Abbott, Carl.
    Boosters and businessmen.

    (Contributions in American studies ; no. 53
ISSN 0084-9227)
    Bibliography: p.
    Includes index.
    1.   Cities and towns--Middle West--Growth.
2.   Middle West--Economic conditions.   I.   Title.
HT371.A23   307.7'6'0977   80-1795
ISBN 0-313-22562-1 (lib. bdg.)

Library of Congress Catalog Card Number: 80-1795
ISBN: 0-313-22562-1
ISSN: 0084-9227

First published in 1981

Greenwood Press
A division of Congressional Information Service, Inc.
88 Post Road West, Westport, Connecticut 06881

Printed in the United States of America

10 9 8 7 6 5 4 3 2 1

CONTENTS

MAPS

TABLES

ACKNOWLEDGMENTS

Every scholar keeps a private roster of individuals and institutions whose assistance has facilitated or improved his or her own research. My own list starts with Richard Wade, whose work on the urban frontier catalyzed my own interests. Neil Harris, Robert Fogel, Daniel Boorstin, William Pattison, and other members of the Chicago faculty provided valuable advice and raised pointed questions which helped me clarify my ideas. I have also benefited from the comments of Robert Walker, James Madison, Don Doyle, Alan Harris, and Anne Harris on all or parts of the manuscript.

My work was assisted by scores of librarians and archivists as I crossed and recrossed the Middle West. I would particularly like to thank the staffs of the University of Chicago Libraries (especially the interlibrary loan service), the Chicago Historical Society (especially manuscript librarian Archie Motley), the Newberry Library, the State Historical Society of Wisconsin, the University of Wisconsin at Platteville, the Galena Public Library, the Illinois State Historical Library, the Indiana University Libraries, the Ohio Historical Society, the Cincinnati Historical Society, and the Cincinnati Public Library.

Financial assistance from the University of Chicago included a Humanities Fellowship and a William Rainey Harper Fellowship. Old Dominion University's research office provided typing services. R. W. McKay of the Geography Department at Portland State University assisted by preparing several maps.

My wife Marge helped this project at every stage. She counted names in census microfilms, shared research tours through the cornbelt, sorted note cards, read successive drafts, and told me when I did not make sense. If she did not become a middle-western booster, she did bear my enthusiasm for the region with remarkable patience.

Portions of the study have appeared in different form in the *Journal of Urban History* and the *Indiana Magazine of History*.

BOOSTERS AND BUSINESSMEN

INTRODUCTION:
URBAN BOOSTERISM
AND URBAN GROWTH

The years from 1848 through 1857 were an era of decision for almost every city of the Middle West. After a decade in which the region's towns had staggered under the impact of financial panic and depression, the later 1840s brought a new set of conditions for growth. The construction of eight thousand miles of railroad altered each city's access to resources and markets. Accelerating migration and the expansion of agricultural production both in older and younger states presented new economic opportunities and forced quick decisions on urban entrepreneurs. The rapid growth of Chicago and St. Louis, the relative lag of Cincinnati, Louisville, Columbus, and Galena, and the emergence of Detroit, Milwaukee, Cleveland, Dayton, and Indianapolis as major cities were all products of the antebellum decade.[1]

The antebellum boom triggered spirited public discussion about the character of the new commercial opportunities, about the economic needs of each city, and about the measures which might satisfy these wants. Newspapers, corporate reports, directories, pamphlets, and orations considered how each town could best exploit its new opportunities. Residents described current activities, advocated new projects, and detailed strategies for growth in a diverse and substantial body of literature which later commentators frequently lumped under the term "boosterism." In fact, boosterism was the entire process by which business and civic leaders assessed the situation they faced, tried to define a coherent economic program to be carried out by public and private action, and publicized that assessment and program to local and national audiences.

Such single-minded attention to the questions of economic growth accompanied by an excited use of the various media of communication was especially characteristic of the antebellum Northwest. Although David R. Goldfield, Arthur H. Shaffer, and Lyle W. Dorsett have recently explored the large body of booster literature produced in the antebellum South and have discovered a strong interest in urban growth, even southerners themselves in the 1840s and 1850s agreed that the "land of advertising" lay north of the Ohio River and complained that the "books, pamphlets, maps, cards, and descriptive plates" which publicized every town in the Northwest were seldom imitated in the South.[2] Daniel Boorstin has identified the fast-growing "upstart cities" of the antebellum West as the natural habitat of the American booster.[3] Where publicists in the East might dwell on the history or the cultural refinement of their cities and southerners might concern themselves with the political implications of commercial growth, citizens of the antebellum Northwest ignored cultural attainments and social advantages to write about population, money-making, and the volume of trade.[4]

The spokesmen for these several visions of the urban future were first of all the cities' professional publicists—its newspapermen, magazine editors, and authors of gazetteers and guidebooks. Also active in the debates were businessmen whose interests required attention to their city's external trade. Wholesalers, commission merchants, larger manufacturers, real estate developers, and railroad entrepreneurs were all interested in the possibilities of urban growth. Clergymen, physicians, attorneys, and other professionals used their education and access to print to disseminate their ideas on the urban future. Together, these individuals provided most of the elected municipal officials in the antebellum years and formed self-established and articulate leadership groups which assumed the task of directing each city's future.

Popular discussion of economic growth by the educated business and professional classes in the cities of the antebellum Middle West was in fact balanced between the two poles of narrow self-interest and vague generality.

Taking their cue from such satirists as Charles Dickens and Mark Twain, several historians have emphasized the deficiencies of much antebellum boosterism. According to this interpretation, public discourse on urban economic growth usually had the purpose of aiding individual real estate speculations and business enterprises rather than the interests of the larger community. In the words of Daniel Aaron, "what was popularly interpreted as 'vision' meant hardly more than faith in Cincinnati real estate."[5] At the other extreme, many western boosters thought in terms of an urban manifest destiny and expected to read their city's future directly off a map of North America. Such an orientation made it easy to ignore the specific circumstances of each city in favor of a broad enthusiasm about regional growth.[6] William Gilpin and Jesup W. Scott, two writers with elaborately developed theories of western urbanization, found no problem in transferring their predictions of urban greatness from one city to another in rapid succession. If the Valley of the Mississippi was destined to be the final home of empire, it made relatively little difference if its capital was to be Toledo or Chicago, Kansas City, or even Denver.[7]

Businessmen in each city ranged at different points between the two extremes. Although some scarcely peered beyond their own bank balances, others recognized that entrepreneurial success in land dealing, banking, commerce, and transportation was closely linked to the growth of the community as a whole. In some cities it is possible to distinguish clear central tendencies—an unwillingness in one town to look beyond individual concerns toward a "combined exertion for the general good," a strong concern with community growth among opinion leaders in another. Residents in the more successful cities tended to identify their personal future with community growth and believed firmly in the importance of joint action through "the self-imposed labors . . . of earnest-souled, iron-willed, active-minded citizens." The acceptance of clearly stated ideas about future economic directions made it easier for "community-focused" entrepreneurs to discover financial backing and to rally popular support. The same consensus helped these business and civic leaders to coordinate their use of private corporations, commercial organizations, and governmental bodies in pursuit of economic goals for their cities.[8]

The purpose of this study is to analyze the character and impact of popular economic thought during the 1840s and 1850s through detailed examination of four middle-western cities. Cincinnati, Chicago, Indianapolis, and Galena were chosen because they developed contrasting economic specializations within fundamentally the same environment for growth. The Ohio and upper Mississippi valleys and the Great Lakes formed an economic unit in the antebellum decades. Temperate climate, adequate and reliable rainfall, well-drained or drainable soil, and moderate relief combined to make the states from Ohio through Iowa primarily a grain belt. Each raised more than enough cereals to satisfy its own needs and shipped its surplus in the form of raw grain, flour, cornmeal, whiskey, pork, lard, or beef to southern and eastern states and overseas. In return the West imported salt, sugar, coffee, textiles, iron goods, and general merchandise through New York, Philadelphia, Baltimore, and New Orleans. Although the volume of trade in both directions grew in the twenty years before the Civil War, there was little change in the types of goods, the basic patterns of exchange, or the commercial techniques used.

At the same time, the dissimilar economies of the four cities provided the basis for discussion of a wide range of ideas about manufacturing, services, and wholesaling as well as transportation and export trade. Cincinnati, for example, was a city of factories. Although the city had been the chief trading center of the West in earlier decades, observers agreed that its economy had changed by the 1840s. As one outsider said in 1853, "the manufacturers of Cincinnati are a most important element of its past progress and present prosperity." Cincinnatians themselves claimed industrial primacy in the West, and experts on western development often spoke of Cincinnati and Pittsburgh together as the region's industrial centers, contrasting them with the more wholly commercial towns such as Louisville, St. Louis, and Nashville. Just as frequently, Cincinnati was compared to the manufacturing city of Philadelphia.[9]

A number of writers seized on the contrast between Cincinnati's dependence on manufacturing and the importance of commerce to "her great rival in the Northwest—Chicago." One Cincinnati editor stated that it was common knowledge that his city's growth resulted from its industrial development, whereas Chicago had been built up by "grain-dealers and travelers." Indeed, Chicagoans frequently claimed that their city had attained commercial pre-eminence within the West. No other place, they said with finality, could rival Chicago as a center of wholesaling and trade in agricultural products.[10] The difference was summed up by Stephen A. Douglas, who told a group of Cincinnatians visiting his city that "there is no better place than Cincinnati to manufacture, and no better place than Chicago to distribute."[11]

Although the development of Indiana's railroad system gave Indianapolis important commercial functions by the middle of the 1850s, observers focused on its many public institutions and the numerous services it provided for the citizens of the entire state. As one publication said, "all the Political, Judicial, Social, Religious, Educational, Monetary, Commercial, and Industrial interests of the State center here. . . . Owing to the facility of access to this city, State conventions, in the interests of the various societies and parties, are held here, almost weekly, during the year." Another writer, less favorably disposed, noted that Indiana's merchants transacted their business largely in towns on the periphery of the state, while Indianapolis attracted "the politicians, the speculators in companies and town lots, and others without pressing business."[12]

Whereas contemporaries defined the economic base of Chicago, Cincinnati, and Indianapolis in terms of a general function, Galena's economy was thought to revolve around a single commercial interest. From the very first, the city's prosperity was identified with the trade in lead from the upper Mississippi mines. Observers in the 1820s noted that it "was ushered into existence on account of the mineral business consequent to the rapid increase of population throughout the Mining District" and called it "the place of deposit for lead and provisions, etc., for all the mining country." Through the 1840s, the lead trade was viewed as "the cause of the present growth of Galena, and to a considerable extent, the foundation of her future prosperity." Even in the 1850s, despite some diversification of its economy, residents and outsiders alike maintained that the lead interest remained the city's mainstay.[13]

The analysis of economic thought and economic growth in these four cities builds on the ideas of several historians who have been interested in the relation between attitudes and economic development. Blaine Brownell, in a recent study of southern cities in the 1920s, concentrated on the content of ideas expressed by their "commercial-civic elites," local leadership groups comparable to the boosters and businessmen of antebellum cities. He defined an "urban ethos," a guiding complex of beliefs about the nature of cities that dominated public discussion. The urban ethos, in his view, was not itself a coherent policy for dealing with particular situations, but rather an internally consistent set of ideas that helped to set the terms for debating problems. Brownell's study is primarily concerned with the "more or less consistent conception of the city" and secondarily with its impact on specific choices.[14]

Two other historians interested in examining urban growth from the inside out have focused more directly on concrete economic decisions in order to weigh the role of ideas as a determinant of development. Julius Rubin demonstrated that an understanding of urban development "depends as much upon the analysis of the subjective traits of groups as it does upon the analysis of the pressure of objective circumstances" and concludes that different responses in Baltimore, Philadelphia, and Boston to the success of the Erie Canal "are to be explained . . . by differences in the attitudes that decision-making groups brought to the common problem rather than by differences in the problem itself." In another first-rate study, Charles Glaab tried to balance "ideological, geographical, and economic influences" on the growth of Kansas City and to answer the questions: "To what extent were notions and conceptions about the nature of the West and transportation translated into a community ideology and how did this ideology affect community policy?"[15]

The present study falls between that of Brownell on the one hand and those of Glaab and Rubin on the other hand. Its broad goal is to place the literature of popular economic thought within the context of specific urban experiences and of general ideas about urban and national growth. One objective is to test whether residents accurately perceived the economic situations of their four cities by comparing their descriptions of economic base and hinterlands with available quantitative data. A second objective is to examine the effect of popular economic discussion on the perception of urban growth opportunities and on choices among developmental strategies in the four cities during the crucial growth era of the 1840s and 1850s. A particular question is whether the quality or character of urban boosterism played a role in channeling individual activity toward common goals. In this aim, the study follows the suggestion of R. Richard Wohl that historians might investigate the way in which "business communities set in strategic urban centers" have "hitched their destinies and policies to expectations of a region's growth."[16] The third objective is to examine the general themes of economic writing in the urban West and to relate this body of ideas to currents in American thought. The choice of cities of differing sizes and economic types is intended to allow the exploration of the full range of such booster themes.

Urban growth in the antebellum Middle West involved a significant element of collective entrepreneurship expressed through city governments, corporations, and voluntary business associations and requiring consensus on common goals. The study is therefore organized around the entrepreneurial sequence of observation, planning, and implementation of economic ideas. The first three chapters describe the economic situation of Cincinnati, Chicago, Indianapolis, and Galena and test how accurately western urban leaders perceived their environment of economic resources and opportunities. Chapter 1 describes the rates of growth in the four cities as influenced by national economic cycles. Chapter 2 discusses the functional specialization of the cities, and Chapter 3 delimits the size and character of their hinterlands. As a clear evaluation of the economic base of a city and the economic opportunities available from its hinterland was necessary for the development of an intelligent program for growth, Chapters 2 and 3 both compare contemporary opinions and perceptions with the objective data. The assumption, of course, is that decision-makers operated on the basis of their own understanding of the character of their city and its surrounding territory.

Chapter 4 treats western urban boosterism in more general terms. Through an analysis of contemporary reactions to urban hinterlands, it describes the economic opportunities that city-dwellers thought they faced. It also explores the means of dissemination of booster ideas, their style, and their common themes and omissions. This discussion serves as background for the examination of the specific growth policies that each city evolved during the spurt of regional growth from 1848 to 1857. The concern in Chapters 5 to 8 is the articulation of economic ideas and their implementation in Cincinnati, Chicago, Indianapolis and Galena. The discussion analyzes the strategies each city's leaders evolved, the efforts to put them into operation, and the problems encountered. The analysis demonstrates that the acceptance of clearly stated ideas about future growth made it easier for community leaders to mobilize support and resources and to execute programs of development. In turn, success in such efforts as measured by population and trade statistics aided individual prosperity and provided further material for publicists and promoters.

Within the context of each city, the study finds that the key in judging the role of boosterism in antebellum urban growth is not the flamboyance of its rhetoric but its accuracy of judgment and the scope of its concerns. Popular discussion of a city's future could promote growth to the degree that it involved the realistic analysis of the particular circumstances of that community. The notoriously highflown prose of Chicago boosters thus did not affect the basic accuracy of their economic analysis or its usefulness as a rallying point for city leaders. In St. Louis as well as in Galena and Cincinnati, in contrast, lack of consensus stemming from wishful rather than hardheaded thinking helped to justify conflicting and wasteful transportation projects and investment schemes.[17]

Popular economic thought in the antebellum Middle West was linked to broad American attitudes about the process of national growth as well as to the development of specific cities. The concluding chapter therefore examines the meaning of western growth for antebellum urbanites. A number of historians—Henry Nash Smith, Leo Marx, R. W. B. Lewis, Kevin Starr—have described the meaning of the "West" in the American mind through a reading of imaginative literature and works of leading intellectuals.[18] Just as important is the study of what the movement westward across the continent meant to average Americans. The flood of pamphlets and editorials expressed a deep faith that national expansion promised to fulfill a "grand and noble purpose" and that the erection of great cities was an essential element in this expansion. Boosterism was at one time a response to the concrete problems of urban growth and a literature of prophecy, an affirmation of the great destiny and mission of the American people.

NOTES

1. Douglass C. North, *The Economic Growth of the United States, 1790-1860* (Englewood Cliffs, N.J., 1961), pp. 136-40, 201-14; Walter B. Smith and Arthur Cole, *Fluctuations in American Business, 1790-1860* (Cambridge, Mass., 1935), pp. 55-57, 63; Frederic L. Paxson, "The Railroads of the 'Old Northwest' Before the Civil War," *Transactions of the Wisconsin Academy of Sciences, Arts, and Letters* 17 (1914): 268-75.

2. Lyle W. Dorsett and Arthur H. Shaffer, "Was the Antebellum South Antiurban? A Suggestion," *Journal of Southern History* 38 (February 1972): 93-100; David R. Goldfield, "Pursuing the American Dream: Cities in the Old South," in Blaine Brownell and David R. Goldfield, eds., *The City in Southern History* (Port Washington, N.Y., 1977); Edward Deering, *Louisville: Her Commercial, Manufacturing and Social Advantages* (Louisville, 1859), p. 5; Louisville *Journal,* quoted in Ben Casseday, *History of Louisville from Its Earliest Settlement Til the Year 1852* (Louisville, 1852), p. 6.

3. Daniel Boorstin, *The Americans: The National Experience* (New York, 1965), pp. 113-34, 161-68.

4. Walter S. Glazer, "Cincinnati in 1840: A Community Profile" (Ph.D. diss. Department of History, University of Michigan, 1968), p. 83; Richard Wohl, "Urbanism, Urbanity and the Historian," *University of Kansas City Review* 22 (October 1955): 54; Carl Abbott, "Civic Pride in Chicago, 1844-1860," *Journal of the Illinois State Historical Society* 63 (Winter 1970): 414-15.

5. Daniel Aaron, "Cincinnati, 1818-1838: A Study of Attitudes in the Urban West" (Ph.D. diss., Department of History, Harvard University, 1942), p. 102. Also see Bayrd Still, "Patterns of Mid-Nineteenth Century Urbanization in the Midwest," *Mississippi Valley Historical Review* 18 (September 1941): 197; Leslie Decker, "The Great Speculation," in David M. Ellis, ed., *The Frontier in American Development* (Ithaca, N.Y., 1970), pp. 364-80.

6. James Pullan, Diary, June, 1857, James Pullan Collection, Ohio Historical Society; Luther Bixby to John C. Bixby, April 4, 1850, Luther Bixby Collection, Chicago Historical Society; *Cincinnati Gazette*, March 18, 1851; *Chicago Democratic Press, Review of Commerce for 1855*, p. 4.

7. Charles N. Glaab, "Jesup W. Scott and a West of Cities," *Ohio History* 73 (Winter 1964): 3-12; Charles N. Glaab, "Vision of Metropolis: William Gilpin and Theories of City Growth in the West," *Wisconsin Magazine of History* 45 (Autumn 1961): 21-31; Thomas L. Karnes, *William Gilpin: Western Nationalist* (Austin, Tex., 1970).

8. The quote is from the *Cincinnati Commercial*, June 5, 1855. Also see the description of the "community-focused" entrepreneur in Arthur Cole, *Business*

Enterprise in Its Social Setting (Cambridge, Mass., 1959), pp. 108–109, 124–28, 161–64; and Gunther Barth's discussion of the identification of individual urbanites with the larger community in *Instant Cities: Urbanization and the Rise of San Francisco and Denver* (New York, 1976), pp. 129–35.

9. *The Ohio and Mississippi Railroad: Its Vital Importance to the Prosperity of Cincinnati* (Cincinnati, 1855), p. 6; *Cincinnati Commercial*, September 14, 1859; *Western Farmer and Gardener* 2 (April 1846): 102; *Railroad Record* 1 (April 14, 1853): 102–03; 2 (September 8, 1854) 517; Israel D. Andrews, *Report . . . on the Trade and Commerce of the British North American Colonies and upon the Trade of the Great Lakes and Rivers*, S. Exec. Doc. No. 122, 32d Cong., 1st Sess., 1853; J. G. Buttner, *Der Staat Ohio* (Bayreuth, 1849), p. 42; *Madison* (Ind.) *Courier,* August 8, 1855; *Chicago Press,* January 21, 1858; Charles Cist, *Sketches and Statistics of Cincinnati in 1859* (n.p., n.d.), p. 240; James Hall, *The West: Its Commerce and Navigation* (Cincinnati, 1848), p. 246.

10. *Cincinnati Gazette*, December 18, 1854; *Chicago Press*, January 21, 1858; *Chicago Tribune*, April 17, 1858; *Chicago Magazine* 1 (March 1857): 94; J. G. Kohl, *Reisen im Nordwesten der Vereinigten Staaten* (New York, 1857), p. 154; Pittsburgh, Fort Wayne and Chicago Railroad Company, *Exhibit . . . with Relation to Their General Mortgage of $1,000,000* (New York, 1857), p. 28.

11. *Railroad Record* 7 (June 23, 1859): 205. Also see Indianapolis *Atlas,* December 18, 1859.

12. *Indianapolis Journal*, June 24, 1856, June 10, 1859; Evansville, Indianapolis and Cleveland Railroad, First *Annual Report* (1855), p. 12; *Indiana Gazetteer* (Indianapolis, 1849), pp. vii–viii; Indianapolis Board of Trade, *Indianapolis: Its Manufacturing Interests, Wants, Facilities,* in *Indianapolis Journal*, March 25-26, 1857.

13. *Galena Advertiser*, July 20, 1829; *Galena Miners' Journal*, September 20, 1828; *Map of the United States Lead Mines on the Upper Mississippi* (Galena, 1829), reproduced in Wisconsin State Historical Society, *Collections* 11 (1888): facing p. 400; letter from Horatio Newhall, in *The History of Jo Daviess County, Illinois* (Chicago, 1878), p. 253; *The Galena Directory and Miners' Annual Register for 1847–48* (Galena, 1847), p. 38; *Galena Jeffersonian,* November 16, 1852; *Galena Gazette,* March 19, 1852, April 15, 1856; *Illinois State Gazetteer and Business Directory for 1858 and 1859* (Chicago, 1857), p. 91.

14. Blaine Brownell, *The Urban Ethos in the South, 1920–1930* (Baton Rouge, 1975), pp. xv-xx, 40, 125-34, 153-55, 218.

15. Julius Rubin, *Canal or Railroad? Imitation and Innovation in Response to the Erie Canal in Philadelphia, Baltimore and Boston,* American Philosophical Society *Transactions*, n.s., 51, Part VII (1961): 9, 93; Charles N. Glaab, *Kansas City and the Railroads* (Madison, Wis., 1962), pp. viii, 9. In a parallel study of state policy, Harry Sheiber examined the "set of assumptions, aspirations, information, and misinformation" in which Ohio canal policy was made and compared the expectations to objectively measured results; see Scheiber, *Ohio Canal Era* (Athens, Ohio, 1969).

16. R. Richard Wohl, "The Significance of Business History," *Business History Review* 28 (June 1954): 131, 133.

17. Wyatt W. Belcher, *The Economic Rivalry between St. Louis and Chicago* (New York, 1947).

18. Henry Nash Smith, *Virgin Land: The American West as Symbol and Myth* (New York, 1957); R. W. B. Lewis, *The American Adam* (Chicago, 1955); Leo Marx, *The Machine in the Garden: Technology and the Pastoral Idea in America* (New York, 1964); Kevin Starr, *Americans and the California Dream, 1850–1910* (New York, 1973).

1

PATTERNS
OF URBAN GROWTH

Cities have always been central to the process of economic growth on American frontiers. During the first years of settlement, towns and cities grew more rapidly than the surrounding countryside on each new frontier. Their development not only accompanied the westward movement of population but was necessary to its advance, for the commercial services which urban centers provided were indispensable for organizing economic activity. The frontier city was initially an advanced base of supply. It furnished emigrants with food until the first crops were harvested and provided clothing, tools, and other needed goods. When pioneers become successful farmers or miners or lumbermen, the city marketed their surplus produce, offering credit and transportation and finding outside buyers. As the interregional and international exchange of agricultural products for manufactured goods was the foundation of American growth from the colonial days through the nineteenth century, the collecting and distributing functions of frontier cities were vital both to the expansion of settlement and to the development of the nation as a whole.[1]

Cities continued to guide regional growth even when their hinterlands moved beyond the frontier stage into sustained development. In the second and third generations of settlement they were centers where capital and entrepreneurship were brought together and where new projects were conceived and organized. Especially in the early and middle decades of the nineteenth century, the nation's cities contended for hegemony over the continent. The early rivalry of Boston, New York, Philadelphia, Baltimore, and other Atlantic ports is one of the central themes of America's economic development. By reaching across the Alleghenies with roads, canals, and railroads, these cities "speeded up the transformation of the wilderness into a modern civilization." The transportation system constructed with their funds and leadership furthered western development by making commercial agriculture possible in new areas and more profitable in old. It also led to a vast increase in the volume of intersectional trade and to the development of specialization conducive to economic growth. By 1860 the United States possessed at least the outline of a national economy in which no region was isolated from the others.[2]

The cities of the antebellum Middle West were as important to that region's continued growth as eastern ports were for the progress of the American economy as a whole. Contemporary writers noted the ongoing functions of the dozens of river and lake towns founded from the 1790s through the 1830s. "The growth of our western cities," said a St. Louis magazine in 1851, "is especially necessary to the full and speedy development of the wealth of this region. It is the surest means of diversifying labor, of introducing new pursuits, and of building up a home market." Cities were centers of innovation in manufacturing, the sites for most new factories, and the focal points for efforts to develop mineral resources. At the same time, they furthered agricultural development through efforts to expand their hinterlands. During the 1820s and 1830s their fierce competition provided much of the impetus for various state canal and road systems. The improvement of transportation was even more marked between 1840 and 1860, when middle-western cities took on much of the responsibility for constructing regional railroads. The growth of the rail net from 90 miles in 1848 to 8,758 miles in 1859 extended their influence into previously underdeveloped areas and integrated the entire Northwest into the system of inter-regional trade.[3]

The pace of urbanization in the mid-nineteenth century reflected the importance of cities in the national economy. In the North Central states the rate of urbanization was almost four times as great in the 1840s and 1850s as it had been in the 1830s, and the two decades can be viewed as the start of a burst of rapid urbanization that lasted through the 1870s.[4] In the United States as a whole, urban population grew almost three times as fast as the total population in the 1840s and more than twice as fast in the 1850s. The increase in the proportion of the American population living in towns of twenty-five hundred or more—7.2 percent in 1820, 10.8 percent in 1840, 19.8 percent in 1860, 28.2 percent in 1880—indicates that the two middle decades of the century saw the fastest urbanization in the history of the nation. The percentage change was 48 percent from 1820 to 1840, 88 percent from 1840 to 1860, and 42 percent from 1860 to 1880.

Indeed, the 1840s and 1850s coincided with a single surge of economic growth in the United States. Throughout the nineteenth century, the nation experienced regular cycles of boom and bust. Each cycle involved an increase in productive activity, rising speculation spurred on by the hope of new profits, financial overextension, and collapse. Bankruptcies and several years of high unemployment followed in each case before the development of new business opportunities or changes in market conditions initiated a new boom. Before the Civil War, peaks of economic activity as measured by price levels, bank loans, and the organization of new enterprises came in 1819, 1837-39, and 1857.[5]

In the western states, booms were even more salient than in the rest of the nation because settlement and the opening of new farms occurred in distinct waves corresponding to the peaks of the cycle. The years from 1815 to the panic of 1819 constituted one such flood in the tide of western growth. The period from 1832 to 1837 saw a second wave, during which emigrants thronged to the Northwest and sales of public land increased tenfold. The 1840s and 1850s were a third distinct era of regional development. The year 1839 marked a sharp downturn in business and the onset of severe deflation. Over the next four years, prices of agricultural commodities declined to the levels of 1820, new investment in land and transportation almost ceased, boom towns of the 1830s wasted away, and thousands of individuals and several states found themselves bankrupt. The region began to recover almost as the low point of depression was reached in 1842–43, however, and rode a rising curve of prosperity for the next fourteen years. Agricultural prices rose steadily from 1843 to 1855, immigration increased, and land sales climbed. A small upturn in purchases of government land in 1845–48 anticipated a higher peak in the mid-1850s. Beginning about 1848, the cropping of new farms led to increased grain production in the underdeveloped states of Indiana, Illinois, Iowa, and Wisconsin. The late 1840s and early 1850s also witnessed a boom in railroad construction as citizens of the growing Northwest clamored for better transportation.

The first check to prosperity came in 1854, when the demand in eastern and European markets for western railroad securities slackened and new railroads were unable to raise money. The boom tapered out through 1855 and 1856 as agricultural prices fluctuated and entrepreneurs completed railroad projects already underway. The crisis arrived in the fall of 1857. Financial troubles spreading from New York brought the collapse of mercantile credit and pressed railroad directors to salvage lines already built. Two successive crop failures exacerbated the eighteen months of depression. Indeed, the region had recovered only partially before seccession and rebellion further confused its economic relations.[6]

The histories of Cincinnati, Chicago, Indianapolis, and Galena during the 1840s and 1850s clearly show this pattern of depression, boom, and depression. Cincinnati, for example, had surged ahead of rival cities and established itself as "the commercial hub of the West" in the aftermath of the crash of 1819. Before the War of 1812, the city had been exclusively a commercial center that traded by flatboat and keel boat with New Orleans. The years immediately after the war had seen a campaign to encourage local manufacturing, but most of the new enterprises were killed by the postwar depression. Revival of trade in the 1820s had come with the rapid spread of steamboating on western rivers. By the middle 1830s, the perceptive French traveler Michael Chevalier observed that Cincinnati was again making itself "the capital, or great interior mart of the West" by manufacturing a variety of goods in demand throughout the fast-growing West.[7] During the same decade the city asserted its cultural leadership in the region and established many of the cultural and social institutions that were to serve it until the Civil War. Its 1840 population of forty-six thousand—twice that of Pittsburgh or Louisville—indicated its primacy within the West.[8]

The effects of the depression of the early 1840s were perhaps less persistent than in other parts of the West. The panic of 1837 cut demand for the city's exports but caused few failures among its businessmen. Merchants had therefore been able to take advantage of the rapid recovery, and the city had entered 1839 in glowing health. By the end of the year, however, Cincinnati had caught the virus of hard times. Although mercantile failures were again few, banks drastically contracted their loans and trade largely ceased. As one observer said, "business is torpid . . . and money a nonentity." The years 1840 and 1841 were the nadir of a depression thought by many to be unprecedented in the history of Ohio. Unemployment soared, factories and shops closed their doors, and "general stagnation" clouded the city.[9] The picture brightened in the next two years. Although many workers remained jobless, newcomers crowded the city and construction boomed. Contemporaries estimated that Cincinnati gained ten to fifteen thousand inhabitants during the worst years of the depression and began to assert that it had weathered the crisis better than other American cities.[10]

The ten years after 1843 were the most prosperous the city had known. Growth was checked only by a brief financial stringency early in 1848 and by cholera in the summers of 1849 and 1850. Although the disease chose its several thousand victims largely among the city's foreign-born and poor, it panicked the upper classes and brought business to a standstill. Recovery came quickly, however, and the new decade opened with three years of exceptional growth. Having gained thirty thousand people in the first half of the 1840s and forty thousand in the second half, it added almost fifty thousand in the next three years (see Table 1).[11]

This same decade witnessed the increasing diversification of Cincinnati's economy. While its merchants continued to make fortunes through the export of agricultural goods, the city's newer

TABLE 1
Population of Cincinnati, Chicago, Galena, and Indianapolis

	Cincinnati[a]	Chicago[b]	Galena	Indianapolis
1820	9,642			
—				
1823				600[g]
1824	12,016			
1825				
1826	16,230		150[c]	762[g]
1827				1,066[g]
1828			800[c]	
1829	24,148			
1830	24,831	50		
1831	28,014	100		
1832		200	1,000[c]	
1833	27,546	350		
1834		2,000		
1835	31,100	3,265		
1836		3,820		
1837		4,170		
1838		4,000		
1839		4,200		
1840	46,382	4,479	1,843[d]	2,692[d]
1841		5,000	2,200[c]	
1842		6,000		
1843		7,589		
1844		8,000		
1845	74,699	12,088	4,068[c]	
1846		14,169		
1847		16,859	5,600[c]	4,000[h]
1848		20,023		
1849		23,047		6,500[g]
1850	115,438	29,963	6,004[d]	8,091[d]
1851	132,330	34,000		
1852	145,563	38,754		10,800[h]
1853	165,000	59,130	9,629[e]	

TABLE 1 —*Continued*

	Cincinnati[a]	Chicago[b]	Galena	Indianapolis
1854	170,057	65,872		
1855	172,370	80,023		
1856	174,000	84,113		
1857	174,000	93,000	12,000[f]	15,000[h]
1858	175,968	91,000		
1859	178,315	95,000		
1860	161,044	109,206	8,196[d]	18,611[d]

SOURCES:

[a]Figures through 1833 from Sherry O. Hessler, *Patterns of Transport and Urban Growth in the Miami Valley* (M.A. thesis, Johns Hopkins University, 1961), p. 257; after 1833 from Cincinnati Board of Trade, *Report* for 1869, p. 92.

[b]Homer Hoyt, *One Hundred Years of Land Values in Chicago* (Ph.D. thesis, University of Chicago, 1933), p. 483.

[c]*Galena Directory for 1848-49* (Galena: E. S. Seymour, 1848), pp. 34, 45.

[d]U.S. Census.

[e]*Galena Directory for 1854* (Galena: H. H. Houghton and Co., 1854), p. 6.

[f]Alexander Leslie, unpublished diary, 1857-58, Chicago Historical Society, p. 24.

[g]William R. Holloway, *Indianapolis: A Historical and Statistical Sketch of the Railroad City* (Indianapolis: 1870), pp. 23, 31, 37, 90.

[h]Ignatius Brown, "History of Indianapolis from 1818 to 1868," in *Logan's Indianapolis Directory* (Indianapolis: Logan and Co., 1868), p. 53.

industrialists also enjoyed flush times. It outstripped its rivals in the West in food processing, clothing, furniture, and wood products; the variety of lesser manufactures caused one traveler to report that it was "one great bee hive—exhibiting more activity than New York, and every thing that ever was manufactured I suppose is made here." In the latter 1840s and 1850s, wholesaling of eastern merchandise gained rapidly in importance, as did the distribution of "groceries"—chiefly coffee, sugar, and molasses purchased from New Orleans.[12]

The social structure of Cincinnati changed with its economy. The city received thousands of immigrants, especially from Germany.

As Frederick Gerstäcker noted: "Ask a German, who is traveling to the interior from one of the seaports, 'Where are you going?' and the answer will universally be—'to Cincinnati.' " By 1850, over 65 percent of the city's workers were foreign born, two-thirds of them natives of the German states (see Table 2). Urban growth created new problems calling for civic action, and municipal elections in the 1840s revolved around temperance, annexation, and city debt. The demarcation of distinct neighborhoods also accelerated. The business district centered on Main Street and spread north from the river. Wholesalers and meat packers occupied the banks of the Miami Canal, and heavy industry concentrated on the east side of town.[13] Germans congregated north of the Canal and in adjacent northern townships. The city also spawned industrial suburbs in Fulton and Mill Creek townships along the Ohio and in Covington and Newport across the river.[14]

Cincinnati's population largely ceased to grow in the middle and late 1850s, and trade and manufacturing increased more slowly than before. Basic to the city's problems were failings in its transportation facilities. Extraordinary droughts in 1854 and 1856 embargoed river traffic, destroying the fall trade in produce and merchandise and creating coal famines that shut down many factories. Together with railroad competition and bad weather during the rest of the decade, these disasters bankrupted many packet lines.[15] At the same time, important east-west rail lines bypassed the city, loosening Cincinnati's hold on the trade of Ohio and Indiana.

With its weakened competitive position, Cincinnati suffered seriously from the financial troubles of the 1850s. Excessive speculation and crop failures in 1854 brought on a sharp depression. According to the *Commercial*, "winter found our mechanics out of work, our manufactories silent, our coal yards empty, hunger and nakedness among the poor . . . and distressing embarrassments among the businessmen." The shortness of money reduced the demand for real estate and forced a halt to several railroad projects. The crisis also allowed Chicago to capture much of Cincinnati's wholesale trade and reduced the value of its manufactures. Indeed, Cincinnati did not completely recover until 1856.[16] The new prosperity lasted only a few months before the collapse of the Ohio

TABLE 2
Place of Birth of Labor Force: Chicago,
Cincinnati, Galena, and Indianapolis

	Chicago		Cincinnati		Galena		Indianapolis	
	1850	*1860*	*1850*	*1860*	*1850*	*1860*	*1850*	*1860*
New England	7.5%	7.8%	2.8%	1.9%	4.4%	4.1%	4.1%	3.0%
Mid-Atlantic[a]	20.6	15.1	16.9	10.4	22.3	13.1	23.8	17.6
South[b]	1.2	0.7	3.9	4.1	3.1	1.1	16.8	8.9
Midwest[c]	1.9	1.4	0.8	1.4	5.6	4.4	12.6	9.3
City's Home State	1.6	1.7	9.2	13.1	1.9	7.3	15.3	15.5
Ireland	22.7	27.3	15.0	18.0	21.3	25.7	7.7	13.4
Great Britain	11.9	7.9	5.3	5.5	10.2	7.7	3.5	4.0
Germany[d]	18.5	29.8	43.2	41.6	24.8	31.2	13.7	26.1
Other Foreign	7.3	7.2	1.9	3.6	3.8	4.9	0.5	1.5
Illegible	6.9	1.0	1.1	0.4	2.8	0.5	2.0	0.5

[a]New York, New Jersey, Pennsylvania, Delaware, Maryland, Virginia.
[b]North Carolina, South Carolina, Georgia, Florida, Alabama, Mississippi, Tennessee, Kentucky, Arkansas, Louisiana, Texas.
[c]Ohio, Indiana, Illinois, Michigan, Wisconsin, Minnesota, Iowa, Missouri, but excluding the state in which the city is located.
[d]All German states including Austria.

Life Insurance and Trust Company in August of 1857 brought new troubles. Ninety-six local firms failed in 1857, and fifty-one the following year. Their liabilities totaled over $5 million. Dry goods merchants suffered severely, as did iron manufacturers and other industrialists, many of whom closed their operations or cut to halftime. Many Cincinnatians faced starvation during the winter of 1857-58. Poor crops in 1858 and 1859 allowed only a moderate revival of export trade, and other sectors of the economy remained depressed into 1860.[17]

Despite its difficulties, Cincinnati remained the largest city in the West in 1860. The 161,000 inhabitants reported by the federal census gave the city only a narrow lead over St. Louis, but boosters justly argued that much of its recent growth had occurred in suburbs outside the city limits. Pointing to its diversified economy, its extensive relations with all parts of the West, and continued foreign immigration, Mayor R. M. Bishop claimed that it was still the "Metropolis of the Ohio Valley."[18]

If Cincinnati in 1840 was the acknowledged capital of the West, Chicago seemed to many to have its future behind it. As late as 1832, it had been little but a fur-trading post on the edge of a vast swamp. In 1833 and 1834 migration to northern Illinois had incited a building boom that raised the prices of available lots. Continued immigration and outside capital attracted by the promise of the Illinois and Michigan Canal had fixed a mania for speculation on the town by 1835. At the same time, the opening of a federal land office made Chicago the great market for town lots in plats scattered throughout the Northwest. "As the gentlemen of our party walked the street," wrote Harriet Martineau at the peak of the enthusiasm in June, 1836, "store-keepers hailed them from their doors, with offers of farms, and all manner of land-lots, advising them to speculate before the price of land rose higher."[19]

The crash of 1837 had come like "the day of wrath and retribution." The city's population, which had climbed to over four thousand by 1837, stagnated in the next three years as "confidence and credit, too long abused, refused any longer to lend their aid" to speculation. Leading businessmen protested their inability to meet their real estate debts, and William B. Ogden wrote that "the town's ancient dynasty have mostly fallen. . . . It seems as if there was scarce one left to escape the blight and mildew of 1836."[20] The renewed crisis of 1839, along with the suspension of expenditures on the canal, further lowered land prices. The nadir came in 1842, when dozens of businessmen declared bankruptcy or abandoned the city and its population swelled with unemployed canal workers. As Governor Thomas Carlin sadly reported, "the tides of emigration and wealth have ceased to flow into the state. All the channels of trade are completely obstructed, and the vitality of business seems almost extinct.''[21]

The depression lifted almost as rapidly as it had descended. In 1843 and 1844, Chicago began a long surge of growth which carried it into third place among western cities. The town tripled its 1840 population by 1847. It nearly tripled again in the next six years of "unexampled prosperity" and more than doubled between 1852 and 1857, despite the financial panic of 1854, which ruined four of its banks, caused minor unemployment, and temporarily disordered its commerce.[22]

Chicago's basic activity during this period of growth was commerce. In the mid-1840s, it carried on a prosperous trade with the surrounding countryside, exchanging dry goods and lumber brought by lake boats for the grain and provisions of northern Indiana and Illinois. The completion of the Illinois and Michigan Canal and the opening of the city's first railroad in 1848 changed this "thriving country town" into the "grand depot, exchange, counting-house, and metropolis of the prairies." In 1850, the *Chicago Democrat* announced that "we have but just now entered on our life as a city.[23] The continued development of its railroad system in the 1850s and its importance as a lake port made it a conduit for tens of thousands of emigrants, all of whom left money in the hands of hotel keepers and store owners. The rage for real estate also reappeared, for Chicago was *the* boom town of the 1850s and outsiders clamored to participate in its growth. A traveler reported in 1856 that "land is the great topic of conversation in the streets, hotels, and liquor saloons . . . the acquisition of wealth by its sale and purchase is the ruling passion among the citizens of the prairie city.''[24]

In the same decade, Chicago developed many of the attributes and problems of a mature city. Natives pointed proudly to the thousands of new buildings, which served as "tangible proofs of the growth of Chicago." Boosters delighted in describing the increase in the "number and value of permanent residences, business blocks, and public buildings." Just as often, they remarked the replacement of rotten tenements by "magnificent piles of brick and stone." The city opened public schools, built bridges, established omnibus lines, and installed gas lights. Despite the trial of various pavements and persistent loud complaints, however, it was unable to keep its streets out of the mud or build an adequate hydraulic system. Its new water pipes delivered fish and sewage as well as water, and the *Tribune* suggested that "the sort of mixture, by courtesy called water, because it is a little damp, which is furnished to the people from the Water Works, ought to be analyzed."[25]

Social patterns changed along with Chicago's appearance. Its location made it at least the temporary stopping place for many immigrants from abroad. As early as 1850, 60 percent of its labor force was foreign born. By the end of the decade, 30 percent of its workers were Germans, 27 percent were natives of Ireland, and 15 percent from other foreign countries. Germans demanded recognition from political slate-makers as early as 1846 and led the creation of labor organizations in the mid-1850s. The city's first wave of strikes came in 1853 and 1854 as unions appeared in almost every trade.[26]

In 1856 perceptive Chicagoans noted that their economy was beginning to soften. Real estate prices leveled off, and the demand for foodstuffs slackened with the end of the Crimean War. Money was scarce by the following summer, and businessmen complained of hard times. A disastrous panic followed these forewarnings in the fall of 1857. Several large banks collapsed, and over a hundred firms closed their doors. Employers who did not shut down during the winter could scarcely obtain money to pay their hands.[27] The situation improved only slightly in 1858. Because businessmen in its hinterland felt the full crisis months after the worst had passed in Chicago, the failure of hundreds of interior merchants combined with unusually poor crops to reduce the demand for Chicago products and imports.[28] Many factories operated on only a token level, and the lumber trade, one of the mushrooms of the mid-1850s, collapsed totally.[29] A second year of "failure and destitution of all crops" prevented any general recovery, and real estate prices plunged in 1859 and 1860 after holding for almost a year. Investment in new construction in the latter year was only one-sixth that of 1857.[30] However, the census of 1860 confirmed that Chicago's population had passed the one hundred thousand mark and now ranked ninth among American cities.

Chicago and Cincinnati together dominated their region by the 1850s. Their largest rivals—Louisville, St. Louis, Milwaukee, Detroit, Cleveland, Pittsburgh—were all in some way peripheral to the heartland of the Middle West. Their hinterlands penetrated only short distances into Ohio, Indiana, and Illinois, and only St. Louis had equal potential to control the economy of the entire West. In addition, most of the smaller cities of Ohio, Indiana, and Illinois operated within the shadow of Cincinnati and Chicago. Among others, however, both Indianapolis and Galena had managed to establish a sort of economic independence by 1840. Though not particularly wealthy, each was old enough and far enough removed from rivals to have developed a distinct economy guided by local decisions.

The legislature of Indiana had breathed first life into Indianapolis in 1821 by accepting the newly surveyed site as the seat of government. After four years of desultory growth the town had boomed briefly when the state offices were moved to the new capital. Population jumped by several hundred, but the expectations proved greater than results. Between 1827 and 1835, it was little more than a country town with a larger and more interesting court session than most. One visitor found it "utterly forlorn" and "few expected a brighter future."[31]

The city had felt a second surge of hope in the mid-1830s when the state's internal improvements program promised to end its mud-bound isolation with canal, railroad, and turnpike connections. Citizens speculated in Indianapolis lots, population rose to an estimated four thousand, and the town prospered until disbursements for public works ceased in 1839.[32] During the next several years, "a deranged and ruined currency, a universal prostration of credit and confidence, [and] deep and unmitigated pecuniary distress" drove away many inhabitants and again reduced the city's ambitions. In the 1840s, Indianapolis was "a mere country town" which regained a population of four thousand only in 1847. "Its business was purely local," wrote one native later. "It produced little, and it distributed little that it did not produce. . . .The manufacturing, except for home demand, was even more trifling than the mercantile business."[33]

Through the 1840s, Indianapolis was more village than city. Unlike Cincinnati or Chicago, it drew much of its population from the surrounding states of Indiana, Ohio, and Kentucky. Few of its inhabitants were European-born. Only Germans were present in sufficient numbers to form a distinct ethnic neighborhood on the east side of town. Apart from this district, there was little differentiation among the various sections of Indianapolis, nor did the city's few thousand citizens create any serious social or civic problems. Indeed, a number of residents attempted to abolish the municipal government entirely in 1842, and Indianapolis was not organized as a city until 1847.[34]

The city's career changed dramatically in September of that year. The completion of the Madison and Indianapolis Railroad stimulated all branches of trade and brought "new life and animation" to the town. Contemporaries were of one mind that the event marked a new era.[35] This first line stimulated a railroad fever and attracted connecting roads. In 1852, 1853, and 1854, seven new railroads were finished between Indianapolis and other Indiana cities. New industries appeared in response, and "business showed its growth in its divisions" as merchants began to experiment with a jobbing as well as a retail business. By the middle of the decade, the town's population had tripled and natives were styling it the "Railroad City."[36]

The growth of Indianapolis slowed when the panic of 1854 killed several additional railroads. The crisis also disrupted its financial system by destroying many of Indiana's free banks. Although poor crops made 1855 another bad year, the city recuperated with a moderate boom in real estate in 1856. The financial troubles of 1857 again damaged new enterprises and threatened serious unemployment, but the ensuing depression was probably less disastrous than in Chicago or Cincinnati. Taken as a whole, 1854 to 1860 was a period of slower growth in which the city continued to build on the foundations laid in the previous years.[37]

Indianapolis by 1860 was the focus of Indiana. As the node of the state's transport network it lay within a few hours' journey of eighty of its ninety-six counties. Indeed, the city's railroads provided the only physical bond which tied together the corners of the state. At the same time, it was the nerve-center where Indiana's churchmen argued dogma, its reformers planned their crusades, its politicians scratched each others' backs, and its farmers admired the exhibits at the state fair. In recognition of its importance, its citizens claimed a population of 20,000, 25,000, or even 29,000 by the end of the decade.[38] The 18,611 inhabitants counted by the census still matched it with Dayton and Columbus as one of the largest inland towns in the West.

Galena's growth was concurrent with the sustained exploitation of the lead mines of the upper Mississippi Valley after 1822. The first permanent settlers had arrived in Galena in 1823, and the first lots were staked off in 1826. Between 1825 and 1828, the production of lead rose from 332 tons to 5,533 tons as four thousand prospectors swarmed over northwestern Illinois and southwestern Wisconsin. According to John Mason Peck, "the country was almost literally filled with miners, smelters, merchants, speculators, gamblers, and every description of character."[39] Galena's site at the head of navigation on the Fever River, a slack water tributary of the Mississippi, gave it easy access to the interior of the region and made it the point of deposit for imports and the shipping point for lead. The city had rapidly grown toward the thousand mark and impressed visitors with its prosperity. Morgan Martin noticed that "there was that 'snap' about the place that gave promise of great things in the future."[40]

Galena's growth had slowed in the 1830s. In 1829, overproduction abruptly cut lead prices in half; inhabitants of the region complained of the "depressed price of lead, and the oppressed situation of the people in their mining country." Many adventurers left to seek their fortunes elsewhere, and the Black Hawk War of 1832 scared away still more miners. In 1834, Charles Fenno Hoffman noted that many mines were still abandoned, although business was beginning to recover and Galena was "for its size . . . one of the busiest places in the Union." The crash of 1837 again lowered the price of lead after a brief rise and brought mining to a temporary standstill. Through the end of the decade, business in Galena remained "horrid dull."[41]

Federal land policy had been an additional obstacle to the development of both Galena and the lead region. As it had done already in Missouri, the government chose to withhold valuable mineral lands from sale. In Illinois and Wisconsin, the superintendent of mines required prohibitive terms for outright leases, substituting a system under which miners received permits that allowed them to roam the region at will and dig ore where they found it. Any mineral they raised had to be sold to licensed and bonded smelters, who collected 10 percent of the product as the federal rent. Carrying the policy to extremes, the government had even reserved title to the plat of Galena, allowing lot holders only a permit revocable at thirty days' notice.[42]

After several years of rigorous application, enforcement of the permit system had grown lax in the 1830s. Federal officers charged with its supervision were unenthusiastic, while spokesmen for local interests argued that it discouraged investment in internal improvements. Indeed, the negligence or the collusion of the superintendent of mines and the Mineral Point land office had allowed thousands of mineral-rich acres in Wisconsin to pass into the hands of local capitalists under the guise of agricultural lands. In 1836, the government also acceded to the petitions of the Illinois legislature and authorized the sale of lots in the town of Galena with preemption rights for current occupants. A new set of officials attempted to re-institute the lease and permit system between 1840 and 1842, but the region's farmers, smelters, and speculators refused to tolerate such a threat to their position. Their resistance made it impossible to evict illegal landholders or to collect back rents, as local juries refused to return convictions. In 1846, Congress finally opened all lands to outright sale, to the delight of Galena's business community.[43]

The 1840s were the flush decade. Lead production climbed from twelve thousand tons in 1839 and 1840 to twenty-six thousand tons annually between 1845 and 1848. The city began to regain its prosperity in 1840 and 1841, and population tripled by 1847. A dozen or more vessels often crowded the narrow river in front of the town, and lead was sometimes stacked so high on its wharves that the boats were unable to tie up. The streets that squeezed underneath the high bluffs were just as crowded with business.[44] Galena carried on a livelier and perhaps more valuable commerce than Chicago and was equally cosmopolitan. Despite its small population of six thousand, three-fifths of its workers were of foreign origin. Germans alone were numerous enough to transform the staid American Sunday into a day of festivity.[45]

In the 1850s, lead production fell by about 40 percent as hundreds of miners left for California gold fields. Superficial lead deposits accessible to crude mining techniques were rapidly exhausted, and few businessmen chose to sink their capital in a deep shaft that might or might not strike ore.[46] Galena itself, however, found a new activity to supplement the declining lead trade. The settlement of northern Iowa, western Wisconsin, and Minnesota created a large market for merchandise and manufactures, which Galena merchants undertook to satisfy with goods received via the Mississippi. Through the first two-thirds of the decade, Galena's size again doubled, its businessmen continued to make money, and it was justly described as a "rich, thriving, and enterprising city."[47]

Unfortunately for Galena, this new trade depended on its position astride the only artery of transportation between the older United States and the new settlements to the north. The completion of several railroads from Lake Michigan to the upper Mississippi in the later 1850s destroyed the town's monopoly and exposed its merchants to the competition of the lake ports. Simultaneously, the panic of 1857 devoured the capital of many Galena businessmen and left the town without the resources to fight back.[48] At the end of the decade its population had already fallen several thousand below its peak.

The patterns of growth in the four cities corresponded closely to the long economic upswing of the 1840s and 1850s and reflected even minor fluctuations in the national cycle of boom and bust. Between 1840 and 1847, Cincinnati, Chicago, Indianapolis, and Galena each launched independently into a distinct phase of development. Although the crash of 1857 arrested growth for the nation as a whole and sharply affected each of the cities, three of them recovered to a degree by 1859 or 1860. The secession of the South provided a more definite end to this period of urban development in the Northwest, for the Civil War altered the conditions of growth for almost all western cities and opened new eras for Cincinnati, Chicago, Indianapolis, and Galena.

Towns dependent on the river trade found the war a disaster. Although Galena was already in decline, the disruption of traffic on the Mississippi and the stoppage of trade through St. Louis destroyed hope of revival. With its wholesalers unable to obtain supplies, its hinterland was absorbed by Chicago and Milwaukee, which could ship needed goods by rail. Nor did a war-incited rise in the price of lead help the city; by the end of the war, only one worker in twenty through the region earned a living in the lead industry.

Galena's population continued to shrink while its upriver rivals grew, and many of its most enterprising citizens fled the city during the 1860s.

Cincinnati in 1860 depended not only on river transportation but also on southern markets and southern debts. In the fall of 1860 and in 1861, its businessmen faced the future with fear. Its newspapers offered gloomy forecasts, its manufacturers ceased to expand their plants, and its chamber of commerce reported that "the future looks so dark none can contemplate it without a shudder." For two years, trade was crippled and manufacturing depressed, retailers desperate for business and workers for jobs. Government orders sparked a revival of trade in the later years of the war, but the return of peace showed that neither the river trade nor the southern market retained their former power to build a great city north of the Ohio.[49]

In western cities with good railroad connections to the East the Civil War stimulated growth. In Indianapolis it ushered in a boom that lasted into the 1870s. The town's central position made it the marshaling point for Indiana's war supplies and soldiers, whose presence at camps near the city increased the demand for imports and local manufactures. In the later years of the conflict, large wholesaling houses and factories appeared as Indianapolis wrested the state's business from faltering Cincinnati merchants. If Indianapolis had been an overgrown town in 1860, it was a city by 1865; if it had been a city, it was fast becoming a metropolis.

Chicago perhaps benefited more from the rebellion than any other city in the Union. The closing of the Mississippi and the suspension of business in St. Louis handed it the opportunity to become the sole supplier of southern Illinois, northern Missouri, Iowa, and Minnesota. As its businessmen rushed to take advantage of the opportunity, outsiders invested their surplus funds in Chicago enterprises and the city sailed out of the commercial doldrums of 1859 and 1860. Its wholesaling expanded, its factories multiplied, and it replaced stricken Cincinnati as the packing center of the country. By 1870, Chicago stood not third but first in the new ranking of western cities.[50]

The surge of regional and national growth that so strongly affected each Middle-Western city also brought important structural changes that opened the era of rapid American industrialization. Despite a national population increment of 14,374,000, the per capita value of national commodity output—the sum of value added in agriculture, mining, manufacturing, and construction—rose by about a third from 1840 to 1860. Changes in the relative importance of economic activities accompanied this increase in the production of goods. The share of commodity output accounted for by agriculture dropped from 72 percent in 1839 to 60 percent in 1849 and 56 percent in 1859, while the share for manufacturing rose from 17 percent to 30 percent to 32 percent. Stanley Lebergott in a parallel study found relatively small shifts in the sectoral distribution of employment in the 1850s but agreed that the 1840s saw the culmination of a movement from farming to manufacturing, trade, transportation, and services. During that single decade, for example, the share of employment in agriculture fell from 64 percent to 54 percent while that in manufacturing rose from 14 percent to 20 percent.[51]

The Middle West shared the pace of economic development during these two decades. In 1840, the North Central states had a lower per capita income than any other part of the Union. During the next two decades, however, the area's per capita income grew faster than that of the nation as a whole, and its share of total national income rose from 14 percent to 19 percent. The growth of western agriculture allowed middle-western grain and provisions to challenge cotton as the chief American export. At the same time, the rapid development of processing and consumer goods industries raised the regional share of American manufacturing employment from 11.5 percent to 14.4 percent during the 1850s alone.[52]

The role played by cities in this process of economic maturation has been relatively neglected by historians. In general terms, the years between the 1830s and the 1870s have been characterized as a time of transition from the commercial to the industrial city, but the complexities of change have been left largely unexplored. Blake McKelvey has thus suggested that 1835 to 1870 constitutes a distinct era during which the nation's cities stabilized their economic position by enlarging their labor force, extending their trade, and developing manufactures. "Whether industry had become a major source of urban growth," he adds, "was still in doubt in most sectors." Allan Pred has explicitly called the two decades after 1850 the "transition period" during which "changes were under way that were bringing the phenomena of urban growth and industrial growth into closer association," while Zane Miller portrayed the entire period from 1840 to 1880 in the same terms.[53]

Historians interested specifically in the trans-Appalachian region have paid greatest attention to the economic activities of cities in their first decades of development. Richard Wade and Floyd Dain, for example, examined middle-western cities at the beginning of the nineteenth century. For the middle decades of the century, such scholars as Kenneth Wheeler, Charles Glaab, Robert Dykstra, Roger Lotchin, and Gunther Barth have followed the urban frontier across the Mississippi River. All of these studies share an emphasis on commerce as the great formative influence, in part because of their choice of cities and in part because of their focus on the first generation of settlement.[54] For the older Middle West in mid-century the most important supplementary perspective comes in the recent work of Alice Smith and Margaret Walsh on Wisconsin towns and the earlier work of Catherine Reiser on Pittsburgh. All three recognize the early importance of manufacturing in western urban growth and help to correct the early assumption that it was not until after the Civil War that "a predominant concern for trade and commerce . . . gave way to the encouragement of manufacturing."[55]

The present study attempts a more systematic comparative picture than is now available of middle-western urban development in the two antebellum decades. The following analysis of verbal and quantitative evidence on the economic base in the four cities supports the idea that the urban West was moving beyond its initial dependence on export trade to perform a more complex set of functions. Indeed, the Middle West had nearly as many urban types as the East. The industrial city of Cincinnati was a western counterpart of Philadelphia, the commercial hub of Chicago corresponded to New York, and the service center of Indianapolis was similar to Washington. Consideration of a different set of western cities—Pittsburgh, Detroit, Lexington—probably would support the same conclusion. As economic historians Eric Lampard and Douglass North have pointed out, such increasing sophistication in the economic functions of antebellum western cities is the expected corollary of the rising income and changing employment shown by gross regional figures.[56]

NOTES

1. Adna F. Weber, *The Growth of Cities in the Nineteenth Century* (New York, 1899), pp. 20–21; Julius Rubin, "Urban Growth and Regional Development," in David T. Gilchrist, ed., *The Growth of the Seaport Cities, 1790–1825* (Charlottesville, 1967), p. 8; Charles N. Glaab and A. Theodore Brown, *A History of Urban America* (New York, 1967), pp. 25, 31; Harvey Perloff et al., *Regions, Resources, and Economic Growth* (Baltimore, 1960), p. 117.

2. Richard C. Wade, "The City in History—Some American Perspectives," in Werner Z. Hirsch (ed.), *Urban Life and Form* (New York, 1963), p. 64; Louis B. Schmidt, "Internal Commerce and the Development of the National Economy before 1860," *Journal of Political Economy* 47 (December 1939): 800–820; George R. Taylor, *The Transportation Revolution: 1815–1860* (New York, 1951), pp. 132–48, 158–69, 396–98.

3. *Western Journal and Civilian* 5 (March 1851): 287; Frederick L. Paxson, "The Railroads of the 'Old Northwest' before the Civil War," *Transactions* of the Wisconsin Academy of Sciences, Arts and Letters 17 (1914): 268–75.

4. Jeffrey G. Williamson, "Antebellum Urbanization in the American Northeast," *Journal of Economic History* 25 (December 1965): 598–600; Weber, *Cities,* p. 22.

5. Thomas S. Berry, *Western Prices before 1861: A Study of the Cincinnati Market* (Cambridge, Mass., 1943), pp. 530, 585–89; Arthur H. Cole, *Wholesale Commodity Prices in the United States, 1700–1861* (Cambridge, Mass., 1938), pp. 94, 109; Walter B. Smith and Arthur H. Cole, *Fluctuations in American Business, 1790–1860* (Cambridge, Mass., 1935).

6. Berry, *Western Prices,* pp. 433, 471, 530; North, *Economic Growth,* pp. 136–40, 201–7, 212–14; Smith and Cole, *Fluctuations,* pp. 55–57, 63, 185; Paxson, "The Railroads of the 'Old Northwest,' " pp. 268–75; Albert Fishlow, *Railroads and the Transformation of the Antebellum Economy* (Cambridge, Mass., 1965), p. 397; A. L. Kohlmeier, *The Old Northwest as the Keystone in the Arch of American Federal Union* (Bloomington, Ind., 1938), p. 167; George Van Vleck, *The Panic of 1857: An Analytical Study* (New York, 1967), p. 83; Edward J. Morgan, "Sources of Capital for Railroads in the Old Northwest before the Civil War" (Ph.D. dis., University of Wisconsin, 1964), pp. 221, 301, 329.

7. Timothy Flint, *The History and Geography of the Mississippi Valley* (Cincinnati, 1832), p. 410; Isaac Lippincott, "A History of Manufactures in the Ohio Valley to the year 1860" (Ph.D. diss., University of Chicago, 1914), pp. 71, 78; Richard T. Farrell, "Cincinnati, 1800–1830: Economic Development through Trade and Industry," *Ohio History* 77 (Autumn 1968): 111–15, 122; Wade, *Urban Frontier,* pp. 53–56, 59, 189–91, 196–97; Michael Chevalier, *Society, Manners and Politics in the United States* (Boston, 1839), pp. 202–5.

8. Daniel Aaron, "Cincinnati, 1818–1838: A Study of Attitudes in the Urban West" (Ph.D. dis., Harvard University, 1942), pp. xii–xiv; Wade, *Urban Frontier,* pp. 190–93, 243.

9. James S. Buckingham, *The Eastern and Western States of America* (London, 1842), 2:394–95; William D. Gallagher, "Ohio in 1838," *Hesperian* 1 (July, 1838):

188; Reginald McGrane, *The Panic of 1837* (Chicago, 1924), pp. 123-25; *Proceedings of a Public Meeting of the Citizens of Cincinnati on the Subject of a Western National Armory*, H.R. Doc. No. 149, 27th Cong., 2d Sess., 1841, p. 17; David Schaffer, *The Cincinnati, Covington, Newport and Fulton Directory for 1840* (Cincinnati, 1839), p. 483; Friedrich Gerstäcker, *Streif- und Jagdzüge durch die Vereinigten Staaten Nordamerikas* (Jena, 1901), p. 165; Thomas Corwin, Governor of Ohio, *Annual Message* (1842), p. 4; *Cincinnati Republican*, April 8, 1841; *Liberty Hall and Cincinnati Gazette*, April 30 and August 6, 1840; Berry, *Western Prices*, pp. 450-53, 468-69.

10. Edward D. Mansfield, *Personal Memories: Social, Political and Literary* (Cincinnati, 1879), p. 307; *Cincinnati Enquirer*, April 23 and 24, 1842; *Liberty Hall and Cincinnati Gazette*, October 21, 1841, October 6, 1842; Hall, *Commerce and Navigation*, p. 311; Charles Cist, *The Cincinnati Directory for the Year 1843* (Cincinnati, 1843), pp. 3-6; *Cincinnati Commercial*, November 5, 1842, quoted in Berry, *Western Prices*, pp. 468-69.

11. Cincinnati Chamber of Commerce, *Report* for 1848, pp. 4-6, for 1850, p. 1, for 1851, p. 1, for 1852, p. 3; *Cincinnati Enquirer*, September 8, 1849; Rufus King to Mrs. William Peter, July 18, 1849, King Family Papers, Cincinnati Historical Society; Margaret Lytle to Elias Haines, August 27, 1849, Lytle Family Papers, Cincinnati Historical Society.

12. William Sherwood to Lois Sherwood, October 6, 1848, Sherwood Letters, Cincinnati Historical Society.

13. Gerstäcker, *Vereinigten Staaten*, pp. 164-65; *The Ohio Railroad Guide* (Columbus, 1854), pp. 6-10; *Liberty Hall and Cincinnati Gazette*, February 27, 1845; Cincinnati, Wilmington and Zanesville Railroad Company, *Special Report* (January, 1857), map; Walter S. Glazer, "Cincinnati in 1840: A Community Profile" (Ph.D. diss., University of Michigan, 1968), pp. 222-27, 258-59; Carl Abbott, "The Location and External Appearance of Mrs. Trollope's Bazaar," *Journal of the Society of Architectural Historians* 29 (October, 1970): 256-57.

14. Franz Löher, *Geschichte und Züstande der Deutschen in Amerika* (Cincinnati, 1847), pp. 330-32; Gerstäcker, *Vereinigten Staaten*, p. 165; Henry Howe, *Historical Collections of Ohio* (Cincinnati, 1847), p. 216; George Conclin, *Conclin's New River Guide* (Cincinnati, 1854), pp. 32, 36; Cist, *1843 Directory*, p. 4; Chevalier, *Society, Manners and Politics*, p. 193.

15. Louis Hunter, *Steamboats on the Western Waters* (Cambridge, Mass., 1949), pp. 207, 330; Berry, *Western Prices*, p. 60; Cincinnati *Price Current*, July 18, 1855; *Cincinnati Commercial*, January 15, 1852, January 12, 1857; Cincinnati Chamber of Commerce, *Report* for 1857, pp. 3, 10.

16. *Cincinnati Commercial*, July 20, 1855, April 4 and 9, 1856; *Cincinnati Gazette*, August 25, 1855; Cincinnati, Hamilton and Dayton Railroad Company, Sixth *Annual Report* (1856), p. 7; Cincinnati Chamber of Commerce, *Report* for 1854, p. 4, for 1856, p. 3.

17. *Bankers' Magazine* 13 (February 1859): 641; Cincinnati Chamber of Commerce, *Report* for 1858, p. 5; Lewis A. Leonard, *Greater Cincinnati and Its People: A History* (Chicago, 1927), 1:253; *Cincinnati Enquirer*, December 9, 1860.

18. Mayor R.M. Bishop, Annual Message, in *Cincinnati Commercial*, April 12, 1860; *Cincinnati Gazette*, January 1 and November 27, 1858, September 10 and

November 6, 1860; *Cincinnati Price Current,* in *DeBow's Review* 29 (December 1860): 780–84.

19. Harriet Martineau, *Society in America* (New York, 1837), 1:259–60; Thomas Ford, *History of Illinois,* ed. by Milo M. Quaife (Chicago, 1945), 1:179–80; A.T. Andreas, *History of Chicago from the Earliest Period to the Present Time* (Chicago, 1884), 1:133–38; Homer Hoyt, "One Hundred Years of Land Values in Chicago" (Ph.D. diss., University of Chicago, 1933), pp. 27–38; Pierce, *Chicago,* 1:55–67; Joseph N. Balestier, *The Annals of Chicago: A Lecture Delivered before the Chicago Lyceum, January 21, 1840,* Fergus Historical Series no. 1 (Chicago, 1876), p. 28.

20. J.W. Norris, *General Directory and Business Advertiser of the City of Chicago for the Year 1844* (Chicago, 1844), pp. 14–15; Balestier, *Annals,* p. 31; William B. Ogden to James Allen, January 15, 1840, Ogden Collection, Chicago Historical Society. Also see: Gurdon S. Hubbard to Mrs. A.H. Hubbard, 1840, Hubbard Collection, Chicago Historical Society; Archibald Clyborne to Arthur Bronson, January 14, 1839; William Egan to Orasmus Bushnell, December 12, 1837, October 12, 1838, all in Bronson Collection, Chicago Historical Society.

21. Mayor B. W. Raymond, Inaugural Address, in *Chicago American,* March 9, 1842; William B. Ogden to B. Mayer, June 21, 1841, Ogden Collection, Chicago Historical Society; Elias Colbert, *Historical and Statistical Sketch of the Garden City* (Chicago, 1868), pp. 46–47; Gov. Thomas Carlin, Message to Illinois General Assembly, December 7, 1842, in *Illinois Reports* (1841/42), p. 10.

22. Jesse Thomas, "Statistics Concerning the City of Chicago, 1847," in *Chicago River-and-Harbor Convention,* Fergus Historical Series no. 18 (Chicago, 1882), p. 181; Henry Brown, *The Present and Future Prospects of Chicago: An Address Delivered before the Chicago Lyceum, January 20, 1846,* Fergus Historical Series no. 9 (Chicago, 1876), p. 16; Norris, *1844 Directory,* p. iii; *Chicago Democrat,* August 13, 1845; *Chicago Democratic Press, Review of Commerce* for 1852, p. 1, for 1853, p. 60, for 1854, pp. 4, 27, for 1855, pp. 4–7; Weston A. Goodspeed and Daniel D. Healy, *History of Cook County, Illinois* (Chicago, 1909), 2:160–62.

23. James Parton, "Chicago," *Atlantic Monthly* 19 (March 1867): 327–30; *Chicago Democrat,* February 19, 1850, in Goodspeed and Healy, *Cook County,* 1:207.

24. *Chicago Tribune, Review of Commerce* for 1860, p. 54; William Hancock, *An Emigrant's Five Years in the Free States of America* (London, 1860), pp. 257, 261, William Carter to George Carter, November 2, 1853, Carter Collection, Chicago Historical Society; Hoyt, "Land Values," p. 67.

25. *Chicago Democratic Press, Review of Commerce* for 1854, p. 57; *Chicago Times,* March 16, 1855, December 25, 1858; *Chicago Tribune,* April 18, 1856; Carl Abbott, "Civic Pride in Chicago, 1844–1860," *Journal of the Illinois State Historical Society* 63 (Winter 1970): 410–12.

26. Arthur C. Cole, *The Era of the Civil War, 1848–1870* (Springfield, Ill., 1919), p. 369; Theodore C. Pease, *The Frontier State, 1818–1848,* p. 395; Goodspeed and Healy, *Cook County,* 1:235, 259; *Chicago Democratic Press,* April 6 and August 10, 1853.

27. Patrick Barry, *The Theory and Practice of International Trade of the United States and England* (Chicago, 1858), p. 22; *Chicago Magazine* 1 (June 1857): 361–64; *Chicago Democratic Press, Review of Commerce* for 1856, p. 17; *Chicago*

Press, December 3, 1857; *Bankers' Magazine* 13 (February 1859): 641; James Lawrence to brother, December 25, 1857, Lawrence Collection, Chicago Historical Society; Tolman Wheeler to Jonathan Hoyt, October 26, 1857, Wheeler Collection, Chicago Historical Society.

28. James Caird, *Prairie Farming in America* (London, 1859), pp. 34–35; Chicago Board of Trade, *Report* for 1858, pp. 5, 38, 43; Chicago, Burlington and Quincy Railroad Company, Eighth *Annual Report* (1857/58), p. 13.

29. *Chicago Press and Tribune, Review of Commerce* for 1858, p. 3; I.D. Guyer, *History of Chicago: Its Commercial and Manufacturing Interests and Industry* (Chicago, 1862), p. 182; *Chicago Tribune,* May 10, 1860; Charles Mears Diary, April 19, May 5, August 17–18 and 27, 1858, Chicago Historical Society.

30. Chicago and Northwestern Railroad Company, First *Annual Report* (1859/60), p. 7; *Chicago Press and Tribune, Review of Commerce* for 1859, p. 3; Hoyt, "Land Values," pp. 74–76; Colbert, *Garden City,* pp. 21, 24, 74–75.

31. William R. Holloway, *Indianapolis: A Historical and Statistical Sketch of the Railroad City* (Indianapolis, 1870), pp. 16, 25–30, 36; Ignatius Brown, "History of Indianapolis from 1818 to 1868," in *Logan's Indianapolis Directory* (Indianapolis, 1868), p. 19; Hugh McCulloch, *Men and Measures of Half a Century* (New York, 1900), p. 71.

32. Berry R. Sulgrove, *History of Indianapolis and Marion County, Indiana* (Philadelphia, 1884), p. 114; "Historical Sketch," in *Indianapolis Directory City Guide and Business Mirror* (Indianapolis, 1855), pp. 37–39; Indianapolis *Indiana State Journal,* November 10, 1838; Holloway, *Indianapolis,* p. 48; Indianapolis *Indiana Democrat,* May 30, 1838, in Jacob P. Dunn, *Greater Indianapolis* (Chicago; 1910), 1:99–100.

33. Gov. David Wallace, Message to the Indiana General Assembly, December 3, 1839, in *Messages and Papers relating to the Administration of David Wallace,* ed. Dorothy Riker, Indiana Historical Collections, vol. 43 (Indianapolis, 1963), p. 323; Brown, "History of Indianapolis," p. 34; Holloway, *Indianapolis,* pp. 52–53, 73.

34. Albert E. Dickens, *The Growth and Structure of Real Property Uses in Indianapolis,* Indiana Business Studies, vol. 17 (Bloomington, Ind., 1939), pp. 19–24; George T. Probst, "The Germans in Indianapolis, 1850–1914" (M.A. diss., Indiana University, 1951), p. 14; Sulgrove, *Indianapolis,* p. 111.

35. Calvin Fletcher Diary, October, 1847, Indiana Historical Society; Joseph Mix to William Gray, February 18, 1848, William Gray Papers, Indiana State Library; Indianapolis *Indiana State Sentinel,* October 9, 1847, in Wylie J. Daniels, *The Village at the End of the Road: A Chapter in Early Indiana Railroad History,* Indiana Historical Society Publications, vol. 13, no. 1 (Indianapolis, 1938), p. 41; *Indiana Journal,* November 2, 1847, in Daniels, *Village* p. 41; Indianapolis Board of Trade, *Indianapolis;* Holloway, *Indianapolis,* pp. 4–5.

36. Oliver H. Smith, "Address Delivered before the Agricultural Society of Marion County," in Indiana, State Board of Agriculture, Fifth *Annual Report* (1856), p. 256; *Indianapolis Directory* (1855), p. v; Brown, "History of Indianapolis," p. 52; Victor Bogle, "Railroad Building in Indiana," *Indiana Magazine of History* 58 (September, 1962): 215–16; Holloway, *Indianapolis,* p. 83.

37. Indianapolis *Locomotive,* January 26, 1856; Indianapolis *Indiana Republican,* May 24, 1855; *Indiana Journal,* November 11, 1853, November 24, 1857, March 24, 1858; Indianapolis *Freie Presse von Indiana,* November 5, 1857; Oliver H. Smith, "The Railroads of Indiana," in Indiana, State Board of Agriculture, Fifth *Annual* Report (1856), p. 458; Holloway, *Indianapolis,* pp. 103, 300.

38. *Indiana State Gazetteer and Business Directory for 1860 and 1861* (Indianapolis, 1860), pp. 175-77; *Indiana Sentinel,* June 11, 1851; *Indiana Journal,* August 3, 1857; *Indiana State Gazetteer and Business Directory for 1858-59* (Indianapolis, 1858), p. 126; *Indianapolis City Directory and Business Mirror for 1860-61* (Indianapolis, 1860), p. 286.

39. John M. Peck, *A Gazetteer of Illinois* (Jacksonville, Ill., 1834), pp. 20-21. Also see: Reuben G. Thwaites, "Notes on Early Lead Mining in the Fever (or Galena) River Region," Wisconsin State Historical Society *Collections* 13 (1895): 286-91; "Galena and Its Lead Mines," *Harper's Monthly* 32 (May 1866): 686-87; *History of Jo Daviess County,* p. 247; James E. Wright, *The Galena Lead District: Federal Policy and Practice, 1824-47* (Madison, Wis., 1966), pp. 17-18.

40. "Narrative of Morgan L. Martin," Wisconsin State Historical Society *Collections* 11 (1888): 398. Also see: *History of Jo Daviess County,* p. 253; Henry Schoolcraft, *Summary Narrative of an Exploratory Expedition to the Sources of the Mississippi* (Philadelphia, 1855), pp. 562-63; Glenn T. Trewartha, "A Second Epoch of Destructive Occupance in the Driftless Hill Land," *Annals of the Association of American Geographers* 30 (June 1940): 132.

41. "Memorial of the Inhabitants of the Mining Country, 1829," in Clarence E. Carter (ed.), *The Territorial Papers of the United States,* vol. 12: *The Territory of Michigan, 1829-1837* (Washington, 1945), pp. 95-96; Charles F. Hoffman, *A Winter in the West* (New York, 1835), 2: 40-42; Cadwallader Washburn, July 11, 1839, in Galliard Hunt, *Israel, Elihu and Cadwallader Washburn, A Chapter in American Biography* (New York, 1925), p. 306. Also see Peck, *Gazetteer of Illinois,* pp. 20-21; *Galena Advertiser,* July 20 and August 3, 1829; Schoolcraft, *Summary Narrative,* p. 569; William Hempstead to D.B. Morehouse, April 9, 1837, Hempstead Papers, Illinois State Historical Library; *Galena Gazette,* September 30, 1837; Anonymous Diary, 1839, Chicago Historical Society, p. 50.

42. John W. Taylor, "Reservation and Leasing of the Salines, Lead and Copper Mines of the Public Domain" (Ph.D. diss., University of Chicago, 1930), pp. 102-12; Wright, *Lead District,* pp. 17-18; *History of Jo Daviess County,* pp. 266-67.

43. Memorials in Carter, *Territory of Michigan,* pp. 93-98, 411-14, 450-53, 1096-97, 1121-24; *Galena Advertiser,* January 13, 1830; James A. Lake, *Law and Mineral Wealth: The Legal Profile of the Wisconsin Mining Industry* (Madison, Wis., 1962), pp. 38-40; Wright, *Lead District,* pp. 35-46, 52-67. 72-97; Joseph Schafer, *The Wisconsin Lead Region* (Madison, Wis., 1932), pp. 114-20; *History of Jo Daviess County,* pp. 330-35; "Application of Illinois for Donation of Land to Citizens of Galena, Jo Daviess County, in that State, January 20, 1829," in *American State Papers, Public Lands,* 5: 620; Ann M. Keppel, "Civil Disobedience on the Mining Frontier," *Wisconsin Magazine of History* 41 (Spring 1958): 190-92; *Galena*

Jeffersonian, July 20 and September 28, 1846; *Galena Directory for 1847–48,* pp. 44, 47.

44. *Galena Gazette,* April 7, 1841; Orin G. Libby, "An Economic and Social Study of the Lead Region in Iowa, Illinois and Wisconsin," *Transactions* of the Wisconsin Academy of Science, Arts, and Letters 13 (1900): 210; S.W. McMaster, *Sixty Years on the Upper Mississippi* (Rock Island, Ill., 1893), pp. 107–8; Stephen H. Hayes, "Letters from the West in 1845," *Iowa Journal of History and Politics* 20 (January 1922): 44; William R. Smith, *Observations on Wisconsin Territory* (Philadelphia, 1838), pp. 106–7.

45. Augustus L. Chetlain, *Recollections of Seventy Years* (Galena, 1899), p. 46; Charles Cleaver, *Early-Chicago Reminiscences,* Fergus Historical Series no. 19 (Chicago, 1882), p. 46; Hunt, *Washburn,* p. 172; Moritz Wagner and Carl Scherzer, *Reisen in Nordamerika in den Jahren 1852 und 1853* (Leipzig, 1857), 3: 96–97.

46. *Scientific American* 7 (March 6, 1852): 194; J.D. Whitney, *The Metallic Wealth of the United States* (Philadelphia, 1854), pp. 416–17; Edward Daniels, *Report on the Geological Survey of the State of Wisconsin* (1854), pp. 40–43.

47. Alexander Leslie Diary, 1857–58, Chicago Historical Society; *Galena Gazette,* February 21, 1849, April 10, 1855, January 15, 1856; *Galena Jeffersonian,* November 16, 1852; *The Galena City Directory* (Galena, 1854), p. 6; Chetlain, *Recollections,* pp. 46–47; Conclin, *River Guide,* p. 71; Kenneth Owens, *Galena, Grant and the Fortunes of War,* Northern Illinois University Research Series (DeKalb, Ill., 1963), pp. 6–7; Daniel S. Curtiss, *Western Portraiture and Emigrants' Guide* (New York, 1852), p. 85.

48. Chetlain, *Recollections,* pp. 46–47; Owens, *Galena,* p. 18; *Galena Courier,* October 24, 1857; Alexander Leslie Diary, 1857–58, Chicago Historical Society, pp. 44–45; Bernard H. Schockel, "Settlement and Development of Jo Daviess County," in Illinois State Geological Survey *Bulletin* no. 26, 1916, p. 222.

49. Cincinnati Chamber of Commerce, *Report* for 1861, pp. 5–8; *Memorial of the Chamber of Commerce in the City of Cincinnati . . . in Relation to a National Armory West of the Alleghenies,* H.R. Rep. No. 43, 37th Cong., 2d Sess., p. 115; Edward Dicey, *Six Months in the Federal States* (London, 1863), 2: 53–54; Charles E. Wilson, "The Cincinnati Daily Enquirer and Civil War Politics: A Study in 'Copperhead' Opinion" (Ph.D. diss., University of Chicago, 1934), pp. 52–60; Carl M. Becker, "Miles Greenwood," in Kenneth W. Wheeler (ed.), *For the Union: Ohio Leaders in the Civil War* (Columbus, 1968), p. 282; Kohlmeier, *Old Northwest,* p. 214; Leonard P. Curry, *Rail Routes South: Louisville's Fight for the Southern Market, 1865–72* (Lexington, Ky., 1969), pp. 51–54.

50. Chicago Board of Trade, *Report* for 1862, p. 7; Wyatt W. Belcher, *The Economic Rivalry between St. Louis and Chicago, 1850–1880,* Columbia University Studies in History, Economics and Public Law, no. 529 (New York, 1947), pp. 139–57.

51. Robert Gallman, "Commodity Output, 1839–1899," *Studies in Income and Wealth* (New York, 1960), 24: 13–16, 26; Stanley Lebergott, *Manpower in Economic Growth: The American Record since 1800* (New York, 1964), pp. 101, 510; Alfred Chandler, "The Organization of Manufacturing and Transportation," in David T.

Gilchrist and W. David Lewis, eds., *Economic Change in the Civil War Era* (Greenville, Del., 1965), pp. 148-50.

52. Richard Easterlin, "Regional Income Trends, 1840-1950," in Seymour Harris, ed., *American Economic History* (New York, 1961), pp. 527-31, 535; Douglass North, *The Economic Growth of the United States, 1790-1860* (Englewood Cliffs, N.J., 1961), pp. 69-70, 140-41, 209-12; Margaret Walsh, *The Manufacturing Frontier: Pioneer Industry in Antebellum Wisconsin, 1830-1860* (Madison, 1972), p. vi; Perloff, *Regions*, p. 210.

53. Blake McKelvey, "American Urban History Today," *American Historical Review* 57 (July 1952): 923; Blake McKelvey, *American Urbanization: A Comparative History* (Glenview, Ill., 1973), pp. 39, 51; Allan Pred, *The Spatial Dynamics of U.S. Urban Industrial Growth, 1800-1914* (Cambridge, Mass., 1966), pp. 11, 145-51; Zane Miller, *The Urbanization of Modern America* (New York, 1973), pp. 26-33; Maury Klein and Harvey J. Kantor, *Prisoners of Progress: American Industrial Cities, 1850-1920* (New York, 1976), pp. 93-98; Glaab and Brown, *History of Urban America*, p. 27.

54. Richard C. Wade, *The Urban Frontier, 1790-1830* (Cambridge, Mass., 1959); Floyd Dain, *Every House a Frontier: Detroit's Economic Progress, 1815-1825* (Detroit, 1956); Kenneth Wheeler, *To Wear a City's Crown: The Beginning of Urban Growth in Texas, 1836-1865* (Cambridge, Mass., 1968); Charles Glaab, *Kansas City;* Robert Dykstra, *The Cattle Towns* (New York, 1968); Roger Lotchin, *San Francisco, 1846-1856: From Hamlet to City* (New York, 1974); Gunther Barth, *Instant Cities: Urbanization and the Rise of San Francisco and Denver* (New York, 1975).

55. Alice Smith, *Millstone and Saw: The Origins of Neenah-Menasha* (Madison, 1966); Walsh, *Manufacturing Frontier;* Catherine Reiser, *Pittsburgh's Commercial Development, 1800-1850* (Harrisburg, 1951); Bayrd Still, "Patterns of Mid-Nineteenth Century Urbanization in the Midwest," *Mississippi Valley Historical Review* 28 (September 1941): 198-200.

56. Eric Lampard, in Perloff, *Regions*, pp. 117-19; North, *Economic Growth*, pp. 153-55; McKelvey, *American Urbanization*, pp. 46-47.

2

NEW FIELDS OF ENTERPRISE: THE ECONOMIC BASE OF CINCINNATI, CHICAGO, INDIANAPOLIS, AND GALENA

According to local observers, Cincinnati, Chicago, Indianapolis, and Galena represented different economic types in the two decades before the Civil War. As successful growth decisions required the clear observation and evaluation of each city's circumstances, a first step in evaluating the character of popular economic thought is to test whether westerners were correct in their analysis of dominant economic activities. Impressionistic writing on economic development by local boosters can first be compared for consistency. The consensus of antebellum observers that emerges from this analysis can then be checked against quantitative evidence. The general conclusion is that contemporary arguments and assertions were conscientious efforts to assess available information. Even a city's own boosters usually abstained from flights of fancy and gauged accurately the development and importance of industry, wholesaling, export trade, and services.

Contemporary debates about urban growth were assisted by an impressive array of numerical data that were available in printed form before 1860. The increasing importance of manufacturing in the 1840s and 1850s, for example, caused a number of writers to inventory the industrial establishments in their cities, especially in the years between or immediately preceding the decennial census. These surveys not only described the different types of local manufacturing but also assembled estimates of employment, capital investment, and value of product in each industry. When used with data published in the federal census, they provided a rough picture of the composition and amount of local manufacturing. Newspaper reporters and trade organizations similarly compiled substantial information on the volume of trade in order to assess the commercial importance of different imports and exports.

Contemporary descriptions can be tested further by reconstructing the distribution of workers by occupational category using manuscript returns of the federal census. In 1850, census takers recorded the occupation of every employed male fifteen years old or older, and in 1860, that of every employed person fifteen or older. In the published census reports, this information is aggregated only by states. Sampling of the original census returns, however, allows the determination of the occupational distribution of employed persons in each city. The result is an accurate measure of economic structure that directly reflects the activities in which their residents engaged.

According to local opinion, Chicago "in the way of manufactures . . . had practically nothing to show until 1853." Before that date, its editors complained, the city had made at best "small beginnings" and had nurtured no large firms. Most of its manufacturers operated with only two, three, or four employees, producing building supplies, foodstuffs, and tools for nearby farmers or basic consumer goods required by local residents.[1] Only beef packers conducted their business on a larger scale and sold to customers outside Illinois. As early as 1846, the industry employed 250 hands at peak season. Five years later it had doubled its employment and accounted for almost a third of the city's industrial sales.[2]

The next three years opened a new era. Between 1852 and 1854, the tighter weaving of the Illinois rail net opened new markets at the same time that the doubling of the city increased local demand. The *Democratic Press* and other newspapers broadcast the growing importance of manufacturing. "At this moment," they complained in 1853, "there is a very large proportion of the actual residents of the city who have not a correct apprehension of her real position. . . ." Boosters asserted that Chicagoans could pride themselves that workshops and factories were now vital to the city's prosperity.[3]

Such writers had reason for their sudden enthusiasm. Whereas Chicagoans in 1851 claimed a total investment in manufacturing of $2,000,000 and a total product of $2,500,000, boosters of 1855 claimed an investment of close to $8,000,000 and an output of over $10,000,000.[4] Estimates of employment in Table 3 also show a substantial increase in industrial workers in the early 1850s. Metalworking plants making locomotives, railroad cars, engines, machinery, and agricultural implements and woodworking establishments producing furniture and building supplies for all parts of the rapidly growing Northwest were prominent among the new factories. Figures compiled by the *Democratic Press* indicate that these activities accounted for about half of Chicago's industrial sales in 1855 and 1856. At the same time, new entrepreneurs began to furnish a greater variety of consumer goods and the processors of agricultural commodities struggled to keep pace with the growth of the city. Production at times lagged behind demand, as during the Beer Famine, which lasted through four sweltering days in the summer of 1854.[5]

After several years of rapid growth, Chicago's manufacturing languished in the later 1850s. Editors began to remark that "the only item in the prospect of Chicago that has not kept pace with the otherwise unexampled progress and success of the city is that of manufacturing." To a degree they were reacting to a shift toward goods that were less obvious in the local marketplace. Vehicles, machinery, and furniture grew relatively less important, accounting for only 30 percent of industrial sales in 1860 and 1861. At the same time, capitalists were building the city's first rolling mill, laying the foundations for a huge pork-packing industry, and beginning to manufacture clothing, shoes, and other light consumer goods. More obviously, the panic of 1857 and the ensuing depression reduced the sales of Chicago factories. Reflecting either slackened growth or more realistic methods of counting, the Eighth Census

TABLE 3

Cincinnati and Chicago Employment in Manufactures, 1840-1860

	Cincinnati	Chicago
1840	10,287[a]	414[a]
1841	10,866[b]	—
1843	11,394[c]	506[e]
1846	—	1,134[f]
1850	15,638[a]	2,081[a]
1851	—	1,649[g]
1854	—	5,000[h]
1858	23,615[d]	—
1860	29,501[a]	5,360[a]

SOURCES:

[a]U.S. Census.

[b]Charles Cist, *Cincinnati in 1841* (Cincinnati, 1841), pp. 38-43.

[c]*Cincinnati Enquirer*, August 28 and 29, 1843.

[d]Ohio Commissioner of Statistics, *Report* for 1858, p. 96.

[e]David D. Griswold, *Statistics of Chicago, Illinois* (Chicago, 1843), p. 7.

[f]J. W. Norris, *Norris' Business Directory and Statistics of the City of Chicago for 1846* (Chicago, 1846), p. 7.

[g]Chicago *Tribune, Review of Trade* for 1851, in *Hunt's Magazine*, XXVI (April 1852), p. 510.

[h]Chicago *Democratic Press, Review of Trade* for 1854, p. 55.

reported that Chicago produced only $11,740,000 of manufactured goods in 1860 and Cook County only $13,555,000; both figures were considerably less than the supposed total for 1856.[6] The Census also reported the same industrial employment total as claimed by the *Democratic Press* in 1854 (Table 3).

Cincinnati entered the 1840s as "the greatest manufacturing place in the Western country" with an industrial employment of more than ten thousand (Table 3). During the next fifteen years, Cincinnati boosters reveled in "unparalleled," "astonishing," and "altogether unequalled" industrial growth. They also argued that factories and workshops were the great engine of their city's extraordinary economic expansion, providing a living for "the largest portion of its people." Cincinnati was "essentially a manufacturing city. It depends upon its manufactures mainly for its power." According to one statistically minded booster, "the products of manufacture here, constitute more than one-half of the business operations of Cincinnati, and the profits not less than three-fourths of the rewards of industry in all its branches." Toward the end of the decade, when the growth of Toledo, Chicago, St. Louis, and other rivals confined the Queen City's commerce, writers found solace in the conviction that industry would sustain its preeminence in the West.[7]

The growth of manufacturing was in part a result of sophisticated organization and receptiveness to innovation. In the 1830s and the first years of the 1840s, most of Cincinnati's manufactures were produced by individual mechanics and artisans working alone or in small shops, for businessmen were still unwilling to spare the capital required for larger operations.[8] Its few large factories were inadequately powered by water from the Miami Canal. By the middle of the decade, in contrast, Cincinnatians started to notice larger plants and the introduction of machinery for the production of items previously made by hand. The change was facilitated by the use of 50 steam engines in 1835, 200 by 1847, and 350 or 400 ten years later.[9] Annual consumption of coal from mines along the upper Ohio rose from about 40,000 tons in the early 1840s to 180,000 in 1850 and 600,000 by 1860. By mid-century the city's smokestacks emitted a perpetual blanket of smoke as dense and black as that over the mill towns of England.[10]

Cincinnati's woodworking industry showed the effects of steam power. In the late 1840s, the mechanization of furniture, sash, and door factories cut finished prices by about a third, allowing Cincinnati goods to undersell handmade products throughout the Mississippi Valley. The result was the creation of "immense establish-ments" which sold two-thirds of their product outside the city. In the late 1850s, furniture makers further reduced costs by shipping their goods in pieces designed for easy assembly at their destina-tion. Together, these innovations enabled the industry at least to triple its output in the 1850s.[11]

The iron industry was a complex of related pursuits that dis-played the technological advantages of large-scale operation with few of its organizational drawbacks. At its core were foundries and machine shops that cast and assembled stoves, sugar mills, steam engines, and the like for individual consumers and for boat yards, vehicle and implement makers, and other factories. Rolling mills in Cincinnati and its suburbs turned out hoops, sheets, and plates of wrought iron for blacksmiths, coopers, hardware factories, and tool makers. New enterprises fed on the skills developed in existing factories. As one example, the several firms that built almost two hundred locomotives during the railroad boom of the 1850s were run by businessmen who had previously operated foundries or ma-chine shops in the city. Many workers simply transferred from the old activity to the new.[12] As one of the city's first major industries, iron manufacturing employed over one thousand Cincinnatians in the 1830s. Twenty years later, the output of the various ironwork-ing establishments was worth perhaps $5 million, and the dozens of firms together employed about five thousand workers.[13]

By popular reputation, pork packing was Cincinnati's leading in-dustry. The central activities of killing and packing were themselves lucrative enough to allow profits to dozens of separately owned slaughterhouses and packing houses. During the hectic winter season, the industry employed over a thousand temporary laborers and scores of independent carters who hauled the live pigs and gut-ted carcasses. It also took much of the output of the city's several hundred tool makers and coopers. Other Cincinnati enterprises manufactured leather, brushes, glue, chemicals, lard oil, soap, and candles from the refuse of the industry. The demand for by-products enabled local packers to pay up to a tenth more for hogs than their competitors in other western towns.[14]

During the 1840s, meat packing itself grew as fast as western ap-petites. As roads and canals improved connections with the interior, the number of pigs pickled in Cincinnati rose from an average of 150,000 per year in the late 1830s to over 400,000 in 1848 and 1849. In the 1850s, however, the city's annual pack stablized near an average of 380,000 and entrepreneurs turned more and more to utilization of waste products. Hooves, hides, bristles, and viscera became so profitable that slaughterhouses paid ten or twenty-five cents for the right to clean each hog. By 1860, the manufacture of soap, candles, and lard oil, all made from fat rendered from the carcasses, ranked as the city's third industry in value of product.[15]

Cincinnati's highly competitive clothing business contrasted sharply with the internally cooperative packing interest. Output in the industry rose from perhaps $2 million at the start of the decade to an estimated $15 million or $16 million at its end, when Cincinnati turned out half the ready-made clothing produced in the West. In contending for a share of the expanding trade, the several dozen manufacturers were unable to lower raw material costs or to increase sales by product differentiation, for they bought their cloth from the same eastern factories and made standarized goods for a uniform and nondiscriminating market of farm hands, workers, and slaves. They competed by reducing labor costs. In the early and middle 1850s they employed five thousand or six thousand part-time seamstresses who worked long hours at home for appallingly low wages.[16] Their exploitation was so notorious that a short-lived effort to organize for higher wages in 1853 received at least verbal support from many of the city's leading citizens and several of its newspapers. In the later 1850s, clothing manufacturers achieved the same effect while somewhat raising wages by installing perhaps a thousand sewing machines kept in continuous operation by shifts of female workers.[17]

Despite their importance, these four industries accounted for less than half of Cincinnati's manufacturing output. Along with its foundries and chair factories, its sweatshops and shambles, the city boasted other million-dollar businesses in flour milling, boot and shoe making, printing, distilling, and production of finished foods. As Cincinnatians liked to point out, hundreds of small firms turned out finished commodities varying in size from watches to steamboats and intermediate products for other western manufacturers ranging from rectified alcohol and bagging to varnish and white lead. No unbiased observer could argue with the booster who wrote: "we make almost everything, and . . . claim to stand in the first rank of American manufacturing, as well from the variety and excellence of our fabrics, as from their aggregate annual value."[18]

The exact value of this aggregate is hard to determine, for figures available are contradictory. The various contemporary estimates can be divided into high and low series. The former indicates sales of $17,395,000 in 1841, $54,564,000 in 1851, $71,000,000 in 1855, and $112,259,000 in 1859.[19] The latter ranges from $7,848,604 in 1840 to $28,328,690 in 1849, $20,790,743 or $35,739,377 in 1850, $48,900,500 in 1858, and $46,436,648 in 1860.[20] The second series seems the more realistic. Its 1840 values are reasonable for a city where manufacturing had been developing steadily for only a decade. Its totals also show an expected decline at the end of the 1850s.

Even the relatively low census figures for Cincinnati manufacturing in 1860 gave the city a total output four times that of Chicago and an employment over five times as great. Local publicists also reflected the differing importance of manufacturing in the two cities. Chicagoans were pleased with their factories, but their descriptions were often defensive, with more pride in the potential for industrial development than in accomplishments. Cincinnatians, on the other hand, bubbled without restraint, searching for the wildest adjectives. They had no doubts that their town was "the manufacturing mart of the Great West," and only the eccentric doubted that it was destined to be the industrial capital of the Union.[21]

Cincinnati's commerce developed in close association with its manufacturing. Its large industrialists customarily sold their own carriages, furniture, machinery, and medicines directly to retailers throughout the West. Book publishers developed an elaborate system of distribution involving advertising, mail orders, and traveling agents, while the clothing industry was controlled by wholesale houses with branches throughout the West. The availability of so many different manufactures in the city also attracted customers for its importers of eastern and southern goods.[22] At the same time, much of Cincinnati's export of agricultural goods consisted not of raw products but of processed foodstuffs—whiskey, pork and pork products, dairy products, and flour.

Surprisingly enough, in view of the common image of Cincinnati as Porkopolis, meat, hogs, and lard furnished only 15 percent of total receipts and shipments by the middle 1850s. All indigenous agricultural commodities supplied only 34 percent of its imports and 40 percent of its exports. About 13 percent of its imports were groceries, 44 percent merchandise, and 9 percent manufactures. As about a quarter of the groceries and merchandise were consumed locally and as the city produced large amounts of manufactured goods for sale elsewhere, the figures for exports were 8 percent, 32 percent, and 20 percent respectively.[23]

Scattered data show that the annual value of agricultural exports rose from about $4 million in the late 1830s to $10 million in the late 1840s. From 1852 through 1856, the average receipt of agricultural goods was worth about $20 million and shipments about $16 million, the latter figure passing $20 million toward the end of the decade. Although there was little change in the share for pork and lard, the share for grain, flour, and whiskey gradually increased during the 1850s.[24] The real development of wholesaling came with the prosperity of the mid-1840s and reached a plateau in the early 1850s. Cincinnati merchandise wholesalers grew prosperous enough to establish agents in New York and New Orleans, while the construction of railroads in Indiana and Illinois expanded the city's market and enabled its grocery dealers to undersell Louisville and New York. Local writers welcomed the new age of wholesaling with enthusiasm, and local publishers issued the *Cincinnati Business Mirror* in 1851 and the *Cincinnati Wholesale Business Directory* in 1853, both of which were compilations of advertisements directed to western retailers.[25] Despite poor years in mid-decade caused by low water, poor sugar crops, and financial crises, Cincinnati's wholesaling through the 1850s kept pace with the growth of its export trade.

All of these increases in the 1850s came despite severe problems of capital and credit. The closure of four of Cincinnati's six chartered banks between 1852 and 1856 marked the virtual disappearance of incorporated institutions interested in local commercial needs. Two dozen private bankers and scores of exchange dealers took their place, many using funds sucked out of legal banking. Noted in 1851 as "an interesting feature in the growing commercial operations of our city,'' their capital quickly surpassed that of chartered banks and their loans were soon given credit for much of Cincinnati's growth. Although these institutions performed the necessary banking functions of holding deposits, furnishing exchange, and making loans and discounts, they charged uncontrolled interest and often preferred to finance speculation in pork, whiskey, and other agricultural goods rather than imports. Because the private banks issued no currency, the city depended on Indiana or Kentucky notes that bought exchange only at a high discount.[26] Through the 1850s the *Cincinnati Commercial* and the *Cincinnati Gazette,* the town's leading business-oriented papers, responded with constant complaints. The chamber of commerce likewise stated that ''every business man knows that the growth of our city, large as it is, has been materially retarded by the want of Banking capital.'' In fact, a portion of the western pork business was forced to other cities when Cincinnati packers were unable to obtain short-term discounts. Similarly, many Cincinnati manufacturers and wholesalers lost customers because they were unable to supply liberal credit.[27]

The city was also slow to develop other commercial facilities. Created in 1839, the chamber of commerce functioned within a narrow interpretation of its charter, which allowed it ''to collect information in relation to commercial, financial, and industrial affairs . . . to secure uniformity of commercial laws and customs, to facilitate business intercourse, and to promote . . . the adjustment of differences and disputes in trade.'' Its most useful activity through the 1850s was an annual review of trade, and not until 1861 did it attempt such a simple measure as the establishment and enforcement of uniform grades for flour. Facilities for handling goods were inadequate. Despite its dependence on riverboats, the city owned only fifteen hundred yards of public landing equipped with floating wharves and spent only five thousand dollars per year on its upkeep and supervision. The lack was especially severe because the dry goods and pork trades made their heaviest shipments in the spring, when high water submerged private docks.[28] The city's eastern and northern railroads lacked a common terminal or belt line and the Miami Canal had only a small public basin, giving an advantage to businesses in buildings along its length.

Chicago's commerce differed from Cincinnati's in its late start, its rapid growth, and its sophisticated organization. In the 1830s, the city had done little export business and imported largely for its own inhabitants. Over the next eight years, the value of its exports grew to $2,296,000 as more acreage in northern Illinois was brought into cultivation. In 1847, according to one estimate, seventy thousand teams arrived in the city from surrounding farms. The same wagons carried back much of the city's $2,641,000 of imported dry goods, groceries, hardware, and lumber. The small volume of trade was controlled by a few commission merchants, a few lumber yards, and dozens of retail stores.[29]

In the late 1840s and early 1850s, the opening of the Illinois and Michigan Canal and the completion of a railroad net across northern Illinois transformed Chicago's commercial situation and made possible remarkable commercial expansion. Corn exports rose in 1847 and the wheat trade boomed from 1846 through 1849. More permanent gains in agricultural business came in the 1850s. Corn shipments grew rapidly in the early 1850s and more slowly in the second half of the decade. Wheat and flour reversed the pattern, increasing gradually to 1853 and climbing thereafter like an ambitious politician. Annual shipments of grain and flour were on the average nine times as high between 1856 and 1860 as in the years from 1846 through 1850. Meat exports grew at a relatively even pace for a threefold increase during the decade.[30]

The lumber trade received its first real impetus with the opening of the Canal. Its greatest development came in the mid-1850s, when the settlement of the prairies created almost insatiable demand for fenceposts, rails, rafters, and siding. The number of dealers and the volume of shipments more than tripled between 1853 and 1857. Because the merchants held large inventories piled high on acre after acre along the Chicago River, the trade required large amounts of capital. To protect their investments, many dealers gained control of Michigan and Wisconsin mills by making advances on future production. Integrated firms were also established when Chicago merchants purchased mills and ships and when millowners opened their own sales outlets. A prosperous merchant might spend his winter directing Michigan mills, his spring arranging for the construction of new schooners, and his summer supervising and ex-

panding his Chicago lumber yard.[31] Unfortunately for many
dealers, however, the onset of depression sliced demand at the same
time that the construction of new mills sharply increased supply.
The plunge of prices ruined dozens of firms while total sales in
1858, 1859, and 1860 fell to three-fourths their peak level.[32]

Like the lumber business, Chicago's wholesaling was new in the
1850s. The completion of the canal and of the city's first railroads
transferred much of its retail trade to interior towns but "called into existence and sustained wholesale dealers" to supply the new
country stores. Throughout the 1850s, Chicagoans marveled at
rapid increases in hardware, grocery, dry goods, and clothing sales
and wondered: "Can we keep up with the demands made on us?"[33]
The city boasted a total wholesale trade of perhaps $40 million in
1859, about 30 percent in dry goods, 25 percent in groceries, 12 percent in clothing, and 8 percent in iron and hardware.[34] By the decade's end, several local wholesalers felt themselves in a position to
compete not only with Cincinnati and St. Louis, but also with eastern ports, claiming stocks of goods unsurpassed in the union and
dispatching salesmen through the West to drum up business and
undercut New York prices.[35]

Chicago's export commerce was the most complexly organized
branch of trade. In the 1840s, the growing business was carried on
by twenty or thirty commission houses that bought on contract for
eastern mills and merchants. Keeping pace with the volume of
trade, the number of export merchants in the city grew tenfold in
the next decade. Some of the three-hundred-odd dealers were general commission agents, who charged standard fees for transport-
ing a farmer's produce to coastal markets, finding buyers, and collecting payments. Others specialized as warehousemen, provision
brokers, produce forwarders, shipping merchants, or grain
dealers.[36] In accord with developments in other lake ports, many
began to buy directly on their own account, reselling to eastern and
foreign representatives in Chicago or filling eastern orders. Although some merchants continued to rely on credit from the eastern correspondents to whom they shipped their goods, others financed their purchases by local bank loans or by their personal
note. In the latter case, an interior bank usually bought the note at
a discount from the farmer and received payment from the dealer
once his produce had been sold at Buffalo or Oswego.[37]

Chicago merchants also enjoyed superior facilities for storage and transfer. Railroad spurs reached into the dozens of large lumber yards along the Chicago River to simplify handling. Several stockyards along rail lines in the outlying parts of the city served a parallel function. Livestock could be delivered directly to the yards and held until bought by packers or shipped east. The movement of through freight was expedited by the quarter loop of the St. Charles Air Line, which connected all the city's railroads, while railroad executives located all but one of the city's central depots along the river in order to speed the transshipment of goods between land and water. In pursuit of the same goal, the companies built several of the giant grain elevators that loomed over the city. Each of these citadels of commerce used steam-powered scoops and cranes to lift grain from freight cars on one side and delivered it by gravity to boats moored on the other. The typical establishment could empty an eight-car train of its 3,000 bushels in ten minutes and pour twelve thousand bushels into a waiting schooner in half an hour. During the winter or when shipping was scarce, the elevators could also store vast amounts of grain, the city's total capacity passing 5 million bushels in 1860. Immensely proud of this Chicago innovation, local writers attributed the city's triumph over St. Louis as a grain port to the efficiency of the dozen or more elevators. As one said, "the spectacle was almost pathetic, to behold a city without these elevators assuming to compete with Chicago for grain trade."[38]

Chicago's commercial institutions also aided the growth of export trade. Organized in 1848, the Board of Trade had served in its first years as an active pressure group backing the dredging of the Chicago harbor, the deepening of the Illinois River, and the improvement of lake navigation. After 1855, the Board altered its function, hiring a permanent secretary to prepare an annual review of commerce and purchasing telegraphic reports of eastern markets. It also began to enforce a grading system, which grew out of the technical requirements of the elevator system. Along with the Buffalo Board and similar associations in other lake cities, Chicago's merchants after 1854 participated in a campaign to convince New York buyers to accept grain by weight alone. Following an unsuccessful essay in 1856, the Chicago organization in 1858 defined wheat and corn grades, obtained the cooperation of most elevator owners, and appointed inspectors. Early in the next year, it obtained a new charter that made its inspection certificates legal evidence of grain ownership. In practical terms, grading removed the necessity of separate storage for lots of grain and allowed eastern buyers to purchase by telegraph, since there was no longer any need to inspect particular lots. By logical extension, the system facilitated trading in futures, since easterners could now buy and sell Chicago grain in the abstract rather than as a physical commodity. Although Chicago was already the site of considerable buying of wheat and corn "for future delivery," the new arrangements institutionalized the speculation and helped to make the city a haven for floating capital.[39]

Both Chicagoans and Cincinnatians were pleased with the growth of their wholesale business. In neither city, however, did publicists claim it a key role in local growth, focusing instead on trade in agricultural commodities. In the 1840s, Cincinnatians were convinced that they lived in "undoubtedly the largest provision market in the world." Early in the next decade, in contrast, writers turned fearful eyes to Chicago, which was beginning to call itself "The Greatest Primary Grain Port in the World," a contention it proved with elaborate tables comparing the shipments of Odessa, St. Petersburg, Riga, Danzig, St. Louis, and Milwaukee. Chicagoans thought their agricultural trade "almost incredible when the age of the town is taken into consideration" and agreed that the city's real growth depended not on manufacturing but on the development of its export commerce. Cincinnatians replied with tables demonstrating primacy for their town if whiskey, flour, and pork were reduced to a grain equivalent.[40]

A comparison of figures on the total value of trade in each city shows that Cincinnatians had good reason to feel threatened. Whereas Chicago's export and import trades each amounted to less than a tenth of Cincinnati's in the mid-1840s, they had climbed to roughly half the Queen City's levels by 1854. Each city exported about $20 million of agricultural products in 1858 and about $25 million in 1859. Both cities also distributed about $40 million of groceries, merchandise, and manufactured goods in 1859, although Chicago probably lagged slightly. Within these totals, Cincinnati exported almost four times the quantity of manufactured goods, while Chicago's good communications to New Orleans and New York gave it twice the grocery trade. As many of the Queen City's industrial exports were not included in published data, its shipments of manufactures were in fact much higher than the figures indicate. The two tons were roughly equal in shipments of flour and of livestock. Chicago, however, exported over ten times as much grain as Cincinnati, while the latter shipped ten times as much whiskey and almost twice as much meat.[41]

In contrast to the larger cities, neither Indianapolis nor Galena residents considered manufacturing an important part of their local economy. Important newspapers such as the *Indianapolis Journal, Indianapolis Sentinel, Galena Gazette,* and *Galena Courier* frequently clamored for the promotion of local industry, but they only occasionally praised its current development and never claimed manufacturing as an important source of their cities' prosperity.

The judgment of Indianapolis publicists seems to have been realistic. The few mills which survived the panic of 1837 operated with only a few hands and produced only a few thousand dollars' worth of flour, paper, lumber, or textiles.[42] The arrival of the Madison Railroad set off an industrial boom as entrepreneurs installed steam engines whose fuel could now be obtained at reasonable prices. As it developed during the next several years, Indianapolis manufacturing resembled that of Chicago in its varieties. Most of its factories and mills processed the agricultural products of nearby counties or furnished sawed lumber, furniture, machinery, and agricultural implements to local farmers and townspeople.[43] By 1853 and 1854, boosters pointed with pride to the "wonderful progress" of the last several years. Frequently enunciated hopes for continued growth drew little response, however, for the city commanded only small markets and its businessmen in the later 1850s were unable to raise capital to expand its existing plants or to prosecute successfully such ambitious projects as a large rolling mill. Although a new boom started in 1860, the city's two hundred establishments had an approximate annual output of a million dollars. Not until the Civil War did manufacturing assume an important place in the Indianapolis economy.[44]

In Galena, on the other hand, manufacturing was more important than contemporaries remarked. At the end of the 1830s, the town and its immediate neighborhood had counted perhaps twenty smelteries producing several million pounds of lead annually. The number of smelteries dropped by more than half in the next decade, but a number of large workshops and three factories using steam engines filled their place. The town produced lead, flour, whiskey, clothing, leather goods, and a whole range of consumer goods of iron and wood.[45] From these foundations Galena entrepreneurs expanded the city's industrial capacity in the 1850s. Apart from its flour mills and smelteries, it produced about $430,000 of manufactured commodities in 1853 and $460,000 in 1854. Clothing accounted for about a quarter of the output and hardware, iron, and farm implements for about half. The eighth Census confirmed that manufacturing had continued to grow in the later part of the decade. Excluding flour and lead, Jo Daviess County produced $690,000 of manufactured goods, a highly creditable showing for a town with less than half the population of Indianapolis.[46]

The commercial development of Indianapolis was also slow. The city's central location was initially a commercial disadvantage, since the farmers of middle Indiana normally wagoned their produce directly to the Wabash or the Ohio or floated it down the White River. In the early 1840s, the city had no specialized produce dealers and few retail establishments that were more than general stores.[47] However, the Madison and Indianapolis Railroad enabled the city to attract the exports of surrounding counties and allowed the establishment of a number of commission houses. The railroad between 1846 and 1848 reported an increase in southward freight amounting to twenty-four thousand barrels of flour, 200,000 bushels of wheat and corn, and a million feet of lumber, much of which must have come from the new connection at Indianapolis. Exports on the railroad showed an even larger increase in 1851 and 1852, years when the completion of lines north and west of the city expanded its commercial range. The number of hogs rose by seventy-five thousand, barrels of flour by seventy thousand, and bushels of grain by close to a million. In the unlikely case that all this increased trade was furnished by Indianapolis merchants, their export commerce in the early 1850s was worth $2,000,000 to $3,000,000, or about a sixth that of Cincinnati.[48] Indianapolis retailers also began to furnish goods for storekeepers outside Marion

County. By 1856 and 1857, perhaps as many as seventy retailers and forty manufacturers did at least some wholesaling, but no firms devoted exclusively to jobbing survived more than a few months. The total value of Indianapolis's import commerce for 1860 was erratically estimated at $400,000 and $1,200,000.[49]

Galena, of course, carried on an export commerce unique among western cities. In the 1830s, the entire mining industry and lead trade required almost no local capital. The miners themselves needed money only for tools and food, since they paid for the privilege of digging with a percentage of any mineral found. Smelters bought the ore they processed with a portion of their output or with advances from Galena merchants. Galena exporters depended in turn on advances from St. Louis or Alton. In 1840, Galena's seventeen commission houses reported an average capital of only five thousand dollars, while the establishment of a smeltery required at the most six thousand dollars.[50] During the next decade, growing capital enabled a number of Galena exporters to purchase lead on their own account and sell it for a direct profit. Other merchants used their accumulating wealth to establish banks or to purchase land and smelteries.[51] Despite such investments, mining itself remained underfinanced. It was done usually by groups of two, three, or four persons, many of whom dug ore only during the winter. Few holes were extended more than thirty or forty feet, because few enterprises could afford the steam engine necessary for draining deeper shafts.[52]

One consequence of this financial imbalance was a steady decline in Galena's mineral trade after 1847. Production plummeted, and the volume of exports fell to half the 1847–48 level by 1853–54. Because prices increased, the value of lead shipments fell more slowly, from $1,523,000 in 1848 to $1,300,000 in 1854. The total value of all exports, however, remained roughly constant, as the city shipped an increasing volume of grain, flour, and provisions. Worth only $75,000 in the mid-1840s, this trade was valued at $383,000 in 1851 and $619,000 three years later. In 1857, food exports neared the $1,000,000 mark and passed lead in value.[53] The shifting balance can be traced in the statements of Galena publicists. Barely noting the agricultural trade in the 1840s, they claimed an important but subordinate role for it in the early 1850s. In the later years of the decade, in contrast, they suggested that Galena could become the chief grain port on the upper Mississippi. At the same time, one paper referred to the commerce in lead as an activity of the past rather than the present and thought it a fit subject for a series of historical sketches.[54]

Even more important than agricultural exports in replacing Galena's declining lead trade was the development of wholesaling. In the mid-1840s, when the import commerce was confined to "the supply of the mining region and the pineries of Wisconsin," it was considered merely "an important branch" of the city's economy. During the next several years, however, the trade expanded with settlement along the upper Mississippi. Steamboat captains found it easy to pick up cargoes for upriver towns from Galena merchants, and publicists by 1853–54 claimed for the town the title of "Commercial Metropolis of the Northwest." The city reportedly received twenty thousand tons of goods worth $4,361,000 in 1853 and imported commodities valued at $2,888,000 a year later.[55]

As much of the output of Galena's manufacturing sector was sold to the same customers served by its importers, it seems unarguable that wholesaling had replaced the lead trade as the city's central activity by the early 1850s. Recognizing the shifting economic opportunities, many of its commission merchants had added wholesaling to their list of activities or had shifted entirely to importing. By mid-decade, the city had only a few export merchants but perhaps forty wholesalers or retailer-wholesalers.[56] Galena's import commerce of the 1850s was thus financed to a large degree by lead profits from previous years.

In addition to exporting manufactured goods and handling the trade of their surrounding territory, all of the cities under study furnished personal and professional services for westerners living outside their boundaries. In the two westerly cities this activity was of relatively minor importance. In 1839, a traveler to Galena noted some of the excitement one would expect in a mining center:

Walked along streets—examining main buildings among number a gaming house—where numbers are nightly and daily fleeced—Roulette—Pharo Bank—dice—Chip-Billiards, etc.—etc.—Many young men attend and are ruined—farmers even who come to buy land are lead into the snare and frequently lose much—Much vice and dissipation going on.[57]

In the next decade, Galena's vice resorts faded from sight as the city matured and adventurers left for the Sierra gold fields. Chicago's several colleges attracted a number of students from other parts of the West during these same years, but its many large hotels were used more by transient emigrants and travelers than by tourists.

Cincinnati, in contrast, was the West's leading intellectual center. Although it lacked distinguished institutions of higher learning, the city contained dozens of academies for young ladies and gentlemen, as well as "commercial colleges" that drew ambitious young men from throughout the region. Its publishing houses issued most of the books printed in the West, including millions of volumes of McGuffey's Eclectic Readers. Together with its numerous magazines and its dozens of newspapers, these firms attracted the region's established and aspiring writers. The city's size and the willingness of leading citizens to support cultural activities also assured the city a place on the itinerary of traveling entertainers.[58]

Recognizing these "many inducements for a sojourn within its limits," Cincinnati residents from time to time argued that their town could easily be a center for tourism. The city fathers were urged to build parks, establish public concerts, and plan festivals, while the body of citizens were encouraged to cultivate "the fine arts . . . healthful recreations . . . or refined amusements." With little effort, the city could be made a "Paris of the West," drawing westerners wishing to sample the cultural enticements of a big city and southerners hoping to escape the heat of summer. Although never as popular as Niagara Falls, the city's educational and recreational facilities indeed attracted hundreds of visitors each year, especially from the South. Some Cincinnatians claimed that the city's admittedly fine hotels and superior transportation made it a natural site for western conventions, but residents made little effort to attract such sessions. In 1850 and 1856, for example, its citizens largely ignored the state agricultural fair held near the city, giving it neither the verbal nor the financial support that such a fair received in other locations.[59]

Only in Indianapolis were service activities a vital part of the local economy. In its first decades, hotel owners, saloon keepers, and retailers looked forward to the $30,000 that lobbyists and legislators could be expected to spend during each meeting of the general assembly. Merchants made all debts payable at the time of the session, when hard cash was plentiful. As the state capital and the site of a federal land office, moreover, Indianapolis was the place where Hoosier lawyers gathered throughout the year to transact their most profitable business and swing their biggest deals. The economic base was further enlarged in the 1840s by the decision to build state schools for the deaf and the blind and a public hospital for the insane in its vicinity. Together, state expenditures for asylums, permanent officers, and public printing amounted to perhaps $200,000 per year in the 1850s.[60]

In the same decades, Indianapolis's central location and its excellent railroad system made it the place "where the delegates of the different benevolent societies converge twice a year, and the Legal, Medical, and Clerical Professions are frequently together in a body." In one month of 1865, for example, the city hosted the Indiana Medical Society and the General Conference of the Methodist Episcopal Church. In another, it held a meeting of the General Association of the old-school Presbyterians and a convention of Indiana Episcopalians. Although many of these meetings were considered newsworthy by out-of-town papers, the city's most important conventions were the fairs held six times before the Civil War by the State Board of Agriculture. Each year twenty-five thousand sightseers crowded the city's trains, packed its fifteen-odd hotels, and spent perhaps $100,000.[61]

Indianapolis was also a financial center for Indiana. Since the 1830s it had been the headquarters of the State Bank and in 1854 was proposed as the site for a "Union Bank" intended to support the currency of the state's other banks. Most of the state's free banks, though officially located in other towns, did their business through "agencies" in the capital. Several fire insurance companies transacted a statewide business from Indianapolis headquarters, and formal and informal business organizations normally convened there.[62]

Indianapolis's citizens were very aware of the importance of these service activities. To be sure, spokesmen denied that the city depended on state expenditures when it was challenged by jealous rivals. At all times, however, they regarded its public institutions with pride and frequently acknowledged that the removal of the government offices would bring disaster to many businessmen.

"Aut Caesar, aut nihil," wrote one editor. Contemporaries also recognized that its function as state capital aided the city by attracting railroads and drawing the attention of outsiders.[63]

One can conclude from the scattered discussions of Indianapolis industry, commerce, and services that the city served basically local needs. A metropolis like Chicago or Cincinnati had extensive relations with a quarter of the nation and the smaller city of Galena carried on specialized trades of regional or national importance, but Indianapolis provided professional and personal services almost entirely to Hoosiers. There was little about the size and character of its manufacturing, wholesaling, and commission businesses, moreover, to distinguish it from numerous other northwestern towns which served the needs of surrounding agricultural counties.

Because of the fragmentary character of published information for the antebellum decades, it is necessary to turn to the original census returns for 1850 and 1860 for systematic comparative data on the balance of pursuits in the four cities. Table 4 thus shows the distribution of employment in each city as obtained from random samples of all employed persons listed in the returns of the two censuses (Appendix A). Contrary to their specific instructions, some of the census enumerators in 1850 listed jobs for a number of women. Ten years later, the employment of all women fifteen years old or older was recorded along with that of men. To eliminate any inconsistency resulting from these variations in procedure, Table 5 shows the occupations of the employed males in the eight samples. Comparison with Table 4 shows no significant differences between the two sets of figures for 1850. For 1860, the figures for men are strikingly lower in personal services and slightly lower in consumer goods manufacturing, reflecting the importance of female domestics and seamstresses. The adjustment of the percentages to these differences makes the figures for males slightly higher in all other categories. Table 4 is most appropriate for comparisons among the several cities within a single year, as its figures represent a more complete sample of their labor forces. The information in Table 5 is more useful for illuminating changes in each town between 1850 and 1860, as its all-male samples are more directly comparable.

TABLE 4

Occupational Distribution of All Workers in Chicago, Cincinnati, Galena, and Indianapolis, 1850 and 1860 (percentage of total labor force)

	Transportation	Personal Services	Professional Services	Retailing	Commerce & Finance	Building Trades	Laborers	Clerks	Metal Goods Manufactures	Other Basic Manufactures	Food & Consumer Goods	Farming	Mining & Smelting	Illegible or Unknown
1850:														
Chicago	19.5	6.1	4.5	5.9	5.5	11.4	17.0	4.8	4.8	7.9	8.4	2.7	0.1	1.4
Cincinnati	5.2	7.0	3.9	7.1	5.0	12.0	21.9	3.9	8.1	6.0	17.8	0.6	—	1.0
Galena	10.9	6.6	4.8	4.1	7.5	9.1	16.4	5.6	6.7	5.3	16.9	0.5	5.5	—
Indianapolis	2.9	4.3	8.5	3.3	6.5	18.3	20.7	3.7	6.9	6.8	12.4	5.2	—	0.4
1860:														
Chicago	9.3	19.4	5.5	5.2	6.2	11.3	17.6	6.3	5.0	5.1	7.3	1.4	—	0.4
Cincinnati	9.5	12.9	3.6	7.2	3.4	8.8	14.5	4.8	6.8	6.5	21.2	0.5	—	0.4
Galena	10.6	19.6	3.5	5.5	6.4	7.2	7.6	4.3	2.7	6.0	15.1	2.8	8.5	0.3
Indianapolis	8.6	18.6	6.9	5.8	3.4	12.8	11.9	4.4	7.2	5.5	12.8	1.7	—	0.5

TABLE 5

Occupational Distribution of Male Workers in Chicago, Cincinnati, Galena, and Indianapolis, 1850 and 1860 (percentage of total labor force)

	Transportation	Personal Services	Professional Services	Retailing	Commerce & Finance	Building Trades	Laborers	Clerks	Metal Goods Manufactures	Other Basic Manufactures	Food & Consumer Goods	Farming	Mining & Smelting	Illegible or Unknown
1850:														
Chicago	19.6	5.3	4.4	5.9	5.6	11.6	17.2	4.9	4.8	8.1	8.4	2.8	0.1	1.4
Cincinnati	5.3	6.3	3.9	7.2	5.1	12.6	22.0	3.8	8.2	6.1	17.8	0.6	—	1.1
Galena	10.9	6.6	4.8	4.1	7.5	9.1	16.4	5.6	6.7	5.3	16.9	0.6	5.5	0.1
Indianapolis	2.7	3.9	8.5	3.5	6.3	19.0	22.3	3.3	5.5	6.8	12.5	5.6	—	0.3
1860:														
Chicago	11.0	6.8	5.5	6.1	7.2	13.4	21.0	7.5	6.0	6.0	7.5	1.6	—	0.4
Cincinnati	11.3	5.5	3.6	8.4	3.7	10.5	17.4	5.6	8.2	7.5	17.4	0.6	—	0.4
Galena	13.1	6.0	3.6	6.7	7.9	9.0	9.4	5.3	3.4	7.5	13.6	3.4	10.6	0.4
Indianapolis	10.1	8.2	7.1	6.6	4.1	15.2	14.1	5.2	8.6	6.2	12.2	2.0	—	0.6

Chicago and Cincinnati employment patterns differed sharply in 1850 (Table 4). The lake port had a significantly higher proportion of its workers in transportation, while the Queen City had significantly higher proportions of laborers, metal workers, and producers of consumer goods. Galena unsurprisingly had a number of workers associated with the mining industry, as well as in consumer goods manufacturing. In other manufacturing activities, in services, and in commercial pursuits it was near the average of the four cities. Indianapolis differed sharply from the others. The number of workers in transportation was significantly lower than in any of the other cities and the numbers in professional services and building were significantly higher. In retailing, personal services, and consumer goods its percentages were also significantly lower than those of Cincinnati.

Ten years later, Indianapolis still had a higher proportion of its workers in professional services and building than did Galena or Cincinnati and a lower proportion in mercantile pursuits. However, it no longer lagged in transportation, retailing, or personal service. Galena still had many mining workers but now trailed the other towns in metal workers and laborers and Cincinnati in food and consumer goods workers. Cincinnati and Chicago remained far apart in the relative importance of their consumer goods industries and their mercantile activities. Cincinnati was also startlingly lower than the other cities in the number of personal service employees.

The categories of Table 4 can be grouped to represent the manufacturing, commercial, and local service sectors of the cities' economies (Table 6). Although one would expect the larger cities to have been more dependent on local services, the figures show no discernible pattern. In both years, on the other hand, commerce was clearly more important in Chicago and Galena than in Cincinnati or Indianapolis. Manufacturing in Cincinnati also appears to have been significantly more important than in Chicago in 1850 and more important than in any of the other towns by 1860. It is interesting to note that its occupational structure resembled that of Poughkeepsie, a booming manufacturing town of fifteen thousand people in 1860. The percentage of Cincinnati workers in manufacturing was also roughly the same as in Philadelphia, another acknowledged industrial metropolis.[64]

TABLE 6
Distribution of Chicago, Cincinnati, Galena,
and Indianapolis Workers among Major
Functional Categories, 1850 and 1860

	Manufacturing[a]	Commerce[b]	City-Serving Activities[c]
1850:			
Chicago	21.1	29.8	23.5
Cincinnati	31.9	14.1	26.6
Galena	28.9	24.0	19.8
Indianapolis	26.1	13.1	25.9
1860:			
Chicago	17.4	21.8	36.9
Cincinnati	34.5	17.7	28.9
Galena	23.8	21.3	32.3
Indianapolis	25.5	16.4	37.2

[a]Metal Goods, Other Basic, Food and Consumer Goods Manufacturing.
[b]Transportation, Mercantile and Financial Activities, Clerks.
[c]Personal Services, Retailing, Building Trades.

Chicago and Cincinnati showed few alterations in occupational structure during the 1850s (Table 5). The only significant change in the former was a decline in the relative importance of transport workers. In the latter, the only significant changes were an increase in the importance of transportation and a decline in the percentage of laborers. For Indianapolis, on the other hand, a drop in the relative importance of farmers and an increase in the importance of personal services reveal that city's growing maturity, while sharp increases in transportation workers and metal workers reflect the arrival of railroads. Several statistically significant changes in Galena, including a fall in the importance of metal manufacturing and an increase in the importance of farming and lead mining, seem difficult to explain. The increase in retailing, on the other hand, was a change to be expected in a growing city.

One can also try to identify the export-oriented activities in each city by using data on employment patterns in combination with the procedures developed in community economic base studies. This method of analysis assumes that "basic urban functions involve the processing or trading of goods and the furnishing of goods and services for residents or establishments located outside the urban area." On this premise, it divides a city's economic activities among a "basic" category that includes all enterprises producing goods or services for purchasers living outside the city and a "nonbasic" category that embraces enterprises whose products are consumed within the city.[65]

The simplest method for defining a region's economic base involves a comparison of the distribution of workers in a city with the distribution of employment in the nation as a whole. The activities in which the city has more than its proportionate share of employment can be assumed to be those whose output is sold at least partially to outsiders.[66] Such a comparison of the distribution of all workers in the four cities with the distribution of nonagricultural and nonmining workers in the United States as a whole is given in Table 7. In 1860, all of the towns had more than their proportionate share of workers in personal services; and all but Indianapolis, which had not yet developed an extensive trade, had an excess in retailing. The percentages of merchants and clerks in all four towns were roughly equal to the national figure. Except for Indianapolis, the same was true of construction workers. The lack of a textile industry in the West caused the number of workers in "other basic manufacturing" to fall below the national level in all four towns. Only Indianapolis had professional employees who provided services for outsiders, and only Cincinnati had more workers in manufacturing than required for its own needs.

As could be expected when relatively large cities are contrasted with central places ranging in size from hamlets up, all four towns in 1860 exceeded the national average in transportation workers, retailers, and clerks, and all but Cincinnati in personal service workers. In professional services, only Indianapolis had its proportionate share of workers, and only Cincinnati had more than its share of workers in consumer goods manufacturing. Both Cincinnati and Indianapolis appear to have exported metal goods at the

TABLE 7

Comparison of Employment Structure in Chicago, Cincinnati, Galena, and Indianapolis with Employment Structure in United States, 1850 and 1860
(percentage of labor force)

	Transportation	Personal Services	Professional Services	Retailing	Commerce & Finance	Building Trades	Laborers	Clerks	Metal Goods Manufactures	Other Basic Manufactures	Food & Consumer Goods	Other
1850:												
United States (non-rural)	5.4	2.7	5.8	2.8	4.9	10.5	34.2	3.6	6.7	8.6	15.1	—
Chicago	19.5	6.1	4.5	5.9	5.5	11.4	17.0	4.8	4.8	7.9	8.4	4.2
Cincinnati	5.2	7.0	3.9	7.1	5.0	12.5	21.9	3.9	8.1	6.0	17.8	1.6
Galena	10.2	6.6	4.8	4.1	7.5	9.1	16.4	5.6	6.7	5.3	16.9	6.0
Indianapolis	2.9	4.3	8.5	3.3	6.5	18.3	20.7	3.7	6.9	6.8	12.4	5.6
1860:												
United States (non-rural)	4.8	15.8	6.9	3.1	4.3	8.4	25.1	4.0	5.0	5.6	16.8	—
Chicago	9.3	19.4	5.5	5.2	6.2	11.3	17.6	6.3	5.0	5.1	7.3	1.0
Cincinnati	9.5	12.9	3.6	7.2	3.4	8.8	14.5	4.8	6.8	6.5	21.2	0.9
Galena	10.6	19.6	3.5	5.5	6.4	7.2	7.6	4.3	2.7	6.0	15.1	11.6
Indianapolis	8.6	18.6	6.9	5.8	3.4	12.8	11.9	4.4	7.2	5.5	12.8	2.2

SOURCES:
City data from Table 6. United States data from United States Bureau of the Census, Special Reports, *Occupations at the Twelfth Census*, 1904, pp. liii-lxii.

same time they fell below the national figure in mercantile activities. Chicago and Galena, in contrast, had more than their share of merchants and bankers and fewer than their share of manufacturers, mechanics, and artisans.

All of this information substantiates the opinion that Cincinnati and Chicago had sharply contrasting economies, that Indianapolis was weak in its commercial sector and strong in professional services, and that commerce in general was vital to the growth of Galena. Such corroboration of contemporary testimony is an impressive indication of the seriousness of popular economic thought. In a region only a few decades removed from the forest, economic development was clearly a topic of central and overwhelming importance. With the entire future of the West so dependent on cities, it is not surprising that natives of the section paid careful attention to the details of urban growth. Although they delighted in grandiose forecasting, they were unwilling to indulge their taste to the degree that it interfered with the practical evaluation of factors concerned with their future well-being.

The descriptions of the four urban economies also suggest broader conclusions about the distribution of economic functions within the Middle West. Most striking is the ubiquity of manufacturing activity tied to the cities' basic trading function. Certainly the importance of flour mills, packing plants, lead smelters, and rolling mills confirms the common generalization that much of antebellum manufacturing involved the processing of primary products to facilitate the export process. In addition, other urban manufacturing involved the production of finished goods that would otherwise have been imported from outside the region. Galena, Indianapolis, and Chicago thus manufactured personal and household products, furniture, machinery, and other implements in small shops and larger factories for customers within their normal wholesaling hinterlands. In Cincinnati, with its more extensive manufacturing, industries such as clothing and publishing grew by supplying the city's import merchants with local rather than eastern goods, while the growth of the iron business and the packing business both involved the expansion of simple processing into the production of a wide range of finished goods. The experiences of these four antebellum cities thus appear to support the parallel arguments of Margaret Walsh and Edward Muller that secondary manufacturing for state or regional markets had developed an important role within the West by the 1850s.[67]

Service activities also developed with direct ties to commercial functions in three of the four cities. Galena thus served briefly as a recreational center for the mining district at the height of the lead trade. Chicago's transportation network made it an importer of settlers as well as merchandise, while Cincinnati's broader range of educational and professional services drew patrons as a reciprocal flow along the commercial connections established by its import business. Only in Indianapolis did an important economic function develop in isolation from the commercial-manufacturing complex. That city's service activity depended on its central location and its role as a political capital rather than on its trade connections, and local entrepreneurs were unable before 1860 to translate flows of travelers and information into the movement of goods for collection and distribution.

NOTES

1. *Chicago Democrat,* March 11 and 15, 1851; *Chicago Tribune, Review of Commerce* for 1851, in *Hunt's Merchants' Magazine* 26 (May 1853): 510; Everett Chamberlain, *Chicago and Its Suburbs* (Chicago, 1874), p. 64; David D. Griswold, *Statistics of Chicago, Illinois* (Chicago, 1843), p. 7; U.S., *Sixth Census of the United States: 1840, Compendium of the Enumeration of the Inhabitants of the United States,* pp. 302–9.

2. Cleaver, *Early-Chicago Reminiscences,* pp. 48–51; *Industrial Chicago* (Chicago, 1891–94), 3: 585; *Chicago Democratic Press,* December 18, 1852; *Gem of the Prairie,* November 16, 1850; *Chicago Democratic Press, Review of Commerce* for 1852, p. 8.

3. *Chicago Democratic Press,* December 15, 1853, May 20, 1854, February 19, 1855, March 14, 1856; William Bross, *Address before the Mechanics' Institute* (Chicago, 1853), pp. 4, 8.

4. The first figure is in Joel Matteson, Governor's Message to the Illinois General Assembly, January 10, 1853, in *Illinois Reports* (1853), p. 7. The second figure is in *U.S., Seventh Census of the United States: 1850, Statistical View of the United States,* p. 223. Both can be obtained by combining separate listings in the *Chicago Tribune, Review of Commerce* for 1851, p. 510, and the *Chicago City Directory for 1851* (Chicago, 1851), p. 257. The last two figures are from the *Chicago Democratic Press, Review of Commerce* for 1855, p. 49, and James D. Graham, *Report on the Harbors in Wisconsin, Illinois, Indiana, and Michigan,* S. Exec. Doc. No. 16, 34th Cong., 1st Sess., 1857, p. 40.

5. *Chicago Democratic Press, Review of Commerce* for 1854, pp. 29–54, for 1855, pp. 22–23, 33, 49, for 1856, pp. 33, 46.

6. *Chicago Times,* October 11, 1859; *Chicago Democratic Press,* April 28, 1857; *Chicago Tribune, Review of Commerce* for 1860, p. 37, for 1864, pp. 11–12; Chicago Board of Trade, *Report* for 1861, p. 97, for 1862, p. 32; *Chicago Democratic Press, Review of Commerce* for 1857, p. 47; *Chicago Press and Tribune, Review of Commerce* for 1859, p. 4; U.S., *Eighth Census of the United States: 1860,* Vol. 3, *Manufactures,* p. 87, Vol. 4, *Mortality and Miscellaneous Statistics,* p. xviii.

7. Charles Cist, *Cincinnati in 1841: Its Early Annals and Future Prospects* (Cincinnati, 1841), pp. 236–37; *Liberty Hall and Cincinnati Gazette,* December 2, 1841; *Proceedings . . . on the Subject of a Western National Armory,* p. 4; *Cincinnati Republican,* September 24, 1841; *Ohio and Mississippi Railroad: Its Vital Importance,* pp. 6–7; Charles Cist, *Sketches and Statistics of Cincinnati in 1851* (Cincinnati, 1851), p. v. Also see: Alphonso Taft, *A Lecture on Cincinnati and Her Railroads* (Cincinnati, 1850), p. 21; Cincinnati Chamber of Commerce, *Report* for 1850, p. 8; *West American Review* 1 (October 1853): 193; McCulloch, *Men and Measures,* p. 43, quoting a conversation with Alexander Ewing of Cincinnati, ca. 1850; *Cincinnati Price Current,* July 18, 1855; *Cincinnati Gazette,* November 2, 1854, January 1, 1858.

8. *Liberty Hall and Cincinnati Gazette,* May 2, 1844; *Cist's Advertiser,* March 25, May 13, 1846; Morgan Neville, "Returns for the State of Ohio," in U.S., Secretary of the Treasury, *Documents Relative to the Manufactures in the United States,* H.R. Exec. Doc. No. 308, 22d Cong., 1st Sess., 1832, p. 861; *Proceedings . . . on the Subject of a Western National Armory,* p. 18.

9. *The Cincinnati Miscellany* 2 (October 1845): 174; Wilfrid G. Richards, "The Settlement of the Miami Valley of Southwestern Ohio" (Ph.D. diss., University of Chicago, 1948), p. 55; James T. Lloyd, *Lloyd's Steamboat Directory and Disasters on the Western Waters* (Cincinnati, 1856), p. 119; Conclin, *River Guide,* p. 35; Ohio, Commissioner of Statistics, *Report* for 1857, p. 27.

10. *Hazard's Register* 6 (March 9, 1842): 144; Cincinnati Chamber of Commerce, *Report* for 1855, p. 21; Howard Eavenson, *The First Century and a Quarter of the American Coal Industry* (Pittsburgh, 1942), p. 400; Charles Mackay, *Life and Liberty in America* (London, 1859), 1: 199; J. Richard Beste, *The Wabash: or, Adventures of an English Gentleman's Family in the Interior of America* (London, 1855), 1: 181; *Cincinnatus,* 3 (January, 1858), frontispiece.

11. Cincinnati Chamber of Commerce, *Report* for 1850, pp. 9–10, for 1856, pp. 22, 25, for 1857, p. 25; Ohio, Commissioner of Statistics, *Report* for 1857, p. 27.

12. *Hunt's Merchants' Magazine* 13 (January 1850): 111; Cincinnati Chamber of Commerce, *Report* for 1857, p. 24; Edward D. Mansfield, "Cincinnati and Its Future," in George E. Stevens, *The City of Cincinnati* (Cincinnati, 1869), p. 75; *Proceedings . . . on the Subject of a Western National Armory,* pp. 8–10; John White, *Cincinnati Locomotive Builders, 1845–1868,* United States National Museum Bulletin no. 245 (Washington, 1965), pp. 10–11, 91–93, 117–21.

13. William G. Lyford, *The Western Address Directory* (Baltimore, 1837), p. 296; *Sixth Census, Compendium,* pp. 274, 278; Ohio, Commissioner of Statistics, *Report*

for 1857, p. 26, for 1858, p. 96; Andrews, *Report,* p. 711; Cincinnati Chamber of Commerce, *Report* for 1850, pp. 9–10, for 1856, p. 20.

14. Rudolph A. Clemen, *The American Livestock and Meat Industry* (New York, 1923), p. 97; Cist, *Cincinnati in 1851,* pp. 280–88, 358–61; *Liberty Hall and Cincinnati Gazette,* February 7, 1839; Cist, *Cincinnati in 1859,* pp. 261–64.

15. Cist, *Cincinnati in 1851,* p. 280; Cist, *Cincinnati in 1859,* p. 264; *Eighth Census, Manufactures,* pp. 453–56; Berry, *Western Prices,* pp. 223–28.

16. Cist, *Cincinnati in 1859,* pp. 363–64; Ohio, Commissioner of Statistics, *Report* for 1858, p. 96, for 1860, p. 25; *Cincinnati Gazette,* November 3, 1852; *Cincinnati Commercial,* April 7, 1853; *Eighth Census, Manufactures,* p. 454.

17. *Cincinnati Enquirer,* April 6, 1853; *Cincinnati Times,* April 5, 1853; *Cincinnati Commercial,* April 7, 1853; Ohio, Commissioner of Statistics, *Report* for 1858, p. 34, for 1860, p. 25; Cist, *Cincinnati in 1859,* pp. 363–64.

18. *Eighth Census, Manufactures,* pp. 453–56; Hall, *Commerce and Navigation,* p. 315.

19. Cist, *Cincinnati in 1859,* p. 344; Lloyd, *Steamboat Directory,* p. 119; *Cincinnati Gazette,* October 9, 1857; F. W. Hurtt, *Cincinnati Guide and Business Directory for 1857–1858* (Cincinnati, 1857), p. 18.

20. Andrews, *Report,* p. 711; *Western Quarterly Review* 1 (April 1849): 347; *Seventh Census, Compendium,* p. 241; Andrews, *Report,* p. 711; Ohio, Commissioner of Statistics, *Report* for 1858, p. 96; *Eighth Census, Manufactures,* p. 456.

21. *Chicago Tribune,* February 1, 1855; *Gem of the Prairie,* April 28, 1850; *Cincinnati Times,* February 20, 1857; *Cist's Advertiser,* January 4, 1848; Covington and Lexington Railroad, Sixth *Annual Report* (1855), p. 5.

22. *Cincinnati Price Current,* April 30, 1856; *Cincinnati Times,* February 20, 1857; Cincinnati Chamber of Commerce, *Report* for 1859, p. 15; Berry, *Western Prices,* p. 318; Walter Sutton, *The Western Book Trade: Cincinnati as a Nineteenth Century Publishing and Book-Trade Center* (Columbus, 1961), pp. 255–58.

23. Cist, *Cincinnati in 1851,* p. 262. Export percentages from *Reports* of the Cincinnati Chamber of Commerce and import percentages from the same source via Berry, *Western Prices,* p. 552.

24. Lyford, *Western Address Directory,* p. 295; *Monthly Chronicle* 1 (April 1839): 194; U.S. Patent Office, *Report* for 1847, H.R. Doc. No. 54, 30th Cong., 1st Sess., 1848, p. 646; Berry, *Western Prices,* pp. 165–73; Henry H. White, *Wholesale Prices at Cincinnati and New York,* Cornell University Agricultural Experiment Station Memoir no. 182 (Ithaca, N.Y., 1935), p. 8; Cincinnati Chamber of Commerce, *Reports.*

25. *Cincinnati Commercial,* March 29, 1852; Cincinnati Chamber of Commerce, *Report* for 1852, p. 8; *Railroad Record* 2 (September 28, 1854): 517; Berry, *Western Prices,* pp. 238–39, 335–37; Hall, *Commerce and Navigation,* pp. 319–20; *Cist's Advertiser,* January 25, 1848, February 13, 1850; *Cincinnati Gazette,* March 20, 1849; *Cincinnati Wholesale Business Directory for 1853* (Cincinnati, 1853); *Gray and Company's Cincinnati Business Mirror and City Advertiser, for 1851–52* (Cincinnati, 1851).

26. Cist, *Cincinnati in 1851,* pp. 89–91; Charles F. Goss, *Cincinnati: The Queen City, 1788-1912* (Cincinnati, 1912), 1: 179–92; *Cincinnati Commercial,* January 7, 1854; Cincinnati Chamber of Commerce, *Report* for 1853, p. 13; *Bankers' Magazine* 5 (August 1850 and May 1851): 169–70, 852, 8 (October 1853): 359, 9 (July 1854): 17–18, 11 (September 1856): 171–74; Berry, *Western Prices,* pp. 472, 481–82, 492, 498.

27. Cincinnati Chamber of Commerce, *Report* for 1852, p. 10. Also see: Sutton, *Western Book Trade,* pp. 239–42; White, *Locomotive Builders,* pp. 97, 115; Vernon D. Keeler, "The Commercial Development of Cincinnati to the Year 1860" (Ph.d. diss., University of Chicago, 1935), pp. 167, 181.

28. A. N. Marquis, *The Industries of Cincinnati* (Cincinnati, 1833), p. 69; Cincinnati Chamber of Commerce, *Report* for 1861, p. 27; *Report of the Committee Appointed by the City Council of the City of Cincinnati . . . at the Request of the Ohio and Mississippi Railroad Company* (Cincinnati, 1855); *Receipts and Expenditures of the City of Cincinnati* (Auditor's Reports), 1851/52 through 1859/60; *Report of a Special Committee appointed to examine into the Necessity and Cost of the Purchase of Additional Ground for Public Wharves in the City of Cincinnati* (Cincinnati, 1853), p. 4; *Cincinnati Gazette,* January 31, 1854; *Cincinnati Enquirer,* February 12, March 2, April 12, 1853, February 17, March 15, 1854; Mayor David T. Snellbaker, *Annual Message* (1854), p. 6.

29. *Chicago Democrat,* February 16, 1848; *Chicago Democratic Press, Review of Commerce* for 1852, p. 2; Bemsley Huntoon to Josiah Huntoon, December 15, 1857, Huntoon Collection, Chicago Historical Society; Erne Frueh, "Retail Merchandising in Chicago, 1833-1848," *Journal of the Illinois State Historical Society* 32 (June 1939): 164–68.

30. Chicago Board of Trade, *Report* for 1876, pp. 43–45; Andrews, *Report,* p. 219.

31. George G. Tunnell, "Transportation on the Great Lakes of North America," printed as "Statistics of Lake Commerce," H.R. Doc. No. 277, 55th Cong., 2d Sess., 1898, p. 96; *Industrial Chicago,* 3: 206, 250, 274, 307, 321, 373; Robert F. Fries, *Empire in Pine: The Story of Lumbering in Wisconsin* (Madison, Wis., 1951), pp. 79–82; Charles Mears Diary, 1856–60, Mears Volumes, Chicago Historical Society; Chicago *Democratic Press, Review of Commerce* for 1857, p. 22.

32. *Gem of the Prairie,* October 1, 1852; Chicago *Democratic Press,* October 1, 1852; Curtiss, *Western Portraiture,* pp. 45, 51; *Industrial Chicago,* 4: 304; *Chicago Democratic Press, Review of Commerce* for 1852, pp. 9–10, for 1853, p. 67, for 1854, pp. 15–16; Chicago Board of Trade, *Report* for 1858, p. 32, for 1859, p. 61, for 1860, p. 40.

33. *Chicago Democratic Press, Review of Commerce* for 1852, p. 18; *Chicago Democrat,* April 29, 1854, in Robert W. Twyman, "Potter Palmer: Merchandising Innovator of the West," *Explorations in Entrepreneurial History* 4 (October 1951): 60.

34. Chicago Board of Trade, *Report* for 1860, p. 56; *Chicago Tribune, Review of Commerce* for 1860, pp. 34–37; Colbert, *Garden City,* pp. 74–75.

35. *Chicago in 1860: A Glance at Its Business Houses* (Chicago, 1860); Guyer, *History of Chicago;* Twyman, "Potter Palmer," p. 68; *The Stranger's Guide and*

Hand Book to Chicago (Chicago, 1857), p. 33; Case and Co.'s Chicago City Directory for the Year Ending June 1st, 1857 (Chicago, 1856); Chicago Times, November 20, 1857, July 30, 1859; Chicago Democratic Press, Review of Commerce for 1856, p. 31; Chicago Tribune, January 21, 1861; Colbert, Garden City, p. 74; Chamberlain, Chicago and Its Suburbs, p. 64.

36. J.W. Norris, Norris' Business Directory and Statistics of the City of Chicago for 1846 (Chicago, 1846), p. 7; Chicago Tribune, December 28, 1850; Chicago Board of Trade, Report for 1859, pp. 9-27, for 1860, p. 104; Industrial Chicago, 4: 304; Pierce, Chicago, 1: 130.

37. Charles H. Taylor, History of the Board of Trade of the City of Chicago (Chicago, 1917), 1: 147; Thomas Odle, "The American Grain Trade of the Great Lakes," Inland Seas 9 (1953): 163; Thomas Odle, "Entrepreneurial Cooperation on the Great Lakes: The Origin of the Method of American Grain Marketing," Business History Review 38 (Winter 1964): 444-48; John V. Farwell, "George Smith's Bank," Journal of Political Economy 13 (September 1905): 591; Arthur Cunynghame, A Glimpse of the Great Western Republic (London, 1851), pp. 50-51.

38. Carl Abbott, "The Location of Railroad Passenger Depots in St. Louis and Chicago," Bulletin of the Railroad and Locomotive Historical Society, no. 120 (April 1969), pp. 33-36; Chicago Board of Trade, Report for 1860, p. 9; Chicago Magazine 1 (May, 1857): 274; Chicago Democrat, May 27, 1851; Chicago Tribune, Review of Commerce for 1851, p. 429; Chicago Democratic Press, February 3, 1855; [Patrick Barry], Inquiry into the Practicality, Benefit, and Means of Establishing Direct Western Trans-Atlantic Trade, by a Chicago Broker (Chicago, 1857), p. 4.

39. Industrial Chicago, 4: 265-68; Andreas, History of Chicago, 1: 582-84, 2: 325-26, 376; Pierce, Chicago, 2: 104; Taylor, Board of Trade, 1: 146-47, 185-92, 238, 242, 256; Guy A. Lee, "The Historical Significance of the Chicago Grain Elevator System," Agricultural History 11 (January 1937): 18-22; James E. Boyle, Speculation and the Chicago Board of Trade (New York, 1920), pp. 54-56.

40. Cist's Advertiser, April 1, 1846; Hall, Commerce and Navigation, p. 313; Chicago Democratic Press, Review of Commerce for 1854, pp. 11-12; Chicago Tribune, January 23, 1860; H. H. Warden to Sturgis, November 19, 1855, Warden Collection, Chicago Historical Society; Chicago Democrat, September 1, 1849; Stephan A. Douglas, quoted in Galena Courier, June 17, 1859; Cincinnati Chamber of Commerce, Report for 1855, p. 7, for 1858, pp. 4-5.

41. Cincinnati Chamber of Commerce, Reports; Chicago Press and Tribune, Review of Commerce for 1858, p. 36, for 1859, p. 34; John L. Peyton, A Statistical View of the State of Illinois, to Which Is Appended an Article upon the City of Chicago (Chicago, 1855).

42. Sixth Census, Compendium, pp. 290-97; U.S., Secretary of the Treasury, Report . . . Communicating Statistical Information in Relation to the Condition of the Agriculture, Manufactures, Domestic Trade, Currency, and Banks of the United States, S. Doc. No. 21, 28th Cong., 2d Sess., 1845, p. 380; Sulgrove, Indianapolis, pp. 13, 20, 116, 443-44.

43. Indiana Journal, May 8, 1849; "Historical Sketch," in Directory of the City of Indianapolis (Indianapolis, 1857), p. 44; Indianapolis: Its Advantages for Com-

merce and Manufactures, Published and Compiled by the Manufacturers and Real Estate Exchange (Indianapolis, 1874); *Indiana State Gazetteer for 1858-59,* p. 126; Sulgrove, *Indianapolis,* pp. 440-75.

44. *Indianapolis Journal,* August 5, 1853, February 21, April 7 and 20, 1854; *Indianapolis Sentinel,* April 18 and June 7, 1859; Samuel E. Perkins, "Address Delivered before the Marion County Agricultural Society," in Indiana, State Board of Agriculture, Fourth *Annual Report* (1854/55), p. 388. Two hundred firms are listed in *Indianapolis City Directory 1860-61,* pp. 287-88. *Eighth Census, Mortality and Miscellaneous,* p. xviii, lists an output of $780,000 for Indianapolis, while *Eighth Census, Manufactures,* p. 128, lists an output of $1,090,000 for Marion County.

45. U.S., *Sixth Census: 1840, Statistics of the United States of America,* pp. 346-47; *The Galena Directory and Miners' Annual Register for 1848-9* (Galena, 1849), pp. 40-41, 46; Illinois, State Census for 1845, in *Illinois Reports* (1846/47), pp. 65-71.

46. *Galena City Directory* (1854), p. 7; *Galena City Directory, 1855-56* (Galena, 1855); *Eighth Census, Manufactures,* p. 93.

47. Sulgrove, *Indianapolis,* pp. 14, 152, 444; Daniels, *Village,* pp. 16-17; *Sixth Census, Compendium,* p. 289; *Western Cultivator* 1 (January 1845): 18; Calvin Fletcher Diary, October 18, 1840, Indiana Historical Society.

48. Madison and Indianapolis Railroad, Eighth *Annual Report* (1850), p. 17, Eleventh *Annual Report* (1853), p. 24.

49. George W. Sloan, *Fifty Years in Pharmacy,* Indiana Historical Society Publications, vol. 3, no. 5 (Indianapolis, 1903), p. 333; Holloway, *Indianapolis,* pp. 89, 108, 368-87; William and Thomas Silver Business Papers, Indiana State Library; *Indianapolis Journal,* August 3, 1857; *Indianapolis: Its Advantages for Commerce and Manufactures,* p. 13; Dunn, *Greater Indianapolis,* 1: 345-46.

50. D.B. Morehouse to William Hempstead, October 16, 1835, January 23, April 26, May 1, 1836, William Hempstead Papers, Illinois State Historical Library; James T. Hodge, "On the Wisconsin and Missouri Lead Region," *American Journal of Science* 43 (1842): 41-42, 51-52; *Report of Walter Cunningham, Late Mineral Agent on Lake Superior,* S. Doc. No. 98, 28th Cong., 2d Sess., 1845, p. 5; "Journal of William R. Smith," *Wisconsin Magazine of History* 12 (March 1929): 318-19; *Sixth Census, Statistics,* pp. 346-47.

51. *Galena Gazette,* November 21, 1854; McMaster, *Upper Mississippi,* pp. 103-4; *Galena City Directory, 1858-59* (Galena, 1858), pp. 136-37; Theodore Rodolph, "Pioneering in the Wisconsin Lead Region," Wisconsin State Historical Society *Collections* 15 (1900): 342; J.D. Whitney, "Geology of the Lead Region," in A.H. Worthen (ed.), *Geological Survey of Illinois,* vol. 1: *Geology* (1866), p. 155.

52. *Scientific American* 7 (March 6 and April 3, 1852): 194, 226; James Percival, *Report of the Geological Survey of the State of Wisconsin* (1855), p. 91; Wagner and Scherzer, *Reisen in Nordamerika,* 3: 92-111.

53. *Galena City Directory* (1854), p. 8; *Galena City Directory 1855-56,* p. 1, 9-10; *Galena City Directory, 1858-59,* p. 139; *Western Journal and Civilian* 2 (August 1849): 340; *Hunt's Merchants' Magazine* 27 (August 1852): 229; "Letter from Thomas Melville, Secretary of the Galena Chamber of Commerce, February 27,

1844," in *Documents Showing the Annual Amount of the Trade and Commerce on the Upper Mississippi River,* S. Doc. No. 242, 28th Cong., 1st Sess., 1844, p. 7; U.S., Patent Office, *Annual Report* for 1850, H.R. Doc. No. 32, 31st Cong., 1st Sess., 1851, p. 563.

54. *Galena Directory,* 1847–48, p. 38; *Galena Jeffersonian,* November 16, 1852; *Galena Gazette,* January 18, 1856, December 6, 1858; *Galena Courier,* July 18, 1859, August 29–31, September 6–8, 1860.

55. *Galena Directory 1847–48;* Alexander Ziegler, *Skizzen einer Reise durch Nordamerika und Westindien* (Dresden, 1848), 2: 40–41; George B. Merrick, *Old Times on the Upper Mississippi* (Cleveland, 1909), p. 164; *Galena Gazette,* February 21, April 25, December 7, 1849, November 14, 1854, April 10, 1855; *Galena City Directory* (1854), pp. 7–8; *Galena City Directory, 1855–56,* pp. 10–11.

56. *History of Jo Daviess County,* pp. 619, 635, 649, 652; Chetlain, *Recollections,* p. 47; *Galena Courier,* March 19, 1858; advertisements in *Galena Directory 1847–48* and *The Northern Counties Gazetteer and Directory for 1855–56: A Complete and Perfect Guide to Northern Illinois* (Chicago, 1855).

57. Anonymous Manuscript Diary, 1839, Chicago Historical Society, p. 50.

58. *Cincinnati Gazette,* October 11, 1849; *Madison* (Ind.) *Banner,* January 14, 1850; Cist, *Cincinnati in 1851,* pp. 59–62; *The Cincinnati Miscellany,* 2 (September, 1845): 125; *Hazard's Register* 4 (January 13, 1841): 22; Sutton, *Western Book Trade,* pp. 68, 108, 184, 285; Louis L. Tucker, "Cincinnati—Athens of the West," *Ohio History* 75 (Winter 1966): 15–16.

59. *Liberty Hall and Cincinnati Gazette,* December 29, 1836, June 21, 1838; *Cincinnati Enquirer,* July 23 and August 3, 1852, March 29, 1857; *Cincinnati Times,* April 28, 1856; *Cincinnati Gazette,* January 9, 1857; Ohio State Board of Agriculture, Fifth *Annual Report* (1850), p. 26, Eleventh *Annual Report* (1856), p. 14.

60. Dunn, *Greater Indianapolis,* 1: 81; Holloway, *Indianapolis,* pp. 77–78; "Historical Sketch," in *Indianapolis Directory* (1857), p. 27; *Locomotive,* December 9, 1848; *Indianapolis Journal,* June 10, 1859.

61. *Locomotive,* July 25, 1857, February 11, 1860; Cincinnati *Commercial,* May 27, 1856; *Indianapolis Directory* (1855), p. 58; Holloway, *Indianapolis,* p. 95; *Indianapolis Journal,* October 23, 1852, October 8, 1858.

62. *Cincinnati Gazette,* July 18, 1854; *Bankers' Magazine* 12 (August 1857): 152; Stulgrove, *Indianapolis,* p. 230; *The Indiana Annual Register and Pocket Manual* (Indianapolis, 1846), p. 201.

63. *Indianapolis Journal,* September 29, 1853, June 10, 1859; *Locomotive,* March 8, 1851; Smith, "Address," p. 438; *Railroad Record* 2 (December 14, 1854): 693; *Indianapolis Sentinel,* March 14, 1855.

64. Clyde Griffin, "Workers Divided: The Effect of Craft and Ethnic Divisions Differences in Poughkeepsie, New York, 1850–1880," in Stephan Thernstrom and Richard Sennett (eds.), *Nineteenth Century Cities: Essays in the New Urban History* (New Haven, 1969), p. 55; Sam B. Warner, Jr., "If All the World Were Philadelphia: A Scaffolding for Urban History, 1774–1930," *American Historical Review* 74 (October 1968): 30–31.

65. Walter Isard, *Methods of Regional Analysis: An Introduction to Regional Science* (Cambridge, Mass., 1960), pp. 189-236; John alexander, "The Basic-Nonbasic Concept of Urban Economic Functions," *Economic Geograph* 30 (July 1954): 246-61; Charles Tiebout, "The Urban Economic Base Reconsidered," *Land Economics* 32 (February 1956): 95-99.

66. This procedure can easily be adapted to the present study, using Table 6 for the local employment ratios and computing national ratios from published census data. It is necessary, however, to exclude agriculture and mining from the overall United States employment total. As both activities were found almost exclusively outside cites and together accounted for about half of all workers, their inclusion would drastically lower the percentages for employment in services, commerce, manufacturing, and transportation. The calculation of the distribution of workers among the latter categories alone should provide a rough picture of the employment structure of the urban sector of the American economy, since they were functions to a large degree associated with cities or smaller central places.

67. Pred, *Urban-Industrial Growth,* pp. 167-77; Walsh, *Manufacturing Frontier;* Edward Muller, "Selective Urban Growth in the Middle Ohio Valley, 1800-1860," *Geographical Review* 66 (April 1976): 178-99. Cincinnati would appear to be an extreme case of the situation found by Muller in the smaller cities of the Ohio Valley after 1850, when "the factors of selective urban growth shifted from accessibility to local hinterlands for providing commercial services and agricultural processing industries to accessibility to wider regional and external markets for the support of secondary manufactures" (p. 181).

3

VALLEYS
OF UNEXAMPLED FERTILITY:
THE HINTERLANDS
OF CINCINNATI, CHICAGO,
INDIANAPOLIS, AND GALENA

Antebellum businessmen needed accurate knowledge of markets and hinterlands to complete their pictures of economic activity in the new cities of the Middle West. The preceding chapter described the sources of production and supply for goods and services in each city and analyzed the extent to which contemporaries understood their functional differentiation and economic bases. The present chapter poses the same questions about the geographical range of trade in goods, services, and ideas. It defines the size, spatial orientation, and economic capacities of the hinterlands of Cincinnati, Chicago, Indianapolis, and Galena, finding that characteristics of the trade areas can explain a number of differences in the speed and direction of economic development among the four cities. The analysis also concludes that articulate urban residents possessed clear understanding of the economic situation facing each city.

Two considerations are essential in any effort to define urban hinterlands. First, the area tributary to one city shades gradually into the commercial sphere of its neighbors. As many places trade with several towns simultaneously, the boundary between two contiguous hinterlands is seldom sharply marked. Moreover, the trade area of one city may nest within that of a more important metropolis. Hinterland boundaries thus represent zones of equilibrium between the commercial efforts of rival cities rather than absolute dividing lines. In a related point, it is important to remember that the trade area for every product and service is unique. As most activities of commercial centers can be grouped into the major and distinct functions of import and export trade, however, it is useful to define two separate hinterlands for every city. The import hinterland in the case of towns in the early Middle West was the area to which the town provided services, sold locally manufactured goods, and distributed merchandise and foodstuffs imported from the seaboard. The export hinterland embraced the areas that supplied agricultural products and minerals that the city's mills and merchants processed and shipped to markets elsewhere in the West or outside the region.[1]

As with the preceding discussion of urban economic bases, description of the import and export hinterlands of antebellum cities involves the use both of impressionistic testimony by contemporary observers and of available quantitative data. Certainly there was considerable attention to the dimensions of urban trade areas in antebellum writings. The evidence ranges widely from newspaper reports of the current week's trade to blunt assertions about the extent of a city's tributary area. Behind much of this discussion was an "imperialistic" vision of urban growth in which the commercial conquest of territory was viewed as the prime accomplishment.

Numerical data available in printed sources can supplement verbal descriptions of the Cincinnati and Chicago trade areas and help to measure both their size and shape. In each city, reviews of trade issued by newspapers and commercial organizations recorded the quantity of goods received in the city and listed the shipments by the various agencies of transportation. Such information on the volume of commerce in different directions gives a rough indication of the importance of the different sectors of a city's hinterland. It can be used in conjunction with data contained in annual reports of railroads and canals, which sometimes allow a crude estimation of the distance that a city's trading area extended in a particular direction. Especially useful are figures on the amount and destination of goods shipped from each town located along a transportation line; such data allow the demarcation of dividing points at which particular commodities tended to move in opposite directions like streams from a watershed. Some of these figures have previously been digested by A.L. Kohlmeier, T.S. Berry, and John G. Clark, while others have been analyzed specifically for this study (see Appendix B). Although historical geographer Michael Conzen has pointed out the practical problems in using these fragmentary data, they do provide a picture of middle western urban hinterlands similar to that which might have been available to a merchant or public official at the time.[2]

The trade areas for Cincinnati and Indianapolis and those for Galena and Chicago formed two discrete regions in the antebellum decades. Past mid-century, the central Northwest had two systems of internal circulation. In the 1840s, the Ohio and Erie, the Miami-Erie, and the Wabash canals connected Lake Erie with the Ohio River. Lesser canals and roads in Ohio and Indiana fed these major arteries. At the same time, the Illinois and Michigan Canal and the Wisconsin, Rock, and Illinois rivers tied Lake Michigan and its periphery to the upper Mississippi. A few muddy roads furnished the only overland contact between these two systems of transportation. The first railroads followed this pattern etched by canals and rivers. One network of tracks crossed lower Michigan from Lake Erie to Chicago and from there fanned out to the Mississippi. A second rail net sliced from Sandusky, Cleveland, and the upper Ohio across central Ohio and southern Indiana, reaching the river at several points from Cincinnati through Evansville. As late as 1854 these sets of railroads connected in only two places.

The separate transportation systems made Indiana and western Ohio an economic subregion and northern Illinois and southern Wisconsin a second such region. Merchants of Indianapolis, Cincinnati, and other towns of southern Ohio and Indiana traded with the South via the Ohio River, reaching it by the valleys of the Scioto, Little Miami, Great Miami, White, and Wabash rivers. Goods and travelers came from the East over the several canals to Lake Erie and by the Ohio from Wheeling and Pittsburgh. Northern Illinois and Wisconsin traded with the South via the Mississippi River and with the East by lake boats which loaded and unloaded at ports from Chicago to Green Bay. Most of the region's settlers arrived by lake steamer or by railway from Detroit.

The Cincinnati-Indianapolis subregion was thoroughly developed by 1840. Pioneers in the early decades of the century had occupied the fertile valleys north of the Ohio and filled much of the higher land flanking the Miami and White rivers and east of the middle Wabash. By the end of the 1830s, all of southern Ohio and most of south and central Indiana had at least eighteen persons per square mile, and early maps show that villages and towns elbowed each other for room and roads crisscrossed every county.[3] Over the next two decades, the fabric of settlement thickened as farmers cleared and plowed new land, as hamlets became villages and villages became towns. In 1850, seven southwestern Ohio counties and one Indiana county had more than half their area in improved farm land. Ten years later, the figures were fourteen and eighteen and a band of settled land containing roughly 1,250,000 people extended from the Scioto to the Wabash across southern Ohio and the middle of Indiana. A smaller crescent of heavily cultivated land curved from Maysville through Lexington to Louisville. Northwestern Ohio and northeastern Indiana counted an additional 470,000 inhabitants in 1860. Three quarters had arrived in the fifteen years since the completion of the Wabash, Wabash and Erie, and Miami Extension canals had made it economical to clear the swampy and heavily timbered land of the Maumee and upper Wabash basins. What in the 1830s had been "with few and inconsiderable exceptions . . . a wilderness" was now filled with a framework of towns, farms, and fences.[4] (See Maps 2 and 3.)

The intensely utilized land of western Ohio and central Indiana developed into one of the nation's first corn belts by the 1830s, with whiskey and hogs as related specialties. One Ohio editor in 1838 delimited a distinct corn and pork belt south of the National Road and west of the Scioto. A decade later, the president of Indiana's State Board of Agriculture warned that local farmers concentrated to a dangerous degree on corn and hogs. Perhaps in response to over-specialization, the cultivation of wheat increased sharply after 1850. Indiana's crop rose by 170 percent and the center of production in Ohio shifted from northeast to southwest. By 1856, four of the state's five leading wheat counties were in the Miami Valleys,

MAP 2   Improved Farmland in the Middle West, 1850

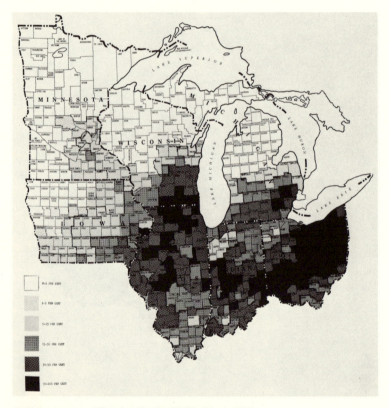

MAP 3   Improved Farmland in the Middle West, 1860

where the acreage in wheat almost equalled that in corn. Contemporaries continued to insist, however, that corn was still the "real staple" of the Ohio Valley.[5]

In the early 1840s, Indiana roads and rivers led away from Indianapolis and the town's export hinterland was measured in townships rather than counties. The situation changed with the arrival of the Madison railroad in 1847. As most of Indiana's surplus grain and pork was sold in New Orleans, counties south of the capital continued to ship directly to the Ohio. Produce from the region between Indianapolis and the Wabash, however, arrived in the Hoosier capital by wagon and rail for transfer to southbound freight cars. Maps of the frequency of stagecoach service also show a hinterland oriented toward the north.[6] The city's trade area extended at the most sixty or seventy miles north and northwest, and one contemporary stated that local merchants expected to control only the area within forty miles. Such a radius would have brought the Indianapolis hinterland roughly to the edge of the area trading through Fort Wayne and Toledo. The opening of the Indiana Central and the Bellefontaine and Indianapolis railroads in the mid-1850s offered new routes eastward. The diversion of trade from counties east of the city was probably balanced by new flows from the area between the city and the Wabash, and there was little basic change in its export hinterland before the Civil War.[7]

Like Indianapolis, Cincinnati in the 1840s shipped most of its agricultural exports through New Orleans, sending pork and whiskey to Atlantic cities, lard to Latin America, and provisions to the plantations of Arkansas, Louisiana, and Mississippi.[8] Whatever their destination, these exports came from a hinterland that local writers thought included equal parts of Ohio, Kentucky, and Indiana. More precisely, they asserted that "the region inseparably connected with, and dependent upon, Cincinnati, Newport, and Covington, as their great commercial and manufacturing mart, embraces the country bordering on the two Miami Rivers, the eastern parts of Indiana, and the adjoining parts of Kentucky, including the valley of the Licking River."[9]

Cincinnati merchants indeed monopolized the Miami country to the north during the years around 1850. The city received agricultural goods from towns as far north as Springfield over the Little

Miami Railroad. After the completion of the Miami-Erie Canal in 1845 enabled Toledo to compete for the exports of western Ohio, the town of Piqua near the head of the Great Miami River roughly marked the northern border of Cincinnati's hinterland. As Toledo controlled the trade of the upper Wabash, there was a clear division of exports by drainage basin. One Toledo spokesman considered the rivalry with Cincinnati to be part of a larger struggle between Ohio River and Great Lakes cities for the commerce of the entire Northwest.[10] Cincinnati was also the major market for the interior counties of southeastern Indiana. The construction of the White-water Canal in the early 1840s facilitated an already established trade and pushed the city's influence north to Muncie. In addition, Cincinnati's hinterland extended into the upper valley of the White River. One native of Rushville reported that his town's "Merchants, Market Men, and Hog Drovers were accustomed to trade in the Queen City."[11] In Kentucky, however, the city's trade area embraced only a narrow strip along the Ohio. The rich bluegrass region largely traded to the south through Louisville and to the east through Maysville. Only from the Licking and Big Sandy rivers did Cincinnati receive animals and foodstuffs throughout the antebellum decades. The city also handled produce from both sides of the Ohio as far upriver as Wheeling, but little from the interior of the Scioto Valley.[12]

The *Cincinnati Chronicle* made the most precise effort to summarize Cincinnati's export hinterland in the 1840s. An article in 1847 claimed that twenty-nine Ohio counties as far north as Shelby, twenty-one Indiana counties, twenty-six in Kentucky, and eleven in Virginia sent the bulk of their produce to be sold in Cincinnati or handled by Cincinnati merchants. These eighty-seven counties would embrace approximately the territories described in the preceding paragraphs (Map 4). The *Chronicle* figures are also compatible with the statement of historian A.L. Kohlmeier that Cincinnati in the mid-1840s drew its exports from an area stretching fifty miles south and west and one hundred fifty miles north and east.[13]

Railroad construction after mid-century altered Cincinnati's export hinterland and helped to account for the slowed growth of its agricultural trade. Since many of the first lines in southern Ohio and Indiana converged on the city, they tightened its hold on its

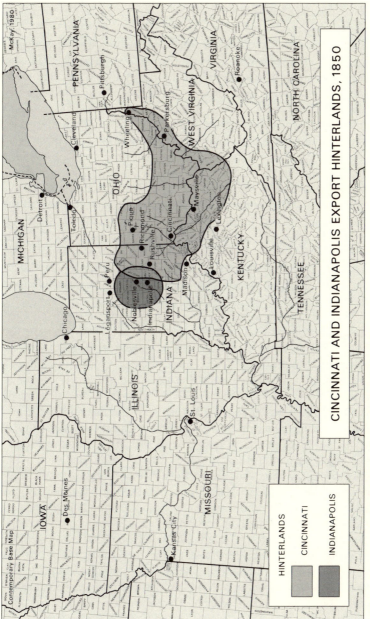

MAP 4 Cincinnati and Indianapolis Export Hinterlands, 1850

current trade area and extended its influence westward beyond Indianapolis and eastward toward the Scioto. Between 1852 and 1854, however, the completion of the Pennsylvania and Baltimore and Ohio railroads and their connecting lines in Ohio sharply changed the direction of trade. Cincinnati merchants began to send their flour, wheat, corn, and whiskey by rail to Baltimore and Philadelphia rather than by boat to New Orleans. The farmers of the upper Ohio likewise found it easy to ship directly eastward.[14] The Marietta and Cincinnati and the Cincinnati, Wilmington, and Zanesville railroads, which ran east-west across the Scioto Valley, hauled only trivial amounts of produce and provisions to Cincinnati markets. Even grain and flour originating along the Little Miami Railroad were carried directly to eastern buyers rather than to the Queen City.[15] At the same time, the northern boundary of Cincinnati's export hinterland shrank from Piqua to Dayton, a point just south of the through rail lines from Indianapolis to the East.[16]

This loss of Ohio trade meant that Indiana supplied an even larger portion of Cincinnati's exports in the 1850s than in the 1840s. Entrepreneurs trying to raise capital for railroad projects argued that southwestern and central Indiana supplied one-third to one-half of Cincinnati's total business and three-fourths of its receipts from north of the river. The Indianapolis and Cincinnati Railroad reported that the region between Indianapolis and Lawrenceburg depended on the Queen City to market its agricultural goods; tables of its freight traffic show that only a minute percentage of the agricultural commodities carried on the line were delivered to Indianapolis. About half the Cincinnati-bound goods delivered to the Cincinnati, Hamilton and Dayton Railroad by the Eaton and Hamilton lines also came from Richmond or beyond.[17]

Indianapolis through the antebellum decades thus lay on the edge of Cincinnati's export hinterland, a location that allowed little room for its own produce trade. In the early 1840s it lay just beyond the reach of the Queen City's roads and canals, and in the later 1840s the rail outlet at Madison put it temporarily outside the control of Cincinnati merchants. However, new railroads brought the two cities into closer contact after 1850. While citizens of the Hoosier capital chafed at their commercial subjugation, many of its agricultural exports found their way to Cincinnati over the direct line of the Indianapolis and Cincinnati road and indirectly by the Indiana Central to Richmond and the Indianapolis and Bellefontaine to Union.

The heyday of Cincinnati's import business came between 1845 and 1855. With Indiana and Ohio canals finished and the growing railroad net working for its wholesalers, the city distributed groceries and dry goods from New Orleans or the East within an area much vaster than its export hinterland. Cincinnati supplied not only the southwest quarter of Ohio but also the Scioto Valley and mining counties near the Ohio where the Cincinnati *Enquirer* had a large circulation.[18] The paper's advertisements and commercial information were read with equal interest by customers in eastern Indiana, the region which Cincinnatians thought was their biggest market for "foreign goods."[19] Wholesalers also shipped northward on the Cincinnati, Hamilton and Dayton Railroad and the Miami Canal. They sold most of this merchandise to the towns and farms of western Ohio but distributed some to Fort Wayne and the upper Wabash, where they fought for business with Toledo. Cincinnati furnished about one-fifth of the westbound freight on the Wabash Canal in 1850 and 1851 and about one-sixth in 1852 and 1853.[20]

At the same time that they reached northern Indiana by canal, Cincinnati importers did business with the lower Wabash Valley by river. Leaping over the immediate hinterland of Louisville, they carried groceries and dry goods as far upstream as Lafayette. The merchants and boats engaged in this trade may also have controlled merchandise shipments to counties along the lower Ohio and the lower stretches of the Tennessee and Cumberland. Directly to the south in Kentucky, in contrast, Cincinnati had to share the trade of the Bluegrass area with Louisville and Maysville.[21]

Cincinnati manufacturers traded even more extensively than its wholesalers. The city's factories drew lead from Missouri and Illinois, salt from Virginia and Pennsylvania, lumber from the Allegheny River, and coal from the upper Ohio. They also bought glass and nails from Pittsburgh and cooperage from southern Indiana and Ohio. The goods fabricated from these raw materials, said one editor, were sold throughout the 100,000 square miles between the Tennessee River and the Ohio-Lake Erie watershed. Another asserted that Cincinnati's industrial products were "found in every city, town, village, and hamlet, from Lake Superior on the north to the Gulf of Mexico on the south, and from the Allegheny Mountains on the east to the Indian Territory on the West." Others defined the trade area as a set of drainage basins (including those of the Miami, the Scioto, the Muskingum, the Kanawha, the Wabash, the Cumberland, the Tennessee, and the Mississippi) or claimed that it comprised a dozen or sixteen states. Within this vast area, Cincinnati writers singled out the "South" as their best customer. They meant in particular the parts of western Kentucky, western Tennessee, northern Mississippi, Arkansas, and southern Missouri that bordered the middle stretch of the Mississippi River and focused on Memphis.[22] Individual manufacturers confirmed these general statements, reporting time and again that they sold their products up and down the Ohio for 300 miles, through the Missisippi Valley, throughout the West and Southwest, or "from Mobile, Alabama, to Marietta, Ohio." Descriptions of individual industries also reported that building materials, books, clothing, and metal goods were taken by customers everywhere along the western rivers.[23]

Information in the annual reports of the Cincinnati Chamber of Commerce allows an approximation of the importance of the various sections of the city's import hinterland in the 1850s (see Appendix B). Between 1850 and 1853, 50 percent of its finished iron goods, 60 to 80 percent of its iron castings, and 90 percent of its "sundry manufactures" were shipped by river to points south and west of the city. Between 1854 and 1857, however, the pattern changed. By the last years of the decade, the southern market still bought 60 to 80 percent of Cincinnati's candles and 80 percent of its furniture but only 10 to 20 percent of its boots and shoes, 20 to 30 percent of its soap, and 30 to 50 percent of its iron goods.

While the lower Ohio and Mississippi valleys took most of Cincinnati's manufactures, the majority of imported merchandise went to the upper Ohio Valley. Canals and railroads carried 60 to 70 percent of all dry goods shipments, presumably to the interior of Ohio and Indiana. Slightly over 20 percent of shipments moved downriver, some to the Wabash, others to the Mississippi, Missouri, Arkansas, and Tennessee rivers. The remaining merchandise was shipped upriver to the mineral districts and to the terminals of eastern railroads. In addition, over 90 percent of the city's sales of molasses and 70 to 80 percent of its sales of coffee were made to points east and north.

The limits of Cincinnati's import hinterland can also be judged from data on the proportion of merchants in each western county who bought on credit at Cincinnati (Map 5). The information indicates the city's dominance in central Indiana and western Ohio and the importance of sales in eastern Ohio, as well as the manner in which the Wabash, Tennessee, and Cumberland rivers shaped its hinterland to the west. Several pockets within Cincinnati's extended trading sphere marked the immediate trading areas of Louisville, of Toledo, and perhaps of Pittsburgh and Wheeling. St. Louis and Chicago blocked Cincinnati from selling groceries and merchandise in the upper Mississippi Valley and western Illinois, but its manufactured goods found steady markets in the same area. As expected, 47 percent of Ohio merchants and 62 percent of Indiana merchants traded in the Queen City. In aggregate, Cincinnati's import hinterland lay equally to the west and east of the city. Of 16,220 merchants trading in the city, 6,578 lived in Ohio and in Kentucky northeast of the Kentucky River, while 6,550 lived in Indiana, Illinois, Tennessee, and southwestern Kentucky. Of the remaining merchants, 896 lived in the other states along the upper Mississippi and 586 in Alabama, Mississippi, Louisiana, and Arkansas. Because many planters dealt directly with Cincinnati factories, the latter figure probably underestimates the importance of the lower Mississippi commerce. On the whole, the data confirm Charles Cist's opinion that Cincinnati's wholesale trade "spread over the whole extent of country between the river Ohio and the lakes, north and south, and the Scioto and Wabash rivers, east and west. The Ohio river line of country in Kentucky, from fifty miles down, and as far up as the boundary line between the state and Virginia, makes it purchases here."[24]

These figures help to explain why the import trade of Indianapolis remained confined to roughly the same sector of Indiana as its export business. As early as the 1830s, Nicholas McCarty, a leading Indianapolis merchant, maintained three branch stores within half a day's ride of the city, another on the Wabash at Covington, and one at LaPorte. All except the last were within sixty miles of the

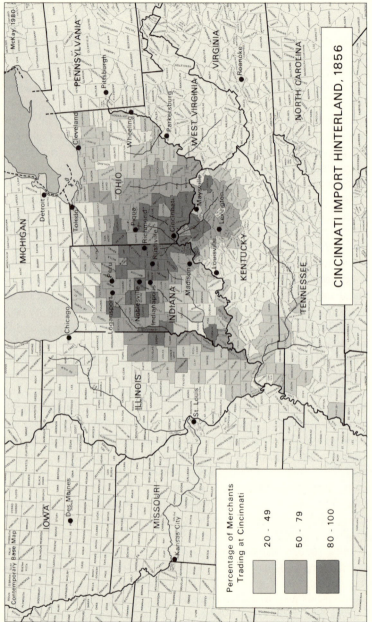

MAP 5 Cincinnati Import Hinterland, 1856

city, the maximum distance that its retail customers were normally willing to travel in the antebellum years. The Indiana legislature similarly included counties within fifty miles in the territory to be served by the Indianapolis Branch of the State Bank. Over the next two decades, the city's import trade grew slowly because its potential hinterland was confined by Cincinnati's sphere of influence. Located between eastern suppliers and Indiana buyers, Queen City merchants controlled the business of many Indiana retailers almost to the grounds of the statehouse and bypassed the city to serve markets along the Wabash. The numerous Cincinnati advertisements in Indianapolis newspapers and directories show that its businessmen expected large sales within the Hoosier capital itself. In competition with Cincinnati, Indianapolis in the 1850s continued to distribute imported goods only within a radius of fifty or sixty miles.[25]

If contemporaries considered the areas around Indianapolis and Cincinnati to be "finished" by the 1840s, they described the hinterlands of Chicago and Galena as part of "The Undeveloped Northern Portion of the American Continent." When the rich and well-cultivated valleys draining into the Ohio were entering their second generation of development, virgin timber and unbroken prairie still covered much of northern Illinois and Wisconsin and most of Iowa. One strip of settlement along the lower shore of Lake Michigan extended inland to the Fox River and north into Wisconsin at the start of the 1840s. A second band stretched southwest from Chicago along the Illinois River. Both sections had felt their first real growth in the boom of 1833–36, and recent emigrants still consumed most of the area's food. Not until 1843 did Chicago's *Prairie Farmer* report that northern Illinois offered a marketable surplus.[26] A third area of settlement was bounded roughly by the Mississippi, Wisconsin, and Rock rivers. As late as the mid-1830s, this region had counted thousands of prospectors but only a few dozen farmers working the bumpy hills and narrow valleys around the lead deposits.[27]

Throughout the 1830s and 1840s, of course, Galena's commerce in lead dwarfed any other trade. Oxcarts laden with newly smelted metal arrived regularly from forty and fifty miles away over the centrally focused road system (Map 6). In 1844, the *Gazette* estimated that 75 percent of the region's area and 70 percent of its smelteries were naturally tributary to the city. Only its northern and

MAP 6 Galena Hinterland, 1840-45 and 1854-58

eastern margins were independent of Galena's commercial facilities, for some of the mineral raised near the Wisconsin River was shipped by flatboat directly to St. Louis, and Lake Michigan ports made strenuous efforts to promote a cross-country wagon trade. Milwaukee in particular had high hopes in 1841 and 1842. Except for a few mines, however, the trade was too expensive for success, and as late as 1848 only one-twentieth of the lead was carted directly east.[28]

All of Chicago's interior trade moved by wagon during the same years. As early as 1834, the *Chicago Democrat* noted that food was "brought from a distance of 100 or 150 miles." Claims in the early 1840s that produce commonly arrived from 200 or 250 miles away seem doubtful, for it would have taken a loaded wagon ten days or more to cover the maximum distance.[29] Moreover, a hinterland stretching 250 miles in all directions would have taken Chicago's sphere of influence to the outskirts of Detroit, Cincinnati, Louisville, and St. Louis. More realistic estimates that few farmers drove for more than four days to reach the Chicago market are supported by the Chicago Directory for 1846, which stated that the city controlled the trade of the Rock, Fox, Des Plaines, Kankakee, and upper Illinois rivers.[30] All of these areas lay within 100 miles of Chicago and had road systems converging on the lake city (Map 7). The city also drew goods from the country lying between 100 and 200 miles southwest and south. Peoria and Springfield, for example, exported at least occasionally through Chicago, and the city's merchants reported business with farmers as far away as Vigo County, Indiana, and Clarke County, Illinois.[31]

Because Illinois's new farmers and townspeople required vast amounts of salt, cloth, tools, groceries, and other merchandise, Chicago's trade in imports developed more quickly than its export commerce. As the "commercial metropolis of Illinois and Wisconsin," Chicago dominated an import hinterland roughly congruent with its trade region for exports. The core of the area lay within 100 miles and its maximum radius was 150 miles. In addition, the city forwarded small amounts of eastern merchandise to all parts of Illinois, to points on the Mississippi, and to the Wabash Valley around Terre Haute.[32]

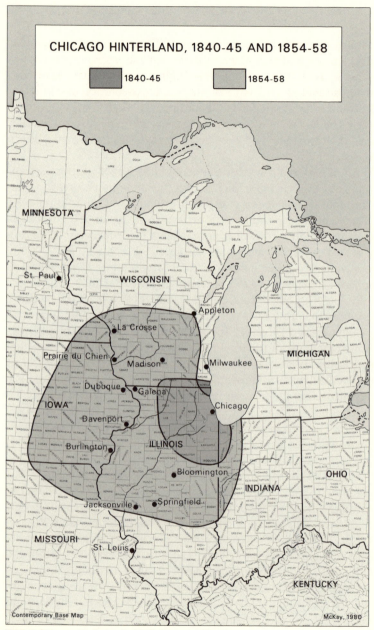

MAP 7 Chicago Hinterland, 1840-45 and 1854-58

After a pause during the depression of the early 1840s, Illinois and Wisconsin attracted new migrants with the return of prosperity and the opening of new transportation facilities. Because the first of these lines tapped areas that offered an agricultural surplus, they furthered growth in the sections already settled. The Illinois and Michigan Canal promoted farming along the Illinois River and the Galena and Chicago Union Railroad along the Fox Valley. When the interest in railroads became an enthusiasm in the early 1850s, however, tracks were also laid into the unoccupied Grand Prairie south of Chicago and into interior counties north and south of the Illinois River. The response to the opening of 2,500 miles of railway in the northern two-thirds of Illinois, in Wisconsin, and in Iowa between 1853 and 1857 was a land boom. The interior of the Illinois Military Tract between the Mississippi and the Illinois rivers, south central Wisconsin, and the parts of east central Illinois penetrated by the Illinois Central all experienced an explosion of speculation and settlement. The amount of land under cultivation in Wisconsin doubled between 1850 and 1857, and it was said of Illinois by the end of the decade that "its hamlets are becoming towns, its towns cities, and its vast prairies occupied and cultivated by a most substantial and respectable farming population."[33] The entire area between the Illinois and Wisconsin rivers had at least eighteen persons per square mile in 1860, with sectors of denser population still evident along the Illinois River and Lake Michigan. The region had attained a degree of agricultural development comparable to that of Cincinnati's hinterland. Only a few counties had less than 30 percent of their area fenced or cultivated and close to a score near the Illinois-Wisconsin border had more than half their acreage improved.

Settlers discovered the lands north and west of Galena in the same decade. The city's immediate hinterland of three Illinois and three Wisconsin counties had added 50,000 residents in the 1840s. This growth was dwarfed after 1850 when an immense tide of migration jammed the ferries into northeastern Iowa and raised the state's population by 350 percent. Another prong of settlement reached up the Mississippi through western Wisconsin into Minnesota, an area with fewer than two inhabitants per square mile at the start of the boom. In the mid-1850s, the latter state was the site of feverish speculation in farm lands and town lots, and a growing steamboat fleet was still unable to cope with the new traffic along the upper river. Although the boom came to a sudden halt in 1857, emigrants had already raised the total population of northwest Wisconsin, northeast Iowa, and Minnesota from 50,000 to 400,000.[34]

Agriculture expanded as rapidly as population. Because it required little capital investment, winter wheat was the first crop for many western farmers. From 1848 through 1851, poor crops forced a switch to other grains or to stock raising. Improved connections to Chicago simultaneously allowed middle Illinois largely to abandon wheat for corn, a change reflected in the hundredfold increase of Chicago's corn exports between 1847 and 1854. Many farmers also experimented successfully with spring wheat, and the increase in foreign demand during the Crimean War set off a second boom. Insects and rust caused several bad years toward the end of the decade, but an exceptional yield in 1860 restored faith in the crop.

The results of these developments were the appearance of a corn belt reaching from the middle Wabash across the Sangamon Valley and the lower Military Tract into southeastern Iowa and the development of a wheat belt in southern Wisconsin and northern Illinois. The latter region stretched into the Driftless Region along the Mississippi and toward the Military Tract, but the ten northern counties of Illinois still raised 45 percent of the wheat grown in the two states in 1859.[35] The predominance of wheat and flour and the lesser importance of meat among Chicago's exports were natural results.

The major effect of the railroads was to double the reach of Chicago's export hinterland (Map 7). It was probably correct at the end of the 1850s to measure its hinterland 150 miles to the south, 100 or 150 miles north, and 250 or 300 miles west. The area included large sections of Illinois, Wisconsin, and Iowa, all of which were thought "necessarily and unavoidably" tributary to Chicago, and small parts of Indiana, Michigan, Minnesota, and Missouri.[36] To the south, more particularly, the new facilities increased receipts without significantly enlarging the radius of trade. Mattoon on the Illinois Central and Springfield on the Chicago and Alton marked lower limits of influence, while the lower Illinois Valley shipped grain either to Chicago or St. Louis depending on market conditions.[37] To the northwest, in contrast, railroads brought new tracts of country under Chicago's influence. Its chief competitors here were the Wisconsin towns of Sheboygan, Racine, Kenosha, and Milwaukee, whose commercial connections pushed the northern boundary of Chicago's export hinterland inland from Lake Michigan.[38] Although Wisconsin railroads enabled these rivals to gain much of the wheat and flour trade of central Wisconsin in the middle fifties, the completion of the Chicago and North Western at a right angle across these lines allowed Chicago merchants to regain export business from areas as far north as Appleton. After 1853, the combined wheat and flour shipments of all the Wisconsin cities remained considerably below those of Chicago.[39]

Further west, the construction of the several Illinois railroads brought a dramatic shift in the fortunes of Chicago and St. Louis. Through the 1840s, St. Louis handled the trade of Illinois, Iowa, and Wisconsin counties accessible by river. Merchants and bankers in St. Louis supplied necessary commercial services and credit, and the city was a break-of-bulk point for trade with the upper Mississippi. It did more trade than Chicago as late as 1852, and during the remainder of the decade confidently promoted facilities for water-borne commerce while neglecting railroads. The initial work on Chicago's own rail system in the 1850s tightened that city's grip on the Rock River country and gave many of the market towns in the Military Tract their first contact with Chicago merchants. New lines to Rock Island in 1854, to Dunleith, Fulton, and Burlington in 1855, and to Quincy in 1856 gave Iowa farmers their first choice of produce markets. By 1856 and 1857, Burlington and Davenport sent most of their grain and flour to Chicago, although St. Louis still received most of Iowa's pork and bacon. In the last years of the decade, the construction of feeder railroads in Iowa and northern Missouri further increased this trade and allowed Chicago in the space of five years to rob St. Louis of roughly half its hinterland.[40]

Figures in the reports of the Galena and Chicago Union and the Chicago, Burlington and Quincy railroads clearly demonstrate the increasing importance of these western portions of Chicago's hinterland (see Appendix B). The portion of the Burlington's eastward freight contributed by stations along the eastern part of its line fell in the late 1850s, while the portion originating west of the Illinois River and at the river ports of Burlington and Quincy increased. The proportion of the Galena railroad's eastbound freight coming from its branches to Freeport and northern Wisconsin similarly decreased, while the proportion from its river terminus at Fulton rose sharply. Taking the two lines together, the volume of freight originating in the river towns increased not only relatively but absolutely between 1857 and 1859, even though economic depression cut total business. Since the Rock Island railroad generally paralleled the Fulton branch of the Galena and Chicago Union and the more northerly line of the Burlington, its freight presumably followed the same pattern.

The relative importance of the several sectors of Chicago's export hinterland in the years immediately before the Civil War can be judged from published figures on total receipts of agricultural goods by its different lines of transportation (see Appendix B for data on selected products). These data show that the editor of the *Democratic Press* was correct in claiming that his city drew the bulk of its exports from the area between Lake Michigan and the Mississippi.[41] Between 1857 and 1861, 55 percent to 85 percent of the city's flour, wheat, corn, cattle, and hogs—products that together constituted about three-fourths of the value of Chicago's exports—arrived by the canal or railroads running between the Illinois River and the Wisconsin border. A tenth to a fifth of this amount originated in Iowa (see Table 10, Appendix B). The remaining receipts divided roughly evenly between railroads running south of the Illinois River and lines into eastern Wisconsin. The contribution of eastern Illinois increased as the lands along the Illinois Central were settled in the mid-1850s. That of eastern Wisconsin rose sharply after the completion of the Chicago and North Western.

The expansion of the western rail net simultaneously increased Chicago's hinterland for imports. By 1860 there was a close correspondence between the areas buying from Chicago wholesalers and the areas selling through its commission merchants. In 1852, the *Democratic Press* stated that Chicagoans sold to country merchants in Peoria and Fulton counties and within a few miles of the Mississippi. The next year it remarked that the city was capturing import business from St. Louis. The same paper circulated in some volume as far south as Jacksonville, Springfield, and Decatur. The opening of the Rock Island Railroad in 1854 further increased the city's customers on the upper Mississippi.[42] Such towns as Dubuque and Burlington received the bulk of their merchandise and manufactures from the Garden City by the middle of the decade, and a Chicago guidebook could say in 1857 that "the great North Western territory, embracing Iowa, Wisconsin, Minnesota, and our own state is now the great field which invites the stocks . . . of our enterprising City Merchants."[43]

The growing importance of the upper Mississippi trade is again confirmed by data on the Galena and Burlington railroads, which delivered an increasing share of their westbound traffic to Fulton and Quincy (see Appendix B). The actual quantity of imports received at the river towns also rose at the same time that the amounts received in eastern Illinois plunged and the amounts received in western Illinois remained steady. In addition, the Illinois Central annually delivered several million tons of merchandise and manufactures to the river at Dunleith.[44] Both the pattern and the trend of Chicago's import trade with western Illinois and Iowa in the later 1850s resembled those of its export commerce with the same areas.

Chicago's lumber trade served a considerably smaller territory, for weight and bulk made the product costly to transport. Most of the lumber shipped by the Illinois and Michigan Canal was used in the Illinois Valley. The area between that river and the Wisconsin border accounted for 80 percent of Chicago's sales in 1857 and 60 percent three years later (see Appendix B). Boards were also carried in growing volume as far south as Mattoon on the Illinois Central and as far east as Plymouth, Indiana, on the Pittsburgh, Fort Wayne, and Chicago. As the Chicago and North Western ran toward the Wisconsin pineries, that line carried lumber only a few miles north of Chicago. The competition of wood floated down the Mississippi from the St. Croix Valley of Wisconsin likewise limited the city's trade to the west through the mid-1850s. By the end of the decade, reductions enabled Chicago dealers to compete on even terms with merchants on the Mississippi and to make occasional sales to points across the river.[45]

As the development of Illinois and Iowa aided Chicago wholesalers, new settlement along the upper Mississippi triggered a brief expansion of Galena's hinterlands (Map 6). Around mid-century, the city drew flour and wheat from the Mississippi and Wisconsin rivers. Local wholesale houses retained customers in the lead region and also extended their influence north into the Wisconsin Valley, east to Rockford, and south to Rock Island. Galenians claimed that the city was the depot for the area west of Madison; and at least one merchant at Portage, on the upper reaches of the Wisconsin River, bought goods from a dozen different Galena businessmen. The city also enjoyed customers west of the Mississippi, perhaps as far south as Davenport and certainly as far north as St. Paul. Almost half the steamboats leaving Galena in 1855 were bound for St. Paul and another third to towns above St. Louis. Ulysses S. Grant, the city's best known though not most successful merchant, reported an experience typical for the 1850s: "I traveled through the Northwest considerably during the winter of 1860–61. We have customers in all the little towns in southwestern Wisconsin, southeast Minnesota, and north-east Iowa."[46]

Galena's grip on this enlarged hinterland depended on its isolation from Lake Michigan. The arrival at the Mississippi of the Illinois Central in 1855, the Milwaukee and Mississippi in 1857, and the La Crosse and Milwaukee in 1858 abruptly terminated Galena's natural hold on the commerce of the upper river. As the railroads adjusted their rates to compete with Mississippi steamers, the new connections allowed Wisconsin towns to trade directly with Lake Michigan markets and made Dubuque, Prairie du Chien, and La Crosse equal competitors with Galena. By the end of the 1850s, Galena's wholesale houses had lost the business of the Rock River country and of the lead region itself. Simultaneously, the railroads turned much of the lead business toward Chicago. Where Galena's slowly sagging export totals in the early 1850s had been the result of declining production, the collapse of trade after 1855 was a function of the new transportation facilities. By 1857 only two-fifths of the lead was marketed through Galena almost half of this shipped east by the Illinois Central rather than downriver.[47] The halving of St. Louis lead receipts between 1852 and 1857 reflected the change. An editor the *Galena Jeffersonian* described the new order:

Our trade is draining into the lakes, even from the shores of the Mississippi and beyond. The river is becoming a mere tributary to the lakes. Our large river towns are threatened with a ruinous diversion of their business and capital—with being a part of the circumference, instead of the centers of trade. Goods brought by way of the lakes can be sold quite as cheap at Madison or Mineral Point as goods brought by the river can be sold at Galena. . . .[48]

In short, Chicago's hinterland had absorbed Galena as the great fish had swallowed Jonah. Like the prophet, Galena could still lament its condition, but the trade remaining to its merchants was for the most part not profitable enough to interest the metropolis of the lake. Barring a miracle, the city's future held promise of digestion within the belly of the whale.

Expansion and shrinkage in the size of the hinterlands of the four cities accounts for many of the differences in their relative prosperity. Dissimilarities among the major resources of their trading spheres explain other obvious differences in their development. In the heart of the middle-western corn belt, Cincinnati exported corn whiskey and corn-fed hogs. Chicago's position on the edge of the wheat belt similarly made it the great emporium for wheat and flour. In a more general view, however, the agricultural products offered by the four hinterlands were remarkably similar by the 1850s. As Chicago drew millions of bushels of corn from the Illinois Valley, wheat replaced corn on hundreds of farms around Cincinnati and Indianapolis. At the same time, the spread of wheat culture along the upper Mississippi added flour and grain to the exports of Galena.

More of the variation among the cities stemmed from differences in the timing of settlement. The delayed development of the region south of the great bend of the Wabash partially explains the smallness of Indianapolis's import and export trades. Aspects of Galena's development are likewise attributable to the age and speed of growth of its hinterland. The town's expansion in the decade after 1845 was a direct result of the boom in Iowa, Wisconsin, and Minnesota. Until the mid-1850s, its hinterland added more territory to the north and west than it lost to the south and east. Galena's growing difficulties also arose in part from its commitment after 1845 to developing a new trade with a new hinterland. In the scant decade before the appearance of competition from more easterly cities it was unable to establish permanent commercial connections in a region marked by rapid change.

Of the larger cities, Cincinnati entered the 1840s with a hinterland already settled and developed, while Chicago held control of largely unsettled territory. Because years of settlement in Ohio and Indiana had led to the creation of excellent facilities for water transportation, the arrival of railroads brought only a slight initial reduction in costs and opened little new land in the area tributary to the Queen City. In northern Illinois and Wisconsin, on the other hand, rails and freight cars replaced dirt tracks and plank roads and drastically lowered the costs of transportation west of the city. The newness of Chicago's hinterland also explains why its import trade so greatly exceeded its export business before 1845, for new settlers required fencing, clothes, plows, and tools before producing a surplus of foodstuffs. In the next fifteen years, the opening of new farms placed an ongoing demand on Chicago importers and mechanics for the same basic goods. Cincinnati's long-settled hinterland had more sophisticated needs for fabricated goods. To fill the orders of Mississippi Valley factories, planters, and merchants, Cincinnati manufacturers produced in greater and greater variety. Whereas Cincinnati in 1840 had been a commercial city that supplied some of its own trade goods, it was a manufacturing city that handled its own sales by 1860.

If the definition of trade areas helps to explain fluctuations and specializations in the economic growth of Cincinnati, Chicago, Indianapolis, and Galena, it also confirms the broad knowledge with which western urbanites approached their economic environment. Descriptions of the several hinterlands have been based on three types of data—general statements by journalists and boosters; specific testimony about their own businesses by factory owners, merchants, and railroad officials; and scattered quantitative data on trade by railroad, canal, river, and lake. Each type of evidence confirms the others, and it is clear that correct information was in general circulation. Few residents of these cities performed the more precise calculations found in statistical reports, but the livelihood of transportation agents, commission merchants, importers, and commercial reporters depended on knowing where the city could buy and sell. Businessmen knew which valleys shipped through their town and which bought their products, which counties were commercial battlegrounds and which lay within the sphere of other cities. Publicists addressing a more general audience also relied on accurate data. Although occasional boosters indulged in the luxury of inflated claims, most took pains to base their projections of future development on undistorted definitions of current hinterlands.

NOTES

1. Otis D. Duncan et al., *Metropolis and Region* (Baltimore, 1960), p. 257; Robert E. Dickinson, *City and Region* (London, 1964), p. 227; Harold Mayer, "Urban Geography," in Preston James and Clarence Jones (eds.), *American Geography: Inventory and Prospect* (Syracuse, N.Y., 1954), p. 148; Harlan Gilmore, *Transportation and the Growth of Cities* (Glencoe, Ill., 1953), pp. 95–97.

2. Michael Conzen, "A Transport Interpretation of the Growth of Urban Regions: An American Example," *Journal of Historical Geography* 1 (1975): 362–64.

3. Flint, *Mississippi Valley,* p. 381; *Liberty Hall and Cincinnati Gazette,* April 4, June 6, 1839; Richards, "Miami Valley," pp. 23, 31, 35, 41; James Hall, *The West: Its Soil, Surface, and Productions* (Cincinnati, 1848), pp. 64–67; Taft, *Cincinnati and Her Railroads,* pp. 18, 48; *Map of Ohio and Indiana* (Philadelphia, 1836).

4. Ohio, Canal Commission, *Report* for 1824, in *Public Documents Concerning the Ohio Canals* (Columbus, 1829), p. 124. See also *Map of Ohio and Indiana; New Map of the State of Ohio* (Philadelphia, 1853); Randolph Downes, *Canal Days,* Lucas County Historical Series, vol. 2 (Toledo, 1949), p. 91; Roger van Bolt, "The Indiana Scene in the 1840s," *Indiana Magazine of History* 47 (December 1951): 353; Harry Scheiber, "State Policy and the Public Domain: The Ohio Canal Lands," *Journal of Economic History* 25 (March 1965): 100–112. From data published in the 1850 and 1860 censuses, the author has constructed maps showing the proportion of the total area in each county in the western states occupied by improved farm land, or land "cleared and used for grazing, grass, or tillage." (Maps 2 and 3.)

5. Gallagher, "Ohio in 1838," pp. 9–10; Indiana, State Board of Agriculture, Second *Annual Report* (1852), p. 5, Sixth *Annual Report* (1857), p. 280; Ohio, State Board of Agriculture, Twelfth *Annual Report* (1857), p. 20; Ohio, Commissioner of Statistics, *Report* for 1858, pp. 15, 69–70, for 1861, pp. 14, 61–64; Percy W. Bidwell and John I. Falconer, *History of Agriculture in the Northern United States, 1620–1860* (New York, 1941), pp. 321–22, 332, 435–38; *Cincinnatus* 3 (September 1858): 406.

6. Holloway, *Indianapolis,* p. 69; Daniels, *Village,* pp. 72, 77–78, 82; Kohlmeier, *Old Northwest,* pp. 89, 196; John G. Clark, *The Grain Trade in the Old Northwest*

(Urbana, Ill., 1966), pp. 149–50; Richard S. Fisher, *Indiana: In Relation to Its Geography, Statistics, Institutions, County Topography, Etc.* (New York, 1852), p. 31; *Indianapolis Sentinel,* June 19, 1851; Conzen, "Growth of Urban Regions," p. 371.

7. *Indianapolis Sentinel,* October 31, 1846, quoted in Daniels, *Village,* p. 35; Charles Poinsette, *Fort Wayne During the Canal Era, 1828–1855,* Indiana Historical Collections, vol. 46 (Indianapolis, 1969), p. 239; Clark, *Grain Trade,* p. 149; Kohlmeier, *Old Northwest,* p. 203. Of twenty-five towns whose flour mills traded largely through Indianapolis, all lay within forty miles of the city *(Indianapolis Sentinel,* November 11, 1857).

8. Drake and Mansfield, *Cincinnati in 1826,* p. 76; William A. Mabry, "Ante-Bellum Cincinnati and Its Southern Trade," in David K. Jackson (ed.), *American Studies in Honor of William Kenneth Boyd* (Durham, N.C., 1940), p. 78; William F. Switzler, *Report on the Internal Commerce of the United States,* H.R. Exec. Doc. No. 6, 50th Cong., 1st Sess., 1888, pp. 203–5.

9. Drake, "Cincinnati at the Close of 1835," p. 28. Also see: Cist, *Cincinnati in 1841,* p. 76; Drake and Mansfield, *Cincinnati in 1826,* p. 99; *Proceedings . . . on the Subject of a Western National Armory,* p. 4.

10. Ohio, State Board of Agriculture, First *Annual Report* (1846), p. 4; Little Miami Railroad Company, Fourth *Annual Report* (1846), p. 59; Kohlmeier, *Old Northwest,* pp. 56, 89, 120, 154, 195; Andrews, *Report,* p. 705; Elbert J. Benton, *The Wabash Trade Route in the Development of the Old Northwest,* Johns Hopkins University Studies in Historical and Political Science, vol. 21 (Baltimore, 1903), pp. 100–105; *Toledo Blade* quoted in *Western Journal and Civilian* 12 (August 1854): 379; Jesup W. Scott, "Westward the Star of Empire," *DeBow's Review* 27 (August 1859): 129.

11. Elijah Hackleman Memoirs, Hackleman Scrapbook No. 2, Indiana Historical Society; Calvin Carpenter Letterbook, Carpenter Manuscripts, Ohio Historical Society; *Report of the President to the Stock-Holders in the Cincinnati and White-water Canal Company* (Cincinnati, 1840), pp. 17–19; *Indiana Gazetteer* (1849), pp. 37–38.

12. *Cincinnati Price Current,* June 23, 1852; Taft, *Cincinnati and Her Railroads,* pp. 47–48; *Cincinnati Gazette,* August 21, 1850; *Cincinnati Chronicle,* June 25, 1845; Freight Book of Steamboat Caledonia, 1859–60, Inland Rivers Collection, Cincinnati Public Library; Clark, *Grain Trade,* 243; Ben Cassaday, *History of Louisville from Its Earliest Settlement Till the Year 1852* (Louisville, 1852), pp. 234–40.

13. *Cincinnati Chronicle,* quoted in *Cist's Advertiser,* May 25, 1847; Kohlmeier, *Old Northwest,* p. 54. As the nation's largest pork market, Cincinnati in the 1840s had a more extended export hinterland for hogs and pork. According to one authority, swine were driven to the city from farms as far as 200 miles away. The same article asserted that 50 percent of the hogs raised within 300 miles of the Queen City were packed in Cincinnati and 30 percent were packed elsewhere but sold by its merchants. *Cincinnati Gazette,* quoted in Hall, *Commerce and Navigation,* pp. 186–87.

14. *Cincinnati Commercial,* November 24, 1852; *Cincinnati Price Current,* March 15, 1854; Clark, *Grain Trade,* pp. 217, 222–24; Berry, *Western Prices,* pp. 87–91; Fishlow, *Railroads,* pp. 290–92; Kohlmeier, *Old Northwest,* pp. 210–12; *Cincinnati Gazette,* August 30, 1859.

15. John Pixton, *The Marietta and Cincinnati Railroad, 1845–1883,* Pennsylvania State University Studies, no. 17 (University Park, Pa., 1966), p. 28; Cincinnati, Wilmington and Zanesville Railroad, Seventh *Annual Report* (1857/58), p. 16; Erasmus Gest, *Receiver's Report on the Cincinnati, Wilmington and Zanesville Railroad* (1859), pp. 16–17; Little Miami Railroad Company, Fifteenth *Annual Report* (1857), pp. 32–33, Eighteenth *Annual Report* (1860), pp. 44–45.

16. *Cincinnati Commercial,* September 14, 1859; Indianapolis *Journal,* April 11, 1856; Kohlmeier, *Old Northwest,* p. 204.

17. Cincinnati, Hamilton and Dayton Railroad Company, Second *Annual Report* (1852), p. 8; Cincinnati and Indianapolis Junction Railroad Company, Third *Annual Report* (1855/56), p. 8; *Report on the Conditions and Prospects of the Cincinnati and Chicago Railroad* (Cincinnati, 1854), p. 9; *Locomotive,* September 27, 1851; Indianapolis and Cincinnati Railroad Company, *Annual Reports* for 1857–58; Eaton and Hamilton Railroad Company, Third *Annual Report* (1855), pp. 26–27; *Railroad Record* 25 (May 25, 1854): 194.

18. Little Miami Railroad Company, Fifteenth *Annual Report* (1857), pp. 32–33, Sixteenth *Annual Report* (1858), pp. 30–31; *Cincinnati Enquirer,* September 11, 1852; Wilbur Stout, "The Charcoal Iron Industry of the Hanging Rock Iron District," *Ohio Archeological and Historical Quarterly* 42 (January 1933): 49.

19. Cist, *Cincinnati in 1841,* p. 49; *Cincinnati Gazette,* August 25, 1854, April 14 and 30, 1856, October 9, 1857; *Cist's Advertiser,* September 14, 1847.

20. *Toledo Blade,* August 13, 1847; *Cincinnati Chronicle,* April 21, 1843; Heffner and Chappel Account Book (1851–52), Cincinnati Historical Society; *Cincinnati Gazette,* September 27, 1849; Kohlmeier, *Old Northwest,* pp. 126–27; Harry Scheiber, *Ohio Canal Era: A Case Study of Government and the Economy* (Athens, Ohio, 1969), pp. 222–23.

21. *Western Tiller* 2 (January 15, 1830): 161; *The Cincinnati Directory and Advertiser for 1831* (Cincinnati, 1831), pp. 206–7; Flint, *Mississippi Valley,* pp. 356–57; *Monthly Chronicle* 1 (May 1839): 243; *Liberty Hall and Cincinnati Gazette,* April 18, 1839; *Cincinnati Gazette,* November 26, 1855; *Cincinnati Price Current,* April 30, 1856; *Lafayette* (Ind.) *Courier,* December 11, 1850; Lawrenceburg and Upper Mississippi Railroad Company, *Exhibit* (New York, 1851), p. 4.

22. Cincinnati Chamber of Commerce, *Report* for 1851, p. 41, for 1856, p. 19. Also see: *Railroad Record* 1 (April 28, 1853): 103; 4 (October 23, 1856): 545; *Memorial . . . in Relation to a National Armory West of the Alleghenies,* pp. 112–13; *Ohio and Mississippi Railroad: Its Vital Importance,* p. 4; Cist, *Cincinnati in 1841,* p. 49; Edward D. Mansfield, *On the Railway Connections of Philadelphia with the Central West* (Philadelphia, 1853), pp. 16–17; Hall, *Commerce and Navigation,* pp. 243–44, 304; *Cincinnati Enquirer,* October 12, 1856, November 17, 1858; Ohio, Commissioner of Statistics, *Report* for 1857, p. 41; *Cincinnati Gazette,* October 13, 1854.

23. See the replies of Cincinnati firms to questionnaires in U.S., Secretary of the Treasury, *Documents Relative to the Manufactures in the United States,* H.R. Exec. Doc. No. 308, 22d Cong., 1st Sess., 1832, pp. 867–72, and in U.S., Secretary of the Treasury, *Report* for 1845, pp. 831–38.

24. Cincinnati Chamber of Commerce, *Report* for 1856, pp. 4–6; Cist, *Cincinnati in 1841,* p. 49; *DeBow's Review* 24 (March 1858): 215; *Sketch Book of St. Louis* (St. Louis, 1858), pp. 77–94; Cincinnati *Times,* May 10, 1857; *Railroad Record* 6 (March 4, 1858): 15; *Ohio and Mississippi Railroad: Its Vital Importance,* pp. 17–18.

25. Sulgrove, *Indianapolis,* p. 99; Sloan, "Fifty Years in Pharmacy," p. 340; William F. Harding, "The State Bank of Indiana" (M.A. diss., University of Chicago, 1895), p. 11; Sawyer and Company Account Book, 1862–63, Indiana State Library.

26. Harlan H. Barrows, *Geography of the Middle Illinois Valley,* Illinois State Geological Survey Bulletin, no. 15 (1910), p. 86; Carl O. Sauer, *Geography of the Upper Illinois Valley,* Illinois State Geological Survey Bulletin, no. 27 (1916), pp. 152, 163; William V. Dooley, *The Settlement of Illinois from 1830 to 1850,* Bulletin of the University of Wisconsin, no. 220, History Series, vol. 1, no. 4 (Madison, Wis., 1908), pp. 379–432, 562–72; A.D. Jones, *Illinois and the West* (Boston, 1838), p. 187 and map; *Prairie Farmer* 3 (April and October 1843): 79, 218.

27. *Map of the United States Lead Mines;* "Narrative of Morgan L. Martin," p. 398; Rodolph, "Wisconsin Lead Region," pp. 343, 362; Pooley, *Settlement of Illinois,* pp. 427–38; *Galena Jeffersonian,* December 1, 1845; McMaster, *Upper Mississippi,* p. 108; "Letter of Thomas Melville," p. 4; "Journal of William R. Smith," p. 312; Schafer, *Wisconsin Lead Region,* pp. 137–39.

28. Schoolcraft, *Summary Narrative,* pp. 562–63; Rodolph, "Lead Region," pp. 342, 377; *Galena Gazette,* January 26, 1844; Trewartha, "Driftless Hill Land," pp. 132–37; *Hazard's Register* 5 (August 1841): 100; Orin G. Libby, "Significance of the Lead and Shot Trade in Early Wisconsin History," Wisconsin State Historical Society *Collections* 13 (1895): 306–23.

29. George Brown, letter, August 28, 1843, George Brown Collection, Chicago Historical Society; D.C. Hall to Dudley Hall, October, 1839, Hall Collection, Chicago Historical Society; *Chicago American,* quoted in *Hazard's Register* 5 (October 1841): 247; *Chicago Democrat,* June 18, 1834, quoted in Goodspeed and Healy, *Cook County,* 1: 105.

30. *Hunt's Merchants' Magazine* 18 (February 1848): 165; James Warnock to William Prentiss, October 19, 1848, Warnock Collection, Chicago Historical Society; Norris, *Business Directory,* p. 18; Jones, *Illinois and the West,* p. 187; *Chicago Journal,* October 13, 1845; Cleaver, *Early-Chicago Reminiscences,* p. 51; J. Seymour Currey, *Chicago: Its History and Its Builders* (Chicago, 1912), 1: 331.

31. Wright, *Chicago,* p. 72; *Prairie Farmer* 2 (September 1842): 77; *Hazard's Register* 5 (October 1841): 262; John M. Peck, *New Sectional Map of the State of Illinois* (New York, 1856).

32. *Chicago Journal,* September 15, 1844; *Western Literary Journal* 1 (September 1836): 247; *Chicago Democrat,* February 17, 1834, December 30, 1835; John Mason Peck to Alexander Grant, February 17, 1834, Peck Collection, Chicago Historical Society; *Chicago Democratic Press, Review of Commerce* for 1853, p. 42–43.

33. Theodore L. Carlson, *The Illinois Military Tract: A Study of Land Occupation, Utilization and Tenure,* Illinois Studies in the Social Sciences, vol. 32, no. 2 (Urbana, Ill., 1951), pp. 97, 100, 109, 117; Pooley, *Settlement of Illinois,* pp. 312, 391–95, 412, 418, 421, 562; John G. Thompson, *The Rise and Decline of the Wheat Growing Industry in Wisconsin,* Bulletin of the University of Wisconsin, no. 292, Economics and Political Science Series, vol. 5, no. 3 (Madison, Wis., 1909), p. 41; Margaret B. Bogue, *Patterns from the Sod: Land Use and Tenure in the Grand Prairie, 1850–1900,* Collections of the Illinois State Historical Library, vol. 34 (Springfield, Ill., 1959), p. 17; quote from *The Illinois Central Railroad Company Offers for Sale Over 2,000,000 Acres Selected Farming and Wood Lands* (New York, 1856), pp. 11–13.

34. Cardinal Goodwin, "The American Occupation of Iowa, 1833 to 1860," *Iowa Journal of History and Politics* 17 (January 1919): 87–88, 96–99; William W. Folwell, *A History of Minnesota* (St. Paul, 1921), 1: 351–63; *Prairie Farmer* 14 (July 1854): 260; Illinois Central Railroad, Tenth *Annual Report* (1859/60), p. 1.

35. *DeBow's Review* 14 (January 1853): 25; *Chicago Tribune, Review of Commerce* for 1852, in *Hunt's Merchants' Magazine* 18 (May 1853): 560; Allan Bogue, *From Prairie to Corn Belt* (Chicago, 1968), pp. 124–27, 145, 217–18; Bidwell and Falconer, *Agriculture,* pp. 329, 336, 339, 348, 409–20; Clark, *Grain Trade,* pp. 154, 208; Sauer, *Upper Illinois Valley,* p. 168; Thompson, *Wheat Growing Industry,* pp. 15–57.

36. *The Northwest—Growth of the Commerce and Necessity for New Outlets,* broadside (Chicago, 1855), John S. Wright, *Investments in Chicago* (Chicago, 1858), p. 5; *Chicago Democratic Press, Review of Commerce* for 1845, p. 3; *Statistics of the City of Chicago, Illinois, for 1856, Showing Its Growth and Improvement* (Chicago, 1857), p. 3.

37. Kohlmeier, *Old Northwest,* pp. 91, 122, 194; *Chicago Tribune, Review of Commerce,* for 1851, pp. 428–30, 436, for 1852, p. 561, for 1860, p. 3; *Western Journal and Civilian* 6 (June 1851): 164; Andrews, *Report,* p. 220; Taylor, *Board of Trade* 1: 152, 161, 205.

38. Herbert Rice, "Early Rivalry among Wisconsin Cities for Railroads," *Wisconsin Magazine of History* 35 (Autumn 1951): 10–13; Wallace Mygatt, "First Settlement of Kenosha," Wisconsin State Historical Society *Collections* 3 (1857): 413–17; *History of Racine and Kenosha Counties, Wisconsin* (Chicago, 1879), pp. 368, 456; *Report of a Committee Appointed by the Trustees of the Town of Milwaukee Relative to the Commerce of That Town* (Milwaukee, 1842), pp. 3–7; King, "Milwaukee to St. Paul," pp. 188–89; *DeBow's Review* 14 (January 1853): 26–27; *Hunt's Merchants' Magazine* 36 (May 1857): 552–57; Edward D. Holton, "Commercial History of Milwaukee," Wisconsin State Historical Society *Collections* 4 (1859): 274–85.

39. Chicago and Northwestern Railroad Company, Third *Annual Report,* (1861/62), pp. 22–23; Thompson, *Wheat Growing Industry,* pp. 113–15; Clark, *Grain Trade,* pp. 56, 239.

40. *Hunt's Merchants' Magazine* 36 (June 1857): 691; Goodspeed and Healy, *Cook County,* 1: 267; George W. Stephens, *Some Aspects of Early Intersectional*

Rivalry for the Commerce of the Upper Mississippi Valley, Washington University Studies, Humanistic Series, vol. 10, no. 2 (St. Louis, 1923), pp. 277, 294–98; Wright, *Chicago,* p. 311; Belcher, *St. Louis and Chicago,* pp. 26–32, 44–52, 72–95, 108–110.

41. *Chicago Democratic Press,* July 16, 1857.

42. *Chicago Democratic Press,* September 28, 1852, October 2, 1852, March 26, 1853, March 3, 1854; *Chicago Democratic Press* account book for 1852–54, Scripps and Bross Volumes, Chicago Historical Society.

43. *Hunt's Merchants' Magazine* 36 (June 1857): 691; *Western Journal and Civilian* 14 (July 1855): 142; *Stranger's Guide and Handbook,* p. 43; Chicago *Tribune, Review of Commerce* for 1860, p. 34.

44. Illinois Central Railroad Company, Eighth *Annual Report* (1858), pp. 19–20, Tenth *Annual Report* (1860), pp. 14–15.

45. *Western Journal and Civilian* 8 (April 1852): 61; *Chicago Magazine* 1 (March 1857): 94; Howard G. Brownson, *History of the Illinois Central Railroad to 1870,* University of Illinois Studies in the Social Sciences, vol. 4, nos. 3–4 (Urbana, Ill., 1915), p. 105; Chicago and North Western Railroad Company, Third *Annual Report* (1861/62), pp. 22–23; Pittsburgh, Fort Wayne and Chicago Railroad Company, Third *Annual Report* (1859), pp. 86–93; *Industrial Chicago,* 3: 43–44, 50; Fries, *Empire in Pine,* pp. 82–83.

46. *Galena Jeffersonian,* September 29, 1852; Chetlain, *Recollections,* pp. 26–28; letters from Galena merchants to C.W. Mappa, Galena Collection, Chicago Historical Society; *Chicago Democratic Press,* February 25, 1853; Galena Steamboat Register, 1855, Galena Public Library; Ulysses S. Grant, *Personal Memoirs* (New York, 1885), 1: 222.

47. *Galena Gazette,* July 18, 1859; *Galena City Directory, 1858–59,* p. 134; Whitney, "Geology of the Lead Region," p. 157; Chicago Board of Trade, *Report* for 1876, p. 44; *DeBow's Review* 24 (March 1858): 212.

48. Lancaster *Wisconsin Herald,* December 31, 1846, in Libby, "Lead and Shot," p. 301.

BOOSTERISM
AND THE EVALUATION OF
ECONOMIC ENVIRONMENT

The evidence is clear that antebellum westerners shared realistic and often precise knowledge about the economic bases of their cities. The preceding chapters have shown that opinions about leading activities hold up well when checked against available quantitative data. The members of the business-civic leadership also provided accurate descriptions of the size and shape of their cities' hinterlands. The objective data of canal, railroad, and steamboat shipments confirm the claims of individual businessmen about the trade of their own firms and the testimony of civic spokesmen in speeches, booster pamphlets, and reviews of trade. There seems little question that residents of Chicago, Cincinnati, Indianapolis, and Galena were able accurately to assess the current economic situation.

The second step in the process of collective entrepreneurship was the evaluation of the further possibilities for growth that could be based on each city's tributary area. To show a profit consistently it was necessary to know not only the size of the trade area but also its economic character. Individual fortunes could depend on properly estimating the market for a particular import or judging the quality of a year's crops. In broader terms, the same sort of analysis of the economic potential of the surrounding country was the basis for developing urban growth strategies. Knowledge of soils, minerals, successful crops, and population was essential for intelligent decisions about the future of western cities. Indeed, there was a correlation between the relative realism of hinterland evaluations in the four cities and the coherence of the economic programs which the cities developed.

Certainly interested urbanites had abundant data on the capabilities of western farms and mines, for boosters in the antebellum Middle West loved to talk about their region almost as much as about their cities. Dozens of gazetteers and guidebooks, which described individual states or the section as a whole, presented a general view of the region's economic capacities for eastern capitalists and amateur geographers and offered specific advice to prospective emigrants. Articles for commercial journals such as *Hunt's Merchants' Magazine,* the *Banker's Magazine,* the *American Railroad Journal,* and *DeBow's Review* summarized similar information. In addition, such magazines provided a ready means of communication among theorists of economic development in East, West, and South.

Publications of state agencies were also intended for a dual audience of westerners and easterners. In the late 1840s and 1850s both Indiana and Ohio printed massive annual reports of their state boards of agriculture. These ill-bound tomes mixed discussions of fruit culture with information on the prosperity of local farmers. From 1857, the reports of Ohio's Commissioner of Statistics summarized data on farming and mining along with statistics on trade, manufactures, and population. Proponents of such annual documents viewed them as beneficial both for local businessmen and for the promotion of economic development.[1] Most western states also conducted one or more geological surveys in the 1830s (Kentucky, Indiana, Ohio, Michigan) or 1850s (Kentucky, Indiana, Michigan, Illinois, Wisconsin, Iowa, Missouri). As well as describing rock strata and publicizing the location of workable mineral deposits, these documents aided farmers by analyzing the soil quality. Their purpose was explicitly defined in promotional terms as the opening of new areas of enterprise and the dissemination of scientific information to "invite population [and] hasten the development of our known resources."[2]

In many ways, assertions about the potential of urban trade areas represented boosterism in its purist form. Indeed, it is this facet of popular economic thought that is most open to ridicule, for it was a more abstract link between the specific description of existing economic patterns and the enunciation of concrete growth strategies. Evaluations of hinterlands could easily be dismissed as flights of fancy until urban leaders took them as the basis for action. Precisely because of this character, however, examination of this body of writing allows initial distinctions among the several cities in the character of their boosterism. On one level, such analysis leads into discussion of the formulation and implementation of growth strategies in the next stages of the entrepreneurial process, as treated in Chapters 5 through 8. On another level, the summary of ways in which westerners described and evaluated each city's hinterland offers the chance to see how specific ideas about urban growth were related to broader national conceptions about the sources of economic growth.

The context for specific booster analysis of urban hinterlands was an informal but widely publicized theory of commerce and city growth. In their most accessible form, these ideas were promulgated by Jesup W. Scott, a Toledo editor who made himself *the* urban growth theorist for residents of the Old Northwest in a score of articles in *Hunt's* and *DeBow's*. Charles Glaab has provided a full analysis of Scott's ideas as he expressed them from the middle 1830s to the Civil War, finding that the key was a stress on the city-building function of internal American commerce. Scott envisioned that a massive and increasing volume of internal trade along the natural routes of the great rivers and lakes would spawn the great American cities in the nation's interior.[3] In some instances, western writers showed their agreement by offering the bold assertion that "cities owe their growth now almost entirely to the relation they sustain to commerce" and in others directly copied Scott's ideas without credit.[4] In still other cases they quoted him explicitly as "one of the ablest statistical writers of the West."[5]

Scott's closest counterpart was Missourian William Gilpin. Living and writing in the Kansas City area in the 1850s, Gilpin also envisioned the emergence of a system of great cities built and tied together by internal trade among the several regions of North America. His essays are filled with a vivid sense of economic activity as the physical movement of goods, of bales on the landing, of flatcars stacked with lumber. The great central plain between the Appalachians and Rockies, with its branching rivers and its ease for railroad building, assured commerce and therefore urban growth on a scale previously undreamed.[6] Chicago boosters who blithely claimed that their city's commercial sphere ranged from Pike's Peak to Hudson Bay provided a more specific accompaniment for Gilpin's grand vision.[7]

If both writers agreed that internal trade would support the growth of a set of commercial cities in the American West, they left largely unanswered the central question of which among several cities with good transportation facilities might expect to supplant New York as the new commercial metropolis. In his own work, Scott was unable to decide for sure among the merits of several nominees, although at different times he offered Cincinnati, Toledo, and Chicago as prime candidates. Gilpin's choice shifted with his real estate investments and political career to Kansas City in the 1850s, and to Denver in the 1860s after his appointment as the first territorial governor of Colorado.

Urban residents who tried to deal with the same question in more concrete terms offered three distinct suggestions that called for different responses to hinterland resources and different strategies for urban growth. One alternative was to emphasize the primary agricultural and mineral resources of the city's hinterland and to argue that the export of foodstuffs and minerals was the key to rapid growth. A second alternative focused on the growth of western markets and the possibilities of import trade and wholesaling. The third option was to stress the combined importance of hinterland resources and markets as the necessary supports for a local manufacturing base. The varying acceptance of these three analyses in each city is one of the differences in boosterism among Cincinnati, Chicago, Indianapolis, and Galena. At the same time, the evaluation of economic environment in each city indicates how antebellum boosters interpreted received wisdom about economic growth in the context of their specific circumstances.

The common economic wisdom in antebellum America was that agriculture was the superior economic activity and the primary source of wealth. The ideas had been fixed in political discourse by Thomas Jefferson's views on the moral and political superiority of the yeoman farmer. The same opinion became a commonplace of rhetoric for politicians of the "Jacksonian persuasion," the set of beliefs in the 1830s and 1840s that ascribed special virtue to the "real people," the farmers, laborers, and mechanics who participated directly in the production of material wealth. The impulse was still strong in the Middle West at mid-century, when state constitutional conventions in Ohio, Indiana, and Illinois placed strict limits on the freedom and opportunities of banks and corporations in the name of the natural agrarian economy.[8]

Beyond the political arena, the primacy of agriculture was a strong theme in the American vision of western growth. As Henry Nash Smith persuasively argued twenty-five years ago, many Americans were motivated by a vision of the Mississippi Valley as a great garden that would support an agricultural society. In Smith's view, many Americans before the Civil War conceived of the Middle West as a "fee-simple empire" to be peopled entirely by virtuous yeomen whose moral superiority depended on their way of life. Statements that confirmed the agricultural bias tended to be accepted as a matter of course. Occasional contrary arguments that the growth of agriculture depended as much on cities as cities depended on agriculture stirred acrimonious debate.[9]

Urban editors, publicists, and civic leaders in the mid-century Northwest responded to the agricultural myth by observing that "every interest traces its life and dependence to that single great source, the productions of the soil." Time and again they asserted not only that agriculture and manufacturing "repose on each other, and suffer or prosper in conjunction," but that agriculture was the foundation for the development of towns. Spokesmen in every city agreed that "the agricultural interests underly [sic] every branch of trade" and that the richness of the surrounding territory was a primary determinant of urban growth. Many westerners would have agreed with the *Chicago Democrat* that "the city of Chicago is completely dependent upon, and, in fact, a mere agency of the surrounding country. It derives every pulsation of its life, and every breath of its existence, from the agricultural region of which it is the depot."[10]

Inhabitants of western cities certainly were careful to keep informed about the progress of local agriculture. During the harvest season, newspapers carried almost daily reports of the status of the year's crops and calculations of their expected yield. Written for produce dealers and speculators, these articles were realistic and precise. In quieter times, urban newspapers filled their columns with letters depicting the trade and agriculture of nearby towns and counties. In addition, agricultural magazines interspersed advice to farmers with information on the status of western agriculture of interest to urban businessmen and western publicists. Among the more important were Chicago's *Prairie Farmer* (1841-   ), Cincinnati's *Cincinnatus* (1856-60), and Indianapolis's *Indiana Farmer* (1840-41), *Western Cultivator* (1844-45), and *Indiana Farmer and Gardener* (1845-48).

Cincinnati writers tended to praise the richness of the entire Ohio Valley in general terms. One called it a "vast area of fertile country," another claimed that the entire region was "unequalled by any in the United States," and a third thought it the largest and most fertile grain-growing area in the world. A more imaginative booster tried to prove that Cincinnati's hinterland was the richest in the West by calculating that the region within 100 miles had a larger population and produced more grain than tracts of similar size around Pittsburgh, Louisville, St. Louis, and Chicago.[11]

Cincinnatians singled out the immediate parts of their hinterland as the most fertile and prosperous. From the early decades of their city's growth, they emphasized that the "exuberant" and "inexhaustible" soil of the Miami Valleys made them "singularly fertile" and productive. After describing this corner of the state, one wrote:

> We no longer wonder at the prosperity and rapid growth of Cincinnati, for although we have examined but *one* district of the vast area of which she is the center and emporium, we have traversed an expanse of country so broad, so rich, so well-cultivated, as to be in itself capable of supporting a great metropolis.

Inhabitants of the Queen City also agreed on the richness of the developed parts of northern Kentucky and believed that the lands along the Whitewater River were "equal in respect to their facilities for agriculture and their degree of cultivation" to those near the Miami.[12] Despite some elements of truth, however, this extravagant rhetoric need not be taken literally. A number of Cincinnati writers operated on the axiom that the entire West was "by far the most extensive, fertile, and productive part of the Union." As a result, many publicists rather illogically applied the same superlatives to section after section of the Mississippi Valley. To some eyes, every region west of the Appalachians was one of the world's "very richest," "most fertile," "finest," "most productive," or most "opulent."[13]

More systematic analysis of the possibilities of export trade was offered by Cincinnatians James Hall and S.H. Goodin. Perhaps reacting to their city's failure to gain its "natural share" of internal commerce, they focused on the importance of increasing the export potential of urban trade areas. Hall in 1848 argued that continued urban growth in the Ohio Valley depended on the filling in of each city's hinterland. Continued settlement and the development of smaller subordinate centers were the keys to future urban growth, and the largest cities would be those dominating the richest hinterlands. Goodin in 1851 offered an argument that anticipated modern central place theory, again asserting that the metropolis that would experience greatest growth would be that which dominated the largest and most productive hinterland. Interestingly, this stress on the richness of tributary areas was the same approach Scott used in 1859 in an effort to explain why Great Lakes cities appeared to be pulling ahead of those in the Ohio Valley.[14]

Galena's chief export was of course lead, not foodstuffs. In assessing the richness of the mines, Galenians started with a levelheaded dependence on scientific surveys. Although one editor claimed in 1835 that numerous veins were yet undiscovered, David Owen's federally financed geological survey, which made the first thorough reconnaissance of the lead region, found no important new lead-bearing areas. On the other hand, he encouraged local interests by asserting that "the district surveyed is one of the richest mineral regions, compared to its extent, yet known in the world" and stating that it offered "rich promise of commercial productiveness." He defined the lead region as eight townships in Iowa, ten in Illinois, and sixty-two in Wisconsin, also suggesting that it might contain workable iron and copper deposits. During the next fifteen years, Owen's report was the basis for discussions of the lead region in the

American Journal of Science, the *Scientific American,* and J.S. Whitney's *Metallic Wealth of the United States,* the most authoritative antebellum volume on American mineral resources.[15]

In the 1850s, declining production created the desire for a new survey. The promoters of the project hoped that scientific authorities could refute Owen's opinion and establish the existence of deep veins of lead, lifting the "general disrepute" in which the region was held by outside investors. In response, the Wisconsin legislature authorized a state geological survey that reached exactly this conclusion in its 1854, 1855, and 1856 reports. In the later 1850s, however, a second Wisconsin survey was conducted on more thorough principles by better-qualified scientists. When published in 1862, its final report without qualification upheld Owen's judgment.[16]

In considering conflicting testimony, many Galenians in the 1850s believed what they wanted to believe. In 1851 and 1852, they claimed that most of the region's lead was yet to be extracted and that deep mining would surely be successful. Under the impetus of the depression at the end of the decade, the city's newspapers again tried to convince anyone who would listen that deep mining would yield good profits and asserted that God had favored Galena as he had favored Moses, making the waters recede from the deeper shafts. Similarly, they tried to revive early interest in local agriculture, promoting such peripheral activities as sheep raising and hay making.[17]

Natives of Indianapolis were more subdued. Neither newspapers nor magazines devoted much attention to the development of farming or the diversification of agriculture in central Indiana. A variety of general descriptions, however, agreed that apart from the valley of the Whitewater, Indiana's best soil was found in the middle of the state along the upper reaches of the White and Wabash rivers. At the same time, these writers held their modifiers under tight control. One, for example, described the state as "tolerably rich" and several simply claimed that Indiana land was as good as that in other parts of the West.[18]

Inhabitants of the Hoosier capital admitted further that much of their agricultural hinterland was incompletely developed. The city's agricultural journals called on farmers to improve their methods of cultivation and to expand production. Newspapers likewise complained about Indiana's backwardness and described the Miami

Reservation between Noblesville and Peru (Indian lands opened to white settlement only in 1847) as virtually unpopulated into the mid-1850s. Even railroad officers resident in Indianapolis admitted to their stockholders that central Indiana was yet in the process of development and admonished Hoosiers to cease wasting their money and energy clearing new land when they were unable adequately to crop acreage already prepared for the plow.[19]

Chicagoans too were relatively realistic about the agricultural potential of their hinterland. Although settlers in Illinois had been reluctant to utilize the state's grasslands in the first decades of occupation, the 1830s had marked a change in attitude as publicists argued the quality of the prairie soils and farmers ventured further from their timbered fringes. By the 1840s, most westerners agreed that the luxuriant pasturage, fertility, and ease of cultivation of prairie land outweighed its disadvantages. Only the wetter prairies requiring extensive drainage were still shunned.[20]

During this decade and the next, Chicagoans appraised the agricultural resources of their state in glowing terms. They seldom singled out particular regions for special praise, as did Cincinnatians, but rather claimed that the entire commonwealth was unsurpassed in its climate, soil, and productions. Editors and politicians agreed that they could find scarcely an acre of uncultivable soil in Illinois.[21] Other enthusiasts contrasted the state's richness to that of the wornout East. So superior was it to other states that all estimates "based on past experience, respecting the results that are here to be worked out, must necessarily fall short of the actual fact."[22]

Within this windstorm of adjectives, however, a number of Chicagoans kept their feet. At times descriptions of the state contained not only ornate prose but also detailed information on farming techniques, soils, topography, stockraising, and crops. Chicagoans also acknowledged that even the best lands in North America were of little value until transportation facilities opened them to settlement and trade. The *Tribune* went so far as to suggest that measures be taken to insure the continued fertility of the soil, unusual advice from one of the chief spokesmen for the rapacious exploitation of the West.[23]

A second answer to the question of which city might become the western metropolis emphasized the need to supplement export trade with banking and wholesaling activity. A leading exponent of this view was Cincinnatian Edward Mansfield, a perceptive economic writer whose *Railroad Record* compared favorably with the *American Railroad Journal* of Henry Varnum Poor. Through the columns of the *Railroad Record* and elsewhere, Mansfield attacked the simple-minded extrapolation of percentage growth rates often practiced by Scott. He argued instead that exporters would use a city's transportation facilities only if it offered complementary imports and adequate credit facilities.[24]

Mansfield argued largely alone, for economic writers in the Middle West had a strong tendency to ignore all aspects of the region's wholesale business. Despite its larger volume, they apparently considered it subordinate to the export trade and said little about its organization, value, or significance. In contrast to their detailed and usually enthusiastic assessments of the primary productions of their trade areas, citizens of the four cities also paid little attention to the quality of the market for goods and services. When they talked about demand at all, they tended to discuss its volume rather than its character and showed interest mainly in the development of new markets. In Cincinnati, whose contiguous trade area was largely settled, writers discussed the need to increase commerce with western Indiana and to expand the city's trading sphere in the South. In Chicago, interest centered on the development of the partly settled region already tributary to the city rather than on its expansion. Editors noted that northern Illinois was rapidly filling with towns, villages, and farms whose inhabitants were certain to buy from the city, and one described the wave of population "rolling a mighty tide of subjugation over the prairies, groves and rivers of the West, consuming, producing, and marshalling into existence a boundless array of wants, dependencies, reciprocities, and business relations."[25]

Only in scattered instances did residents of the four cities discuss the nature of demand within their import hinterlands. One Cincinnati paper noted the special market offered by cotton mills on the upper Ohio and urged local merchants to supply their needs, while Indianapolis writers claimed that the character of their town's hinterland made it a good location for the manufacture of agricultural implements, locomotives, and rails. Occasionally, also, westerners paid attention to variations in the volume of demand. One railroad prospectus noted that northeastern and central Indiana bought more from Cincinnati than did any other tract of similar size. Both Cincinnati and Chicago writers also remarked the obvious fact that prosperity made their hinterlands good customers for local merchants.[26]

What these customers wanted to consume, however, was left unsaid. Perhaps with some justification, given the nature of merchandising in the antebellum Northwest, Chicagoans, Cincinnatians, and Galenians assumed a uniform desire for goods, expecting all the farmers and country merchants who traded in their town to purchase the same things in the same proportions. Newspapers thus encouraged their rural readers to buy from local merchants but saw no need to assure them that any special requirements might be met. The basis for this lack of attention to the character of demand in import hinterlands seems to have been an assumption of reciprocity. City dwellers believed that by describing the richness and prosperity of a region's farms they also described its value as a market. Their frequent references to the interdependence of agriculture and commerce, which were usually followed by a discussion of the former but not the latter, point to the same conclusion.

A third and more common answer to the question of how to assure the growth of one among several cities along a river or railway was that trade in primary products had to be supplemented with manufacturing. Several national writers in widely read publications stated the idea in general terms. John Wright of Pennsylvania argued that the development of local manufacturing was necessary to help a city take full profit from the goods that passed through its warehouses. Such local factories would also provide a trade advantage in the competition among cities with equally good transportation facilities. J. B. D. DeBow offered similar arguments in his efforts to encourage southern urban manufacturing. These ideas reversed Scott, who saw manufacturing as a superstructure reared on the foundation of commercial development.[27]

Westerners enthusiastically adapted these points to their own circumstances. Both the Chicago *Democratic Press* and the *Western Journal and Civilian* of St. Louis asserted that manufacturing provided a more permanent basis for prosperity than did commerce.

The Cincinnati Chamber of Commerce argued that manufacturing allowed the taking of additional profits on goods shipped through the city and supported large numbers of workers.[28] More specifically, each of the four towns under examination was eager to develop manufacturing, a term which tended to summon visions of the iron industry. Despite the importance of agricultural processing industries both in their theoretical formulations and in fact, residents were enamored of sooty foundries, reeking furnaces, and clamorous rolling mills.

As a consequence, Cincinnati, Indianapolis, and Chicago each overvalued the coal and iron resources of its hinterland. Writers in Cincinnati, which in fact was the only one of the three to develop a significant iron industry, judged the extent of the coal fields around the mouths of the Scioto and Muskingum rivers realistically but persistently overstated the amount of iron ore.[29] In Indiana, the state geological survey of 1837–38 had delimited an extensive coal field stretching from the southwestern corner of the state to within seventy-five miles of Indianapolis and had noted workable iron deposits around Terre Haute. Accepting these findings as proof that Indiana was destined to develop extensive manufactures, Indianapolis editors, boosters, and railroad promoters predicted that their city would soon be an industrial center. In fact, Indiana boasted only one operating blast furnace in 1860, and Indianapolis imported its coal from Pennsylvania.[30]

Chicagoans were equally extravagant in expectations of mineral resources, basing their discussion on the "Great Illinois Coal Field" which David Dale Owen had mapped across the lower four-fifths of Illinois in 1839.[31] From the 1840s, Chicago newspapers frequently discussed the closer fields, their richness, accessibility, and value to Chicago industry. In the mid-1850s, the interest in coal merged with a new enthusiasm when the *Democratic Press* tried to convince Chicago businessmen to utilize the copper and iron of northern Michigan. The editors had no doubt that "the mineral treasures of Lake Superior will soon pay tribute to Chicago," working in conjunction with Illinois coal and Galena lead to make it the seat of extensive manufacturing.[32] Before 1860, in fact, little use was made in the city of Lake Superior metals or Illinois coal, especially since production of the latter was inefficient and slow to develop for other than local customers. Perhaps in recognition of this fact, the city's boosters during the 1850s were on the whole more circumspect in discussing the coal mines than were writers trying to promote the settlement of downstate lands.[33]

The foregoing analysis suggests that western urbanites built their discussion of local growth opportunities on common pools of thought. There was close communication among urban theorists in various western cities and in the rest of the United States. There was also a close correspondence between western and national writing in rhetorical techniques and in the recognition of the need to go beyond simple reference to geography and the volume of trade. At the same time, each city made differing use of the prevalent growth theories, and there are differences from one to another in the realism of hinterland perceptions. In descriptions of export hinterlands, for example, Chicago and Indianapolis were the most levelheaded, seeing negative as well as positive aspects. Cincinnati and Galena were more fanciful in their reactions and remained unflinchingly optimistic even when unrealistic predictions proved false. Within the limits already described, Chicago also showed the greatest interest in the development of interior import markets and perhaps was more controlled than the smaller cities in its hopes for heavy manufacturing.

The themes of western boosterism that transcended local variations can easily be summarized. There was considerable interest in heavy manufacturing and in export trade but a curious disregard of import commerce and perhaps an inclination to take processing industries for granted. These tendencies may have been part of a larger interest in economic self-sufficiency. Several historians have pointed out that antebellum westerners approached economic development with a set of priorities that gave attention first to the city and its region, then to the state, then to the nation. In relation to the development of transportation systems the tendency has been called "localism" by Harry Scheiber and "parochialism" by George R. Taylor and Irene Neu. Margaret Walsh focused on the same idea in arguing that the western rationale for manufacturing was not efficiency through specialization of production but rather the search for local and state "autarky."[34] Operating within this context, community-focused entrepreneurs and boosters may have applauded export trade and manufacturing because they brought in money from outside or held local funds in the region but slighted imports because they required external spending.

One related facet of economic localism is that antebellum westerners tended to define regional patterns in terms of urban hinterlands rather than political boundaries. The trade area of Galena overlapped four states and those of Chicago and Cincinnati touched at least six states. It is obvious from contemporary discussions of the "Wabash country" and "Ohio River counties" that urbanites thought of drainage basins as natural units. They realized that economic regions could frequently overlap and that one urban region could nest within that of a larger metropolis. Although urban boosters largely ignored national politics as irrelevant to issues of growth, the perception of regions as spheres of metropolitan influence was potentially a countervailing force to the country's division between politically defined sections.

The emphasis among export, import, and manufacturing activities had a cultural as well as an economic basis. The attention to primary exports involved not only an awareness of the value of a prosperous hinterland but also a more general belief in the primacy of agriculture as the true source of wealth. In a region where Jeffersonian ideals and Democratic Party rhetoric still set the terms of public debate, western politicians were quick to insist that the spread of mining, manufacturing, and commerce had not changed the rural nature of their rapidly developing constituencies.[35] The city-as-importer may have seemed a tool of eastern mill owners and British cotton kings, but the city-as-exporter could be viewed merely as one link in a chain of production that began in the good earth. At the same time, it is important that any common conviction of the central role of farming in the western economy did not weaken the general belief in the necessity and value of urban growth. Scholars who have argued contrary positions, such as Henry Nash Smith, have simply failed to consider the massive body of testimony that described the sources and advantages of growth in Chicago, Cincinnati, and dozens of other booming cities. Like other antebellum Americans, the Citizens of Ohio, Indiana, and Illinois may have salved their consciences by reference to the virtues of the simple life, but they acted according to the ethic of growth.

NOTES

1. Illinois, House Committee Report on Agricultural Statistics, *Illinois Reports* (1840/41), pp. 347–48; Ohio, Message of Governor Salmon P. Chase (1857), p. 9.

2. Walter B. Hendrickson, *David Dale Owen: Pioneer Geologist of the Middle West,* Indiana Historical Collections, vol. 27 (Indianapolis, 1943), p. 26, 84, 116, 124; George P. Merrill, *Contributions to a History of American State Geological and Natural History Surveys,* United States National Museum Bulletin no. 109 (Washington, 1920), pp. 537–38; Indiana, Biennial Message of Governor Abram Hammond to Indiana General Assembly, January 11, 1861, in *Documentary Journal* (1860/61); David Dale Owen, *Report of a Geological Reconnaissance of the State of Indiana* (Indianapolis, 1859), Part 1: 1837, pp. 5–6.

3. Charles Glaab, "Jesup W. Scott and a West of Cities," *Ohio History* 73 (Winter 1964): 3–12; Glaab, *Kansas City,* pp. 10–35.

4. *Gem of the Prairie,* January 1, 1848; *Cincinnati Atlas,* March 22, 1849; *Western Journal and Civilian* 5 (March 1851): 285–86; *Chicago Democratic Press,* June 29, 1854; S.J.B., "The Future Progress of Ohio," *Western Monthly Review* 3 (December 1829): 331–35; Taft, *Cincinnati and Her Railroads,* pp. 5, 18–20.

5. Bebb, *Cincinnati,* pp. 13–16; Wright, *Investments in Chicago* (1858), pp. 7–8; *Exhibit of the Pittsburgh, Fort Wayne and Chicago Railroad,* p. 34.

6. Charles Glaab, "Vision of Metropolis: William Gilpin and Theories of City Growth in the West," *Wisconsin Magazine of History* 45 (Autumn 1961): 21–31; William Gilpin, *The Central Gold Region* (Philadelphia, 1860).

7. *Chicago Magazine* 1 (March 1857): 94.

8. Marvin Meyers, *The Jacksonian Persuasion* (New York, 1960).

9. Henry Nash Smith, *Virgin Land: The American West as Symbol and Myth* (New York, 1957), pp. 141–62, 182–83; *Cincinnati Gazette,* January 9, 1851; James Hall, *Address before the Young Men's Mercantile Library Association* (Cincinnati, 1846).

10. Chicago *Democratic Press, Review of Commerce* for 1856, p. 19; Bellamy Storer, *Address Delivered before the Hamilton County Agricultural Society* (Cincinnati, 1835), p. 8; Cincinnati Chamber of Commerce, *Report* for 1852, p. 4; *Chicago Democrat,* December 9, 1848.

11. Hall, *Commerce and Navigation,* p. 313; *The Cincinnati Almanac for 1840* (Cincinnati, 1840); Drake and Mansfield, *Cincinnati in 1826,* p. 99; Cincinnati Chamber of Commerce, *Report* for 1855, p. 6; U.S., Patent Office, *Report* for 1850, H.R. Doc. No. 32, 31st Cong., 2nd Sess., 1850, pp. 543–44.

12. Hall, *Soil, Surface and Productions,* pp. 162–64; *Report of the Cincinnati and Whitewater Canal,* p. 19. Also see: Flint, *Mississippi Valley,* pp. 399–400; Cist, *Cincinnati in 1841,* p. 76; *DeBow's Review* 3 (February 1847): 130; *Cincinnatus* 2 (June 1857): 256–57.

13. Hall, *Commerce and Navigation,* pp. 28, 197; *Memorial of the Citizens of Cincinnati to the Congress of the United States, Relative to the Navigation of the Ohio and Mississippi Rivers* (Cincinnati, 1844), p. 27; Atwater, *State of Ohio,* p. 48; Conclin, *River Guide,* pp. 31, 37; Cincinnati Chamber of Commerce, *Report* for 1851, pp. 3–5.

14. Hall, *Commerce and Navigation,* pp. 246, 260; Goodin, "Cincinnati—Its Destiny"; Jesup W. Scott, "Westward the Star of Empire," *DeBow's Review* 27 (August 1859): 125-36. Also see Kansas City's Charles Spalding as quoted in R. Richard Wohl and A. Theodore Brown, "The Usable Past: A Study of Historical Tradition in Kansas City," *Huntington Library Quarterly* 23 (May 1960): 244.

15. *Galena Gazette,* October 3, 1835; Owen, *Geological Exploration,* pp. 8, 35, 42, 47-53; Hodge, "Lead Region," pp. 35-72; *Scientific American* 7 (February 28, 1852): 186; Whitney, *Metallic Wealth.*

16. *Scientific American* 7 (March 6, 1852): 194; *Western Journal and Civilian* 7 (March, 1852): 394-95; Lake, *Law and Mineral Wealth,* p. 125; Galena *Jeffersonian,* August 28, September 19, 1851; Edward Daniels, *Report on the Geological Survey of the State of Wisconsin* (1855), p. 4; James Hall and J.D. Whitney, *Report on the Geological Survey of the State of Wisconsin* (1862), 1: 82-85, 416-17.

17. *DeBow's Review* 14 (April 1853): 403; *Galena Jeffersonian,* December 31, 1851, October 12, 1852; *Scientific American* 17 (February 28, 1852): 186; *Galena Gazette,* September 28, 1858, May 3, 1859; *Galena Courier,* August 4, 1857, May 1, 1858.

18. *The Indiana Gazetteer, or Topographical Dictionary* (Indianapolis, 1833), p. 14; Flint, *Mississippi Valley,* p. 370; *Indiana Gazetteer* (1849), p. 4; Owen, *Reconnaissance of the State of Indiana,* pt. 1, 1837, pp. 52-54; John M. Peck, *A New Guide for Emigrants to the West* (Boston, 1837), p. 232; Evansville, Indianapolis and Cleveland Straight Line Railroad Company, *Annual Report* (1855), p. 10.

19. *Indiana Farmer* 1 (February 1840): 18; *Indiana Farmer and Gardener* 1, 24, quoted in van Bolt, "Indiana Scene," p. 349; *Indiana Journal,* May 8, 1848; *Indiana Sentinel,* June 2, 1847; Indianapolis *Indiana Statesman,* November 13, 1850; *Locomotive,* October 6, 1855; *Indianapolis Journal,* April 24, 1851; Madison and Indianapolis Railroad Company, Fourth *Annual Report* (1846), p. 6; Indianapolis and Bellefontaine Railroad Company, Fourth *Annual Report* (1851/1852), p. 6.

20. Douglas R. McManus, *The Initial Evaluation and Utilization of the Illinois Prairies, 1815-1840,* University of Chicago Department of Geography Research Paper, no. 94 (Chicago, 1964), pp. 35-61, 86; Bidwell and Falconer, *Agriculture,* pp. 268-70; Bogue, *Patterns from the Sod,* pp. 31, 36, 117-23.

21. J.W. Norris, *A Business Advertiser and General Directory of Chicago for the Year 1845-46* (Chicago, 1845), p. 137; *Gem of the Prairie,* April 22, 1848; Governor Joel Matteson, Message to the General Assembly, January 1, 1855, *Illinois Reports* (1855), p. 2.

22. Chicago *Democratic Press, Review of Commerce* for 1856, p. 30. Also see: *Prairie Farmer* 2 (April 1842): 33; *DeBow's Review,* 19 (October 1855): 405.

23. See a series of articles in the *Chicago American* in the summer of 1835 and again in the winter of 1836 and *Guide to the Illinois Central Railroad Lands* (Chicago, 1859), pp. 5-11, 24-37, 42-50. Also see *Chicago Democratic Press,* December 20, 1852; *Chicago Tribune,* February 17, 1860.

24. Mansfield, *Ohio and Mississippi Railroad: Value of Its Stock,* p. 9; *Railroad Record,* 1853-1860, *passim.*

25. *Chicago Democratic Press, Review of Commerce* for 1855, p. 5. Also see: Taft, *Cincinnati and Her Railroads,* pp. 9, 31, 33, 45; *Cincinnati Gazette,* August 13, 1847, quoted in van Bolt, "Indiana Scene," p. 341; *Chicago Democratic Press,* August 20, 1855, November 29, 1856; *Chicago Tribune, Review of Commerce* for 1860, p. 6.

26. *Cincinnati Atlas,* July 9, 1846; Indianapolis Board of Trade, *Indianapolis; Locomotive,* April 3, 1852, April 30, 1853; Perkins, "Address," pp. 388–89; *Chicago Democratic Press,* August 22, 1853, March 13, 1857; Cincinnati Chamber of Commerce, *Report* for 1854, p. 5; *Conditions and Prospects of the Cincinnati and Chicago Railroad,* p. 9.

27. John Wright, "Effects of Internal Improvements on Commercial Cities," *Hunt's Merchants' Magazine* 16 (March 1847): 265–66; Jesup W. Scott, "Our Cities, Atlantic and Interior," *Hunt's Merchants' Magazine* 19 (October 1848): 385–86; J.D.B. DeBow, *The Industrial Resources of the Southern and the Western States* (New York, 1854), pp. 2, 122.

28. Cincinnati Chamber of Commerce, *Report* for 1857, pp. 3–4; *Chicago Democratic Press,* August 25, 1854; *Western Journal and Civilian* 5 (March 1851): 286.

29. Flint, *Mississippi Valley,* p. 402; Drake, "Cincinnati at the Close of 1835," pp. 308–09; Gallagher, "Ohio in 1838," pp. 9–10, 100–01; *Western Literary Journal* 1 (July 1836): 146–48; *Western Quarterly Review* 1 (April 1849): 339; Atwater, *History of Ohio,* pp. 19, 23–24; Paul W. Stoddard, "The Knowledge of Coal and Iron in Ohio before 1835," *Ohio Archeological and Historical Publications* 38 (1929): 219–29; Paul W. Stoddard, "Story of the First Geological Survey of Ohio," *Ohio Archeological and Historical Publications* 37 (1928): 126–28.

30. Owen, *Reconnaissance of the State of Indiana,* pt. 1, 1837, pp. 20, 42–47, pt. 2, 1838, pp. 52–55, 62; *Indianapolis Sentinel,* May 23, 1849, June 2, 1853; *Indianapolis Journal,* April 29, 1854; Indianapolis Board of Trade, *Indianapolis;* Oliver H. Smith, *Early Indiana Trials and Sketches* (Cincinnati, 1858), p. 144; Terre Haute and Richmond Railroad Company, First *Annual Report* (1849), p. 14; Lawrenceburg and Upper Mississippi Railroad Company, *Report of the Board of Directors* (1850), pp. 20–22.

31. David Dale Owen, *Report of a Geological Exploration of Part of Iowa, Wisconsin and Illinois,* S. Doc. No. 407, 28th Cong., 1st Sess., 1839, map.

32. *Chicago Journal,* August 2, 1847; *Chicago Democrat,* March 11, 1851; *Chicago Democratic Press,* December 23, 1854, June 29, 1855; *Chicago Democratic Press, Review of Commerce* for 1852, p. 14.

33. *Prairie Farmer* 15 (November 1855): 347; *DeBow's Review* 18 (March 1855): 407, 19 (October 1855): 410; *Illinois State Gazetteer and Business Directory for 1858 and 1859* (Chicago, 1857), p. xxxiv; J.W. Foster, *Report upon the Mineral Resources of the Illinois Central Railroad* (New York, 1856), pp. 10–28.

34. Scheiber, *Ohio Canal Era;* Walsh, *Manufacturing Frontier;* George R. Taylor and Irene Neu, *The American Railroad Network, 1861-1890* (Cambridge, Mass., 1956).

35. See the following annual messages of the Governors of Ohio: Wilson Shannon (1839), p. 4; Seabury Ford (1849), p. 4; Salmon P. Chase (1858), p. 7.

5

CHICAGO: THE PREEMINENT WONDER OF THE NINETEENTH CENTURY

Popular discussion of economic growth in antebellum cities served two functions. In part, it was an affirmation of faith in the urban future of the United States and its western states and territories. As the previous chapter has indicated, editors and businessmen drew on a common set of ideas about regional development and placed expectations for each city in a context of ambitions for American growth. A prosperous Dayton and Chicago and Davenport were viewed as necessary to the full exploitation of the economic potential of the West and to the achievement of national greatness.

Boosterism was also a means for exploring and promoting the economic future of individual cities. The vision of an urban future for the West was balanced by intense competition for trade, investment, and immigration among individual cities. Popular economic writers spoke to specific needs as each town pursued its "imperial" ambitions. They analyzed the particular problems and opportunities of each city, reminded urbanites their own prosperity was bound with that of their neighbors, and debated alternative growth strategies. The following chapters therefore describe the themes and character of popular economic thought about local growth in

Chicago, Cincinnati, Indianapolis, and Galena. The underlying questions are whether such discussion responded to specific local circumstances, whether each city developed a public consensus on growth strategies, and whether civic leaders tried to carry such strategies into action.

Boosterism in Chicago in many ways served as a model for the common description. Chicago was notorious throughout the Northwest as a loudmouthed city, and the pushiness of its spokesmen offered numerous chances to ridicule its "active but gassy people." "Speak to a Chicagoan about any place or any subject other than Chicago," wrote a Toledo editor, "and he knows nothing about it. Chicago, Chicago is the whole theme. What it was, what it is, and what it will be. You cannot divert the mind from it." Other writers pointed out that Chicago's growth was a function of its eagerness to publicize its "advantages of locality, its railroads, its shipping and trade, and its manufactures." One itinerant businessman claimed never to have seen a Chicago newspaper that had not "something in it calling the attention of the stranger to some . . . channel of speculation or other advantage to be derived from investing capital."[1]

Newspapers and magazines were indeed the city's great vehicles for economic discussion and self-advertisement. In the 1840s, the *Journal, Democrat,* and *Prairie Farmer* were deeply interested in projects of advantage to the town. In the 1850s, the *Tribune* and the *Democratic Press* also devoted their energy to impressing the world with the present and future of Chicago. Both the *Journal* and *Tribune* by mid-century printed detailed annual business reviews well larded with trade statistics, but the *Democratic Press* under William Bross was the first to issue its summary of the preceding year in pamphlet form. Sometimes inaccurate and filled with statements that even friends regarded as "pretty highly colored," these reviews were nevertheless extremely popular among Chicagoans and were often quoted in out-of-state papers, in *Hunt's Magazine,* and in *DeBow's Review.*

Chicagoans also took individual responsibility for promoting their city. In 1854 the *Prairie Farmer* reported that bookseller D.B. Cooke, a "live man," was readying a letter sheet whose margins sported a view of Chicago, a map of its railroads, and figures on the increase of population. Many Chicagoans used this sort of stationary for both personal and business correspondence. Several real estate brokers prepared their own pamphlets displaying in small compass the accomplished and anticipated growth of Chicago and incidentally the advantages of the lots they had for sale, while others distributed the *Democratic Press Review of Commerce* under their own cover. Businessmen also financed a German edition of the 1854 *Review.* Under the goad of depression at the end of the decade, Chicago real estate men contrived with several of its railroads to publish the *Western Railroad Gazette.* The paper consisted of a skeleton of articles descriptive of land and railroads and surrounded by a dense tissue of timetables and advertisements.[2] Perhaps the most active booster of all was John S. Wright. In addition to editing the *Prairie Farmer,* he penned numerous articles for the New York *Commercial Advertiser,* the *New York Evening Post,* and the *Boston Courier,* used his own money to print and circulate petitions favoring the Illinois Central Railroad, and published several pamphlets promoting his own real estate interests.[3]

Although one stream of newspaper discussion was intended to introduce particular schemes to a local audience or to incite local businessmen to action, a great flood of words also rolled toward the east. Prominent editors thought that the function of the press was to further the prosperity of Chicago by attracting attention and concentrating capital for deserving enterprises. Few Chicagoans would have disagreed that

> to induce immigrants to come here and settle the vacant lands . . . to control and centre here the trade and travel of the West . . . to induce capitalists to make investments here in works of public and private improvement, are, all of them, objects worthy of the best exertion of her citizens.[4]

Most descriptions of the city were designed to press on outsiders the advantages of identifying their personal fortune with Chicago's. The distinctions between "impartial" discussions, pamphlets serving individual interests, and outright advertisements were blurred. Newspapers often puffed particular enterprises, and real estate notices at times summarized all the common arguments about the city's advantages for growth.

In view of the energy they invested in self-advertisement, it is not surprising that many Chicagoans had a magnified opinion of its effectiveness. The city's chief boosters were convinced that their efforts directly enlarged immigration and developed the resources of the Northwest. Some, indeed, professed to believe that the simple presentation of the facts about the city's condition and prosperity would inevitably rid outsiders of false notions and make them eager to participate in Chicago's growth. "Let it be known what our position and resources really are, and what we annually consume," said one advocate of direct transatlantic trade, "and forthwith the merchants of Chicago can be introduced to the merchants of the United Kingdom, and satisfactory business arrangements made."[5]

In this torrent of discussion, Chicagoans agreed on certain major themes. They were immensely proud of the growth of their city. Its rapid increase amazed even long-time residents familiar with its development. Newspapers filled their columns with stories about the speed of its progress and strained adjectives to the breaking point. Chicagoans, indeed, thought the growth of their city "pre-eminently the wonder of the nineteenth century." A new phenomenon in the progress of the human race, it provided "a sublime illustration of what . . . man can accomplish."[6]

Pride in current achievement was accomplished by a faith that further growth was inevitable. As early as 1834 and 1835, natives had claimed that the human mind could scarcely foretell the magnificent future of the new-found "Key of the West." Although Chicagoans damped their rhetoric during the 1840s, they still asserted that the town was to be one of the important centers of Western America. With widened ambitions in the booming 1850s they forecast a grander destiny as one of the paramount cities of the continent. Even a sober corporation agreed: "Its past growth has been miraculous . . . nothing . . . can apparently arrest or even check its onward progress."[7] So sure were Chicagoans that their city faced decades or centuries of steady growth that many refused to recognize even the possibility of an economic crisis in 1857. Early in the year editors attacked warnings about commercial overindulgence as negative-minded "croaking." After the arrival of depression many natives were willing to acknowledge only a mild disturbance of trade, which in no way threatened the inevitable progress of their commerce. "In the midst of the general financial storm that has swept over the land," they proclaimed, "Chicago has stood firm." By the time the crisis was over, citizens were convinced that their economic performance had fully disproved the calumny that theirs was a "Bubble City."[8]

Chicagoans made everything at hand bear testimony to the city's expansion. Boastful inhabitants interpreted increases in population and in the value of land as indices of economic vitality. The development of the city's physical plant was a further source of pride. As lavish expenditures on public works were both an evidence of past growth and an expression of faith in the future, Chicagoans delighted to read about the number of bridges built, the miles of streets and sidewalks paved, the length of sewer and gas pipe laid. Another evidence of growth was the "number and value of permanent residences, business blocks and public buildings" erected in Chicago. New structures were "the plain and permanent landmarks of the advancing population . . . the definite and explicit response to the demands of her growing trade." Even congested streets were signs of prosperity, and Chicagoans on occasion counted the traffic on their bridges, the business done by the post office, and the number of meals served daily at the Sherman House.[9]

Chicagoans' unbounded confidence was based on the simple axiom that their city's "fortunate geographic position" gave it "commercial advantages inferior to none in the great west." It was not merely that natives were in love with the city's hinterland, believing that its agricultural, industrial and commercial resources promised uninhibited and almost unending growth.[10] Chicagoans also claimed that the Creator himself had marked the city's destiny when he rolled back the waves of Lake Michigan. They thought that Chicago's peculiar location at the head of navigation on the western lakes made it the natural focus for much of the trade of the Northwest. In the 1840s, they declared that the possession of the Illinois and Michigan Canal would make the town the keystone in a vast arch of interregional commerce stretching from New York to New Orleans throught the basin of the Great Lakes and the Valley of the Mississippi.[11] At the same time boosters argued that the city's salient position and the superiority of the lakes as an avenue of export would attract most of the local trade of central Illinois.[12]

In the 1850s, some natives shifted their gaze toward the north. They asserted that the "fixed fact" of Lake Michigan would channel through the city much of the trade and travel of Wisconsin, Minnesota, and Iowa. By extension, the settlement of the continent would add to Chicago's hinterland the territory stretching west to the Rockies and north to the tundra.[13]

Chicagoans placed nearly as much faith in the makers of railroads as in the Maker of the Universe. The Garden City's location, they realized, would make it a focal point in the new system of land transportation. In turn, the new facilities for commerce assured that Chicago would be a great collecting and distributing center with a "commanding influence in the affairs of the great west." An examination of any railroad map, residents maintained, would convince the most skeptical outsider that Chicago was to rank among the great cities of the American continent. In harmony with this opinion, Chicagoans by the end of the 1850s liked to pretend that they lived in the leading rail center in the nation, the continent, or even the world.[14]

Just as Chicagoans gave credit for commercial growth to the simultaneous convergence of vast systems of land and water communications, so they argued that the excellence of transportation would make their town an important industrial center. To a greater extent than in other western towns, they stressed that the city's accessibility to markets and to raw materials was a function of its shipping and especially of its rail lines. "Not only by multiplying customers will our railroads tend to produce the result we are anticipating," said one publicist, "but they will place facilities at our disposal for bringing together the raw material of every description wanted. . . ." This opinion was shared by businessmen as well as boosters, for more than one western factory moved to Chicago precisely because of the superior transportation available there.[15]

If enthusiastic and coherent boosting was the first key to progress, the unity and energy with which Chicago's citizens pursued economic development was the second. There was little dissent from the goal of growth so persistently urged by newspapers and publicists. Although Congressman John Wentworth made his *Democrat* the voice of opposition to many activities of Chicago's business community, his locofoco rhetoric was intended largely for constituents in rural counties and met little positive response in the city itself. Both Wentworth and his newspaper, moreover, were happy to promote the growth of Chicago on what they considered a sound basis. Occasional workers and businessmen feared that a too rapid influx of labor or capital might work against them, but few doubted the value of a steady increase in population and trade.[16] Local medical, religious, and reform publications were also happy to print news about Chicago's prosperity and sometimes directly promoted its growth. Indeed, many reformers believed that Chicago's railroads and commercial connections formed valuable conduits for the dissemination of uplifting influences. The economic growth of the city was thought to make it the "centre of Intelligence and Moral and Religious Influence for the Northwest."[17]

In addition to a common purpose, Chicago lawyers, speculators, merchants, bankers, and journalists shared a common background and a penchant for hard work. Of ninety-five active business leaders who received biographical sketches in the first full-scale histories of the city, three quarters were natives of New England and New York. The same states supplied nine of the first ten mayors.[18] Twenty-eight percent of Chicago's $5000 wealth-holders in 1860 were born in New England, as compared with 10 percent in Cincinnati. If the emphasis in contemporary biographies is an indication, members of the elite were intensely devoted to the prosperity and civic well-being of the town, and over half of the ninety-five served in public offices. Visitors noticed the same characteristics. According to one, Chicago inhabitants were "true enterprising and hardy sons of New England whose energy is unyielding and whose genius knows no successful opposition."[19]

The memories of another visitor in the late 1840s reveal that political differences meant little within the business community. Whigs and Democrats who battled fiercely in Springfield mingled sociably in the Garden City. Members of both parties cooperated in 1846 and 1847 to secure and make successful the great national River-and-Harbor Convention. Even though the meeting was a reply to Polk's veto of an internal improvements bill, Democrats as well as Whigs realized that the attendance of thousands of delegates from all parts of the country served as a great advertisement. Newspapers of both affiliations supported the convention, and all of the city's leading citizens took a hand in its promotion. A few years later, the reciprocal trade treaty with Canada received similar bipartisan support because of its promised benefits for Chicago.[20]

Chicago's business community was open to newcomers. The real estate collapse of the late 1830s had driven many settlers from the city and opened opportunities for men of fresh talents. Half of its antebellum leaders arrived after 1841, and there were few large fortunes as late as 1850.[21] If ratios found in the census samples prevailed through the entire population, Chicago had 27 men worth twenty thousand dollars in real estate in 1850 and 490 a decade later. Both the city and its entrepreneurs were often described as young. The average age of men holding at least five thousand dollars in property dropped from 42.2 to 38.8 between 1850 and 1860.[22] One-third of these wealth-holders were under age 35 in 1860. In turn, the challenge of Chicago drew an excited response from new arrivals. In the 1830s, the land mania had often affected newcomers with Chicagoitis in a matter of days or hours. The same phenomenon could be observed as Chicago's economy moved into a new boom in the late 1840s and early 1850s. Travelers merely passing through sometimes filled their diaries with excited descriptions of its great potential, while young men looking for a place to make their fortune proclaimed to friends and family that "as a place of business Chicago cannot be beat." "I like Chicago very much," went a typical reaction. "I think it is very profitable. I shall take up permanent residence here."[23]

The enthusiasm and unity of purpose that all Chicagoans seemed to share expressed itself in deeds as well as words. Hostile outsiders remarked that the city seemed "mad after money," while more friendly observers noted "the 'Go-aheadism' of this busy and thriving community." All agreed, however, that Chicagoans were "determined to build . . . the finest city of the West." Natives of the city similarly attributed much of its growth to their own "untiring industry and intelligent foresight" and described their neighbors as "full of activity, enterprise, energy and hope—they have strong hands and good hearts and rather shrewd minds."[24]

Chicago entrepreneurs in 1840 had abundant need to display their energy, for the Great Crash had blighted hopes of outside aid. The collapse of the real estate market had frightened away the funds of eastern capitalists, most of whom were satisfied to realize the slightest amount of cash from Chicago holdings. The depression also destroyed the Illinois banking system and its internal improvements program, both of which Chicagoans had hoped would sustain their commercial growth. Goaded by the clear danger that these abandonments might make their city an also-ran in the race of urban greatness, Chicago businessmen in the ensuing decade mounted a vigorous campaign to acquire vital commercial facilities.

Failing in their efforts to maintain work on the Illinois and Michigan Canal because of the "wickedness, ignorance and perversion of an abominable legislature," Chicagoans began to organize a propaganda almost before the workers laid down their shovels. During 1841 citizens variously incubated public meetings, composed newspaper editorials, and published a pamphlet advocating the recommencement of construction. Chicago contractors also attempted without success to devise a plan for finishing the waterway. In the following year Isaac N. Arnold, William B. Ogden, and Justin Butterfield proposed a program in which the holders of canal bonds would participate in the supervision of further work in return for a new loan. While Arnold introduced the idea to the public and pushed it in the Illinois legislature, Ogden and others used their extensive business connections to mobilize support in the East. At the same time, a committee of the Chicago Mechanics Institute developed the engineering suggestions that made possible the completion of the Canal on a shallow rather than a deep cut. The intense lobbying reached a successful climax in February 1843, when the legislature incorporated the various suggestions in a new scheme for reviving the Canal. Once eastern capitalists had accepted the terms offered by the state and work was finally underway, Chicagoans had little to do except call for faster digging and oversee arguments among the Canal Trustees. Actual completion in 1848, however, was celebrated as a kind of civic festival. Nearly every Chicagoan turned out to watch the arrival of the first boat and to listen to grandiloquent speeches, which were too soon echoed in pompous editorials.[25]

Chicago's second great transportation improvement, the Galena and Chicago Union Railroad, was even more exclusively a Chicago enterprise. Chicagoans had first incorporated the railroad in 1836, but the arrival of the depression and a shift of control to New York and Springfield had prevented any work on the road. In the early 1840s, the best efforts of local editors and business to encourage construction met no response from the owners. Late in 1845, however, a group of prominent Chicago entrepreneurs including William H. Brown, Thomas Dyer, Walter Newberry, William B. Ogden, Benjamin W. Raymond, J.Y. Scammon, Mark Skinner, and Charles Walsh began a concerted endeavor to revive the railroad, organizing and rigging a railway convention that met at Rockford in January 1846. Over 300 delegates from northern Illinois dutifully resolved in favor of a railroad from Chicago to Galena and appointed a committee dominated by Chicagoans to receive subscriptions. After further negotiations, the Chicago syndicate purchased the old charter from its absentee owners in return for stock in the reorganized company.[26]

The most active Chicago backers also assumed responsibility for raising cash. Unable to obtain aid from Albany and Boston investors, Ogden and Scammon in the fall of 1847 traveled the entire distance of the line to solicit subscriptions. In support of their efforts Chicago journalists laid down a barrage of articles directed both to local and to eastern investors.[27] Chiefly because of the exertions of its Chicago directors, the company raised about $400,000 and opened its first thirteen miles of track by 1848. In the early 1850s annual dividends averaging 15 percent enabled the line to finance further construction, mainly by stock sales within Illinois.[28]

The campaigns for the Canal and the Galena Railroad received the endorsement of most Chicago businessmen not directly involved. The railroad, its supporters anticipated, would be of special value to export merchants, monopolizing the agricultural trade of northern Illinois and tapping the "accumulated products of the Valley of the Mississippi." The Canal was expected to benefit both exporters and lumber merchants by transforming central Illinois into Chicago's backyard. Grocery dealers looked forward to cheaper access to southern suppliers.[29] Only a few local retailers feared that the completion of the canal and railway would deprive them of their growing trade with farmers in surrounding counties. Other Chicagoans dismissed their apprehension as old-fogyism.[30]

No such disagreement troubled Chicago's drive to obtain legal banking. The mismanaged Bank of the State of Illinois had closed in 1843, leaving the entire state without chartered banks. Anti-bank sentiment aroused by its failure had caused Illinois voters in 1847 to accept a new constitution that forbade special charters and required a referendum on any general banking law. Whig papers began to agitate for the passage of such a law and the Board of Trade drafted a suitable bill. After the 1848/49 session of the legislature failed to adopt the measure, Chicago's businessmen prepared pro-bank memorials and its business-oriented newspapers redoubled their pressure for free banking. At its next session the General Assembly accepted a bill introduced by Thomas Dyer of Chicago. In the required referendum on the proposal held in November, 1851, Chicagoans voted 2,122 to 79 in favor.[31]

The success of these projects drastically altered the conditions of entrepreneurship. As the city shook off the depression and expanded the radius of its commercial influence in the 1850s, eastern businessmen again felt the hallucinogenic effects of Chicago's mushroom growth. As local banks were scarcely able to finance short-term transactions, Chicagoans who wanted to buy land, make permanent improvements, or construct factories had to turn to outsiders for necessary funds. Attracted by the prosperity of the city and by interest rates as high as 50 percent per year, eastern capitalists responded with a flood of money, which floated real estate prices to unaccustomed heights. The distinct profession of mortgage broker developed to handle investments in Chicago land.[32]

Eastern investment was equally responsible for Chicago's railroad boom. Except for the Galena and Chicago Union and two or three other short lines in northern Illinois, the railroads serving prewar Chicago were built mainly by eastern entrepreneurs and almost entirely by Atlantic Coast money. The trunk connections from Indiana and Michigan, for example, were built from east to west. The Michigan Central and the Michigan Southern, the refuse of Michigan's abandoned internal improvements program of the 1830s, were purchased in the late 1840s by separate syndicates of Boston and New York capitalists. Their eastern owners expected both lines to tap the traffic accumulating at Chicago and to become "important portions of the GREAT RAIL ROAD FROM THE ATLANTIC TO THE MISSISSIPPI." Hoping to carry the same traffic, each company fought in the early 1850s to gain first entrance to Chicago and to acquire feeder lines running west from the city. Michigan Southern investors thus gained control of the locally promoted Rock Island Railroad from Rock Island to LaSalle, enlisted other eastern capitalists, and caused the line to be extended to Chicago by 1852. The Michigan Central moved somewhat more cautiously. In the latter year it subsidized the Illinois Central, and its owners began to secure controlling interests in several smaller Illinois railroads, which were consolidated as the Chicago, Burlington and Quincy. The managers of all four companies made it clear in letters and reports that the two weaker lines were adjuncts and tools of their eastern sponsors.[33]

Chicago's third eastern line, the Pittsburgh, Fort Wayne and Chicago, was built under the aegis of the Pennsylvania Railroad. It consisted of three short lines organized locally but aided by the Pennsylvania after 1852. To speed the construction of the segment from Fort Wayne to Chicago, the two easterly lines brought about a union in 1856. During the two years that elapsed before completion, the Pennsylvania extended hundreds of thousands of dollars of additional aid and loaned the new company the services of J. Edgar Thompson as Director and Chief Engineer. Described as a rival of the Michigan Central and Michigan Southern, the railroad was designed largely as a western component of the Pennsylvania.[34]

The great success of the Galena and Chicago Union and the convergence of other lines on Chicago also helped to attract capitalists who viewed Illinois railroads simply as promising speculations. Unlike the entrepreneurs who promoted extensive through systems, these investors had little regard for the grand strategy of transportation development. Instead they sought railroads whose securities could be purchased cheaply and made to return a quick profit. The Chicago and Alton, first promoted by downstate interests, thus became a beanbag to be tossed from one group of financiers to another. The moguls who received the Illinois Central charter were also interested in windfall profits, devising a plan which was essentially a swindle. They hoped to peddle enough bonds in England to complete the road without making more than the minimum assessment on its stock, most of which they held themselves. They of course expected the value of their cut-rate shares to increase rapidly once the road was in operation.[35]

Capitalists who wanted to participate in the western railroad boom without undertaking their own projects invested heavily in the two major railroads in which Chicagoans retained control. In the early 1850s, the Galena and Chicago Union turned to the New York bond market for the several million dollars needed to construct its branch to Fulton. In 1855 William B. Ogden and several other Chicago entrepreneurs assembled the Chicago and Fond du Lac Railroad from two financially embarrassed lines in northern Illinois and Wisconsin. Although Chicagoans managed the road as a feeder for the city's export trade, eastern investors supplied most of the money for its construction.[36]

By the end of the decade it was obvious to Chicagoans and other westerners that the Garden City had to a large degree received its prosperity as a gift from outsiders. "What built Chicago?" wrote one native. "Let us answer, a junction of Eastern means and Western opportunity. . . . Greatness was forced upon Chicago as a golden subjugation." Competing cities complained that the whole surplus capital of New York and Boston had been "turned into the building of highways, towns, and factories along the basin of the lakes" and especially in the giant speculation known as Chicago.[37]

The local reaction to the deluge of money was almost without exception favorable. Although newspapers understandably expressed antagonism toward "Wall Street control" during the panics of 1854 and 1857, they normally made every effort to encourage investment. Boosters considered the influx of funds the only logical response to their strenuous efforts on behalf of the city and thought it proof that "capitalists have placed abundant confidence in our commercial position." Chicagoans were especially proud that the city had never invested a cent of public money in its railroads. Indeed, the choice of their city as a grand junction point seemed to demonstrate that its natural attractions were in fact irresistible.[38]

At the same time they welcomed eastern investment, Chicago's businessmen realized that the massive flow of capital set the terms for their city's development. As the rising land market attracted most of the uncommitted profits of its merchants, for example, the real estate boom ignited by eastern investors rendered futile the persistent efforts of such boosters as William Bross to promote the development of manufacturing. Instead, inhabitants noted, the construction of a web of railroads across the upper Mississippi Valley promised to bring Chicago all the commerce it could handle. To pursue their own lasting prosperity, businessmen were advised to devote their free energy to reforming and developing the city's local facilities for trade.[39]

Whether consciously or unconsciously, most Chicago business-men reacted vigorously to the challenge. Far from growing lazy and satisfied with the free gift of railroads, Chicagoans in the 1850s undertook a vast array of projects. Demonstrating the same force-fulness that had previously characterized the city, they adopted a variety of methods for achieving their goals, often combining pri-vate, public, and quasi-public action on the same issue. The result was an entrepreneurial symbiosis in which Chicago saw to those in-stitutional and physical needs that outsiders ignored.

Chicago's newspapers not only served as civic cheerleaders and advertising agencies but also helped to test new ideas. The construc-tion of railroads by outsiders had removed from Chicago entrepre-neurs the necessity of devising railroad schemes and from editors the burden of publicizing and promoting such plans. Rather than projecting the grand railroad systems envisioned in other western cities, Chicagoans toyed with proposals to change the city's pattern of trade by water. Whether they were proposed by editors or by pri-vate citizens, the reaction to the various suggestions in Chicago newspapers measured both their popular appeal and their practical-ity. A proposal by William B. Ogden to improve navigation on the Illinois River by diverting the waters of Lake Michigan through a deep-cut steamboat canal, for instance, drew serious argument from advocates of alternative methods and led to the establishment of an Illinois River Improvement Company in 1857.[40] Chicagoans also convinced themselves by repetition that there would be "no difficulty in establishing direct Western trans-Atlantic trade." Varied efforts on the part of William Bross and the *Democratic Press* to encourage fuller trade with the upper lakes, on the other hand, met little response. No other newspapers or publicist showed serious interest in somewhat impractical plans to make Chicago the trading center for Lake Superior or to circumvent the Falls at Niagara by building a canal from Georgian Bay to Lake Ontario.[41]

Chicagoans were happy to use the city government in acting on their city's needs. The municipality took energetic measures to im-prove the city's harbor. While newspapers lamented the inattention of Congress, the city fathers straightened and deepened the river and assumed responsibility for dredging a channel to the lake. At one point they created a minor scandal by illegally seizing and operating a government dredge idly anchored in the river.[42] Chicago's civic leadership also had the foresight to attempt to provide adequate streets, bridges, sewers, and water. Although not directly designed to serve the city's trade, these measures prevented it from sinking into the mud under the weight of increasing business.

Entrepreneurs coordinated their private actions through the Board of Trade. Its sessions in the 1850s were an efficient substitute for the time-honored promotional technique of the ad hoc "public meeting." In accord with the general desires of the business community, the board in 1849 successfully petitioned for a rebate of tolls on goods passing between the Mississippi Valley and the East over the Illinois and Michigan Canal. Ten years later it helped to obtain an additional reduction of canal charges. In further pursuit of cheaper water transportation to the south, the organization twice attempted to marshall a cooperative effort on the part of Chicago, St. Louis, and other concerned towns to improve navigation on the Illinois River. In a similar manner the board cooperated with counterparts in other lake cities in efforts to improve navigation at the St. Clair Flats near Detroit, sending delegates to conventions in other cities and sponsoring a meeting in Chicago. The organization also led in mobilizing support of the popular Reciprocity Treaty of 1854, which provided for the free exchange of all primary products between the United States and Canada and the free use of the St. Lawrence and the Welland Canal by American shipping.[43]

Despite the importance of collective activity through the city government and the Board of Trade, the chief responsibility for the development of Chicago's commercial facilities still lay with its businessmen as individuals. No advocacy by local editors was needed to induce the city's commission merchants and exporters to build larger grain elevators or to establish the system of grain grading. Chicago's private bankers and free banks were also eager to furnish the short-term credit necessary for the export of grain and pork. When credit evaporated in the fall of 1857, Chicago commission merchants banded together to purchase and sell on their own account the grain offered in the city.[44] Neither railroads nor banking facilities would have sufficed to make the city a great trading center, moreover, had not Chicago wholesalers, exporters, and lumber merchants worked to develop networks of agents, suppliers, and customers throughout the Mississippi Valley and the basin of Lake Michigan.

The energy with which entrepreneurs pursued personal and collective goals and the forcefulness with which natives proclaimed the magnificence of their town were two facets of the single process by which Chicagoans reacted to opportunities for economic growth. The confidence of businessmen and of boosters were mutually reinforcing. Publicists urged entrepreneurs to action and took the success of their operations to justify ever-heightened enthusiasm. The city's attitude toward its major rivals indicates something of its self-esteem. After fighting with St. Louis to be named the site of the River-and-Harbor Convention and struggling to dominate the St. Louis Railroad Convention two years later, boosters of the Garden City declared open war in the early 1850s and delighted in describing the deficiencies of its rival. A few years, they proclaimed, would see the eclipse of the Missouri metropolis, for the "genius of the age" demanded and assured Chicago's supremacy.[45] In the same decade, Chicagoans virtually dismissed Cincinnati, maintaining that "her citizens may as well make up their minds to yield with a good grace her claims to be the Queen City of the West. Nature has barred the claim and no enterprise on the part of her citizens will be able to set it aside." Chicagoans mocked the "exaggerated statements and incorrect comparisons" by which the Ohio town strove to sustain her former preeminence. The best Chicagoans were willing to allow their rival was a subordinate role as a producer of manufactured goods for Chicago merchants.[46]

Chicago boosterism and Chicago entrepreneurship were also parallel reactions to a distinct phase of the city's growth. In the words of one contemporary, antebellum Chicago was "the type of that class of American towns which have made themselves conspicuous, and almost ridiculous by their rapid growth." According to the typology of historian Charles Gates, Chicago between 1845 and 1870 passed through its "boom stage." In these years, and especially in the 1850s, the development of transportation facilities tied Chicago to the nation's economic heartland and made commercial agriculture feasible for the first time in many parts of its hinter-

land. In turn these developments opened an abundance of new opportunities for the region's cities and towns by creating needs for
manufactured goods and for urban commercial services. Entrepreneurs attempting to satisfy these wants could develop their businesses with little inhibition from established commercial habits or
vested interests. At the same time, initially low land and resource
prices attracted outside capital whose arrival expanded the bubble.
As had earlier been the case in the cities of the Ohio Valley, the
boom stage in Chicago faded into a stage of economic maturity
only when the most lucrative opportunities had been exploited and
potential margins of profit had declined toward levels found in older parts of the nation.[47]

The specific effects of the boom era on antebellum Chicago are
easy to discern. The plethora of chances for making a fortune confirmed Chicagoans' faith in the unrivalled future of their city, incited them to vigorous pursuit of profits in all lines of business, and
attracted the outside capitalists who created new opportunities for
unusual gain by stoking the city's boom. As Chicago faced unexplored possibilities for growth rather than established patterns of
economic activity, its entrepreneurs frequently accepted no limitations on their horizons and caused rivals to complain of "the avari-
cious grasping disposition that manifests itself in every public
movement made by the citizens of Chicago." The city's receptiveness to hard-working newcomers and outside investors and the
complaints about "sharp bargains and over-reaching, undue
coloring and actual misrepresentation" on the part of its businessmen also reflected the openness of boom-stage Chicago to any economic activity. The conditions of growth at mid-century were well
summarized by the Chicagoan who recalled that "these were times
when the coming of great enterprises seemed to fill the air, and the
men were found who were ready to grasp and execute them."[48]

NOTES

1. *Toledo Blade* in *Chicago Journal,* April 11, 1853; *Pittsburgh Post* in *Chicago Democratic Press,* March 24, 1856; John Kirk to *Youngstown* (Ohio) *Free Press,* May 5, 1854, John Kirk Letterbook, Chicago Historical Society. Also see: *Cincinnati Gazette,* November 26, 1855; *Cincinnati Times,* May 27, 1857; *Indianapolis Journal,* August 3, 1857; *Cleveland Plain Dealer,* September 10, 1845; "Chicago in 1856," *Putnam's Monthly Magazine* 7 (June 1856): 606-7.

2. *Prairie Farmer* 14 (March 1854): 125; *Chicago Democratic Press,* December 10, 1856; Cecil K. Byrd, *A Bibliography of Illinois Imprints, 1814-1858* (Chicago, 1966), pp. 396–97, 450, 454, 503.

3. John S. Wright, *Chicago Investments* (Chicago, 1860); John S. Wright, *Investments in Chicago* (Chicago, 1858); Lloyd Lewis, *John S. Wright: Prophet of the Prairies* (Chicago, 1941), pp. 99, 112–14.

4. Norris, *Business Directory,* p. 4. Also see: William Bross in *Galena Gazette,* November 14, 1854; *Chicago Democrat,* December 6, 1851; *Chicago Tribune,* January 14, 1858; John S. Wright in *Boston Courier,* September 23, 1847; *Chicago Press and Tribune,* January 4, 1859.

5. *Chicago Democratic Press, Review of Commerce* for 1855, p. 65; *Chicago Democratic Press,* October 21, 1854; Norris, *General Directory . . . of the City of Chicago for the Year 1844,* p. iii; Norris, *Chicago Directory for 1846-47,* p. 4; *Chicago American,* September 4, 1841; Wright, *Chicago,* pp. xxvii, xxxix; Barry, *Trans-Atlantic Trade,* pp. 9–10.

6. Colbert, *Garden City,* p. 3; Norris, *General Directory . . . of the City of Chicago for the Year 1844,* p. 20. Also see: *Chicago Democratic Press Review of Commerce* for 1855, p. 3; G.M. Dyethus in *Chicago Tribune,* March 24, 1856; Belcher, *St. Louis and Chicago,* p. 56; Junius Mulvey to Oliver Mulvey, June 22, 1854; Harry Kelsey, *Frontier Capitalist: The Life of John Evans* (Denver, 1969), p. 72; Abbott, "Civic Pride," pp. 399–412.

7. *Chicago Democrat,* May 28, 1834; *Chicago American,* August 8, 1835; Gurdon S. Hubbard to E.A. Russell, September 25, 1835, Hubbard Collection, Chicago Historical Society; George Brown to sister, March 2, 1846, George Brown Collection, Chicago Historical Society; Brown, *Present and Future Prospects,* p. 6; Chicago and Fond du Lac Railroad, Second *Annual Report* (1857), p. 10; *Chicago in 1860,* p. 135; *Chicago Democratic Press, Review of Commerce* for 1853, p. 69.

8. *Chicago Times,* March 25, 1858; *Chicago Press and Tribune, Review of Commerce* for 1858, p. 3, for 1859, p. 3; Chamberlain, *Chicago and Its Suburbs,* pp. 65–66; Mayor John C. Haines, Inaugural Address, *Chicago Times,* March 18, 1858; Lewis, *John S. Wright,* pp. 190–91.

9. *Chicago Democratic Press, Review of Commerce* for 1852, p. 2, for 1856, p. 3; Guyer, *History of Chicago,* pp. 9, 26; Mayor Isaac Millikin, Inaugural Address, *Chicago Tribune,* March 16, 1854; *Chicago Times,* December 25, 1858; *Gem of the Prairie,* February 5, 1848; Goodspeed and Healy, *Cook County,* 1: 231, 245; Junius Mulvey to Oliver Mulvey, June 22, 1854, Mulvey Collection, Chicago Historical Society; Hoyt, "Land Values," p. 63.

10. *Chicago Democrat,* September 3, 1834. Also see Brown, *Present and Future Prospects,* p. 9; Chicago Board of Trade, *Report* for 1860, p. 56; Gerhard, *Illinois As It Is,* p. 390; Norris, *Business Advertiser,* pp. 137–38.

11. *Prairie Farmer* 10 (January 1850): 14; Mayor John C. Haines, Inaugural Address, *Chicago Tribune,* March 17, 1858; Thomas, "Statistics Concerning the City of Chicago," p. 178; Walter Newberry, in *Chicago American,* February 20, 1841; *Western Citizen,* July 26, 1842; *Chicago City Directory and Annual Advertiser for 1849-50* (Chicago, 1849), p. 8.

12. *Western Citizen,* July 26, 1842; *Chicago Tribune,* December 28, 1850; Richard P. Morgan, *Report of the Survey of the Route of the Galena and Chicago Union Rail Road,* p. 4; Norris, *Chicago Directory for 1846–47,* pp. 18–19.

13. *Chicago Democratic Press, Review of Commerce* for 1854, p. 24; *Gem of the Prairie,* March 29, 1851; Wright, *Chicago;* John L. Scripps, *The Undeveloped Northern Portion of the American Continent* (Chicago, 1856); Chicago and Fond du Lac Railroad, Second *Annual Report* (1857), p. 16; *Chicago Democratic Press,* June 27, 1855, September 13, 1856; Belcher, *St. Louis and Chicago,* pp. 40, 55.

14. *1851 Directory,* p. 11. See also *Chicago Democratic Press,* January 4 and 6, July 12, 1853; *Chicago Democratic Press, Review of Commerce* for 1852, pp. 19–22; *Chicago in 1860,* p. 149; *Chicago Almanac and Advertiser for 1855* (Chicago, 1855), p. 19; Wright, *Investments in Chicago,* p. 2; *Chicago Tribune, Review of Commerce* for 1864, p. 25.

15. *Chicago Democratic Press, Review of Commerce* for 1854, p. 56. See also: *Chicago Democrat,* October 13, 1848; *Western Citizen,* July 13, 1852; *Chicago Magazine* 1 (March, 1857): 94–97; Chicago Board of Trade, *Report* for 1861, p. 97; *DeBow's Review* 18 (March, 1855): 397; Fritz Redlich, *History of American Business Leaders* (Ann Arbor, 1940), 1: 95; William T. Hutchinson, *Cyrus Hall McCormick* (New York, 1968), 1: 260–70.

16. Don E. Fehrenbacher, *Chicago Giant: A Biography of "Long John" Wentworth* (Madison, Wis., 1957), p. 73; *Chicago Democratic Press, Review of Commerce* for 1854, p. 29; Stanley L. Jones, "Anti-Bank and Anti-Monopoly Movements in Illinois, 1845–1862" (Ph.D. diss., University of Illinois, 1947), pp. 68–70, 173.

17. *Congregational Herald,* quoted in *Chicago Democratic Press,* May 7, 1853. Also see: *Northwestern Christian Advocate,* quoted in *Chicago Democrat,* October 22, 1852; *Northwestern Medical and Surgical Journal,* 4 (May 1851), quoted in Kelsey, *Frontier Capitalist,* p. 72; *Chicago Record,* 1857; *Western Citizen,* 1847–1853; *Watchman of the Prairies,* 1847–1850, especially "Sermon on Railroads," 1 (December 7, 1847).

18. The author compiled a list of ninety-five Chicagoans who were active as business leaders in the 1840s and 1850s and who received biographical sketches in Andreas, *History of Chicago,* or David Ward Wood, *Chicago and Its Distinguished Citizens* (Chicago, 1881). Of the sample members, forty-one were from New England, thirty from New York, ten foreign-born, six from the South, five from Pennsylvania-New Jersey-Delaware, and three from the Middle West. Also see Pierce, *Chicago,* 1: 174–78.

19. Henry Spaulding Diary, 1848, Spaulding Collection, Chicago Historical Society. Also see: J.P. Thompson, letter in Curtiss, *Western Portraiture,* p. 306; *Chicago Magazine,* 1 (March-July 1857): 31–55, 1128–28, 207–8, 305–13, 391–403; Belcher, *St. Louis and Chicago,* p. 24.

20. John L. Peyton, *Over the Alleghenies and Across the Prairies* (London, 1870), pp. 323–51; *Prairie Farmer* 7 (August 1847): 260; William B. Ogden to David Watkinson, July 1, 1847, Ogden Collection, Chicago Historical Society; *Chicago Journal* and *Chicago Democrat,* January-July 1847; *Chicago Democratic Press,* February 3, 1853; *Chicago Democrat,* February 15 and 21, 1851.

21. The arrival dates are taken from the list described in Note 18. The census sample described in Appendix A shows only 3 out of 1078 workers in 1850 with over twenty thousand dollars of real estate.

22. William B. Ogden to James Allen, January 15, 1840, Ogden Collection, Chicago Historical Society; *Chicago Democratic Press, Review of Commerce* for 1857, p. 30; J.P. Thompson, letter in Curtiss, *Western Portraiture*, p. 306; census sample.

23. William Carter to George Carter, November 2, 1853, Carter Collection, and James Warnock to William Prentiss, October 19, 1848, Warnock Collection, both in Chicago Historical Society. Also see: L.C.P. Freer to Lawrence Hamblin, May 23, 1836, Freer Collection; Benjamin Barker to Jacob Barker, September 6, 1832, Barker Collection; Edward Talcott to Hunt Ormsba, June 23, 1835, Talcott Collection; Bemsley Huntoon to Josiah Huntoon, December 15, 1837, Huntoon Collection; John Kirk to Mr. Elliott, May 5, 1854, John Kirk Letterbook; James Lawrence to family, May 20, 1857, Lawrence Collection; Henry Spaulding Diary, 1848, Spaulding Collection; Anonymous Diary, Journey from Boston to Chicago, 1849; Jacob Gross to family, December 28, 1856, Gross Collection, all in Chicago Historical Society; Hutchinson, *McCormick*, 2: 81, 102.

24. William Ferguson, *America by River and Rail* (London, 1856), p. 425; Charles Weld, *A Vacation Tour in the United States and Canada* (London, 1855), p. 191; Anthony Trollope, *North America* (Philadelphia, 1863), p. 157; *Chicago Press and Tribune,* August 25, 1858; William B. Ogden to William H. Swift, November 20, 1846, William B. Ogden Collections, Chicago Historical Society.

25. William B. Ogden to N. Bloodgood, March 26, 1841; to H. Norton, January 5, 1841; to Arthur Bronson, January 19, 1841: William B. Ogden Collection, Chicago Historical Society; *Chicago American,* March 13 and 20, December 22, 1841; [Henry Brown], *a Letter to the People of the State of Illinois, on the Subject of Public Credit . . . and the Illinois and Michigan Canal* (Chicago, 1841); I.N. Arnold in *Chicago Democrat,* November 30, 1842; letter of Ira Miltimore in *Prairie Farmer* 3 (January 1843): 22; "Report of the Committee on Finance," in *Illinois Reports* (1842/43); *Chicago Journal,* June 14, 1845, April 17, 1848; *Chicago Democrat,* February 2, April 18, 1848; John V. Farwell, *Some Recollections* (Chicago, 1911) p. 61.

26. *Chicago American,* September 1, 1841; Walter L. Newberry to Arthur Bronson, September 4, 1840, Bronson Collection, Chicago Historical Society; Ralph W. Marshall, "The Early History of the Galena and Chicago Union Railroad" (M.A. diss., University of Chicago, 1937), pp. 12–29, 35–38; Pierce, *Chicago,* 1: 45; *Chicago Journal,* October 13, December 15, 1845, January 19, 1846.

27. J. Y. Scammon, *William B. Ogden,* Fergus Historical Series no. 17 (Chicago, 1882), pp. 49, 62–72; Galena and Chicago Union Railroad Company, First *Annual Report* (1847/48), pp. 4–5; *Chicago Democrat,* August 10 and 24, September 7, 1847; *Chicago Journal,* July 26, August 23, November 15, 1847; *Prairie Farmer* 7 (September 1846): 269; John S. Wright in *Boston Courier,* August 27, September 23, October 7, 1847.

28. Galena and Chicago Union Railroad, Second *Annual Report* (1848/49), pp. 4–7; *Chicago Democratic Press, Review of Commerce* for 1852, pp. 17–18; Colbert, *Garden City,* p. 64; Pierce, *Chicago,* 1: 116–18.

29. Morgan, *Galena and Chicago Union Railroad,* pp. 15–17; Galena and Chicago Union Railroad, First *Annual Report* (1847/48), p. 7; *Chicago Democrat,* January, 9, 1849; *Chicago Journal,* August 3, 1846; Norris, *Chicago City Directory for 1845-6,* p. 138; *Fisher's National Magazine,* 1 (October 1845): 461; Balestier, *Annals of Chicago,* pp. 38–39.

30. John V. Farwell, speech of December 30, 1850, quoted in Wood, *Chicago and Its Distinguished Citizens,* p. 456; *Chicago Democrat,* March 11, 1851; Brown, *Present and Future Prospects,* p. 9; Lewis, *John S. Wright,* p. 114.

31. Don M. Dailey, "The Development of Banking in Chicago before 1890" (Ph.D. diss., Northwestern University, 1934), pp. 105–110, 139–47; Jones, "Anti-Bank and Anti-Monopoly Movements," pp. 28–43, 78–88, 96, 103; F. Cyril James, *The Growth of Chicago Banks* (New York, 1938), 1: 83–158, 183; George W. Dowrie, *The Development of Banking in Illinois, 1817-1863,* University of Illinois Studies in the Social Sciences, vol. 2, no. 4 (Urbana, Ill., 1913), pp. 102, 113, 132, 135; Pierce, *Chicago,* 2: 118–20.

32. Henry M. Flint, "The Commerce and Banking System of Chicago," *Hunt's Merchants' Magazine* 35 (August 1856): 173; Gerhard, *Illinois As It Is,* p. 391; Luther Bixby to John C. Bixby, April 4, 1850, Luther Bixby Collection, Chicago Historical Society; Alexander Leslie Diary, 1857–58, Chicago Historical Society; Dailey, "Banking in Chicago," pp. 196–201, 233–44, 518.

33. John Jervis, *Report on the Michigan Southern and Northern Indiana Rail-Roads* (New York, 1850), p. 7. For the rivalry between the Michigan Central and the Michigan Southern and their subordinate lines, see: Arthur Johnson and Barry Supple, *Boston Capitalists and Western Railroads* (Cambridge, Mass., 1967), pp. 88–115, 155–80; Richard Overton, *Burlington West: A Colonization History of the Burlington Railroad* (Cambridge, Mass., 1941), pp. 5–72; Paul W. Gates, *The Illinois Central and Its Colonization Work* (Cambridge, Mass., 1934), pp. 44, 90–91; annual reports and special circulars of the Michigan Central, Michigan Southern and Northern Indiana, Chicago and Rock Island, and Chicago, Burlington and Quincy Railroads.

34. Thomas S. Fernon, *Report to J. Edgar Thompson on the Trade of the West* (1852), pp. 11–14; Pittsburgh, Fort Wayne and Chicago Railroad Company, *Exhibit,* pp. 9–13, 28, 43–55, 60–65; Fort Wayne and Chicago Railroad Company, *Report of the President and Chief Engineer* (1854), pp. 5, 9–17; George H. Burgess and Miles C. Kennedy, *Centennial History of the Pennsylvania Railroad Company* (Philadelphia, 1949), pp. 76, 176–81.

35. Gates, *Illinois Central,* pp. 48–50, 66–68; Johnson and Supple, *Boston Capitalists,* pp. 127–28; D.W. Yungmeyer, "An Excursion into the Early History of the Chicago and Alton Railroad," *Journal of the Illinois State Historical Society* 37 (March 1945): 10–20.

36. Galena and Chicago Union Railroad Company, Sixth *Annual Report* (1852/53), p. 6; Eleventh *Annual Report* (1857/58), pp. 23–32; Chicago, St. Paul and Fond du Lac Railroad Company, First *Annual Report* (1856), pp. 8–15, Second *Annual Report* (1857), pp. 3–4, 9, 19–24; *Chicago Democratic Press, Review of Commerce* for 1855, p. 66; Guyer, *History of Chicago,* p. 155.

37. Chamberlin, *Chicago and Its Suburbs,* pp. 171–72; Cincinnati *Gazette,* February 15, 1859.

38. *Chicago Democratic Press, Review of Commerce* for 1853, p. 19; *Chicago Tribune,* April 13, 1860; Chamberlin, *Chicago and Its Suburbs,* p. 171; Wright, *Chicago,* p. 32; Andreas, *History of Chicago,* 1: 262; Dailey, "Banking in Chicago," p. 212.

39. *Chicago Democratic Press,* August 15, October 6, 1853, January 2, November 18, 1854; *Chicago Times,* October 8, 1859; *Chicago Democrat,* November 24, 1848; *Chicago Tribune,* April 20, 1860; William B. Ogden in *Chicago Democratic Press,* March 23, 1854.

40. *Chicago Democratic Press,* March 6, 1854, December, 1856–January, 1857; Pierce, *Chicago,* 2: 39; Scammon, *William B. Ogden,* pp. 49–50.

41. *Chicago Democratic Press,* February 3 and 15, 1853, July 16, 1857; Barry, *Trans-Atlantic Trade,* pp. 3–9; Bross, *The Northwest;* William Bross, *History of Chicago* (Chicago, 1876), p. 66; *The Georgian Bay Canal: Reports of Col. R.B. Mason, Consulting Engineer, and Kivas Tully, Chief Engineer* (Chicago, 1858).

42. Pierce, *Chicago,* 1: 92–93, 2: 69; Andreas, *History of Chicago,* 1: 582; Taylor, *Board of Trade,* 1: 188; Graham, *Report,* pp. 32–33; Mayor John C. Haines, Inaugural Address, *Chicago Tribune,* March 17, 1858.

43. Colbert, *Garden City,* pp. 48–51; Andreas, *History of Chicago,* 1: 582; Taylor, *Board of Trade,* 1: 226, 268; *Chicago Democrat,* November 24, 1848, November 19, 1851; *Chicago Democratic Press,* March 9, 1854; *Chicago Magazine* 1 (April 1857): 184–85; Illinois, Board of Trustees of the Illinois and Michigan Canal, Fifth *Annual Report* (1849), in *Illinois Reports* (1861), p. 9, 44–45.

44. Dailey, "Banking in Chicago," pp. 196–226; Chamberlin, *Chicago and Its Suburbs,* p. 66.

45. *Chicago Democrat,* January 23, 1850; *Chicago Democratic Press,* October 12, 1852, March 30, 1853, May 22, 1855; Barry, *International Trade,* p. 120; Wright, *Chicago,* pp. 66–111, 140–91; Belcher, *St. Louis and Chicago,* pp. 19–74; *Chicago Press and Tribune,* March 10, 1859.

46. *Chicago Democratic Press,* April 6, 1855; Chicago Board of Trade, *Report* for 1858, pp. 44–45; *Chicago in 1860,* pp. 209–10; *Chicago Democratic Press,* April 8, 1856, April 28, 1857; *Chicago Press and Tribune,* June 8, 1859; *Railroad Record* 7 (June 23, 1859): 205.

47. "Chicago in 1856," p. 606; Charles M. Gates, "Boom Stages in American Expansion," *Business History Review* 33 (Spring 1959): 32–42.

48. *Galena Jeffersonian,* November 23, 1851; "Chicago in 1856," p. 612; Bross, *History of Chicago,* p. 121.

CINCINNATI:
THE ABDICATION
OF THE QUEEN CITY

A slow paralysis afflicted Cincinnati enterprise in the twenty years before the Civil War. In the early 1840s, the city still retained the ambition and foresight which had made it the unquestioned Queen of the West. Around mid-century, however, its citizens lost their ability to conceive and carry out projects of benefit to the city as a whole. Over the next decade Cincinnati was tormented by lethargic boosterism and ineffectual entrepreneurship, by decreasingly cogent economic thought, and by the mounting bitterness of internal strife. By 1860, a local editor could lament that the former Queen City was a deposed monarch whose "widow's weeds and discrowned head" attested the effects of "bad advisors, careless agents, and small officers."[1]

Long before Chicago, Cincinnati had developed and refined many of the techniques of self-advertisement. The publication of Daniel Drake's *Picture of Cincinnati* in 1815 had represented "the first systematic attempt to present the development of a Western City in its many dimensions." Its success set a pattern for Cincinnati writers, who periodically inventoried their town's social, physical, and economic growth. In 1826, Edward Mansfield and Benjamin

Drake "undertook to make a little book, descriptive of Cincinnati, as an inducement to immigration." A decade later, the second author followed *Cincinnati in 1826* with an article on "Cincinnati at the Close of 1835." In 1841, Charles Cist published *Cincinnati in 1841,* a book intended specifically to impress on Atlantic cities "the resources, business and prosperity of Cincinnati." The volume was well received by Cincinnati leaders, who were delighted at the broadcast of Cist's enthusiastic praise.[2]

Cincinnatians simultaneously explored other media of publicity. In the 1830s, Timothy Flint and James Hall made Cincinnati the central exhibit in their physical and economic geographies of the West. Along with William D. Gallagher they also changed Cincinnati's literary magazines from pallid imitations of eastern reviews into vehicles for forceful articles and stories about the West and its metropolis. In the 1840s, Cist and Mansfield reduced the political content of the newspapers they edited in order to free space for economic discussion. Hall also helped to set a style for western boosterism by making memorials to Congress about a national armory and about navigation on the Ohio less dry petitions than elaborate expositions of Cincinnati's commercial advantages.[3]

In 1835 and 1836 many of these publicists cooperated with Cincinnati's most vigorous entrepreneurs in a series of open meetings designed to formulate a coherent transportation strategy. A self-designated "Board of Internal Improvements" chaired by Daniel Drake recommended the construction of short roads, canals, and railroads in all directions from the Queen City to supplement a popular plan for a railroad to South Carolina. The unofficial "board" placed special emphasis on ties to the Whitewater and Little Miami Valleys. Endorsed by the city's intellectual spokesmen and newspapers, these improvements were expected to cause the inhabitants of the Ohio Valley "to acknowledge Cincinnati as their common center."[4]

In the next decade, Cincinnatians willingly displayed their "commercial enterprise and liberality." Working to make their city the focus of "an extended circle of business enterprise," they pushed transporation facilities into the surrounding valleys. To the south, they aided a turnpike to Lexington and applauded the improvement of navigation on the Licking River. In Ohio the availability of public funds facilitated more extensive building. Under the so-called Plunder Law of 1837, the state matched private invest-ment in road companies with close to $1,000,000 for macadamized turnpikes leading directly to Cincinnati and almost as much for roads elsewhere in southwestern Ohio. By the mid-1840s, the re-gion's highway system consisted of sunbursts of minor roads cen-tering on each county seat and linked to Cincinnati by half a dozen thoroughfares. The local promoters of the Cincinnati and White-water Canal Company also tapped the state treasury for $150,000 and the municipality for $280,000.[5]

Railroads were pushed with equal energy. The Little Miami Rail-road owed its completion largely to the dedication of the leading men of business in the city. Although little of its stock was pur-chased in Cincinnati, the high standing of its directors enabled it to become the first western railroad to draw on the resources of Boston capitalists. The local influence of its organizers also helped it secure $430,000 from the city and $115,000 from the state. The Cincinnati, Hamilton and Dayton, conceived by Queen City entre-preneurs in 1848, sold $650,000 of stock to Cincinnatians in the first month of its offering. Such enthusiastic support at home made it easy to raise additional funds in New York.[6]

In harmony with their successful pursuit of internal improve-ments, Cincinnatians through most of the 1840s expressed no doubts about the economic health of their city. Repeating ideas of the 1830s, they asserted that the past progress and present growth of the West assured Cincinnati a leading rank among the cities of the Union. The middle as well as the upper ranks of society appar-ently shared this expectation. One workingman reported that any newcomer with ambition and resources could make a fortune. Another wrote that "the country improves very fast and Every one that is industrious and Saving always makes money the Population of our city is now about one Hundred thousand and it is now only 60 years Sins the Read men was in full Possession of all this Coun-try and it was a Dens forest and no white men at all. . . . Just look at this Increse and the Increse is still going on in proportion to the Amt of Population as heretofore. . . ."[7]

Cincinnati in the 1830s and early 1840s had been proud to pos-sess "citizens remarkable for sagacity, intelligence, patriotism and energy; men who perceived what the city might be, and were willing to work for its interests." About 1848, however, newspapers started to complain that businessmen were apathetic about new railroad projects. The spirit of enterprise, they lamented, had become rheumatic and infirm, and Cincinnati merchants lacked the ability to work together for common goals. By the middle of the 1850s the Queen City was infested with lethargy and preferred to "rest supinely upon past laurels."[8]

This decay of civic entrepreneurship that worried boosters was in part a product of changing attitudes among Cincinnati's elite. In the earlier years, successful citizens had indeed cared about the progress and prosperity of their community. Though they dominated local decisions, they had been open to suggestions and participation from below. During the 1840s, however, wealthy Cincinnatians became steadily less interested in public affairs and paid more attention to solidifying their own position in "society." Controlling an increasing share of the city's wealth, they were more and more concerned with enjoying the wealth they had obtained in travel, parties, and balls and in marking themselves off from the middling classes. The Grand Ball to celebrate the opening of the Burnet House, a magnificent hotel building which symbolized civic achievement, epitomized the new order. Where earlier milestones of the city's maturity had been open public festivals, the Grand Soiree of 1850 was a social event attended on invitation only by a self-constituted upper crust.[9]

Two prominent examples show the effects of these changes. The city's interest in improving navigation at the falls of the Ohio dated from the first use of steamboats on the river. The completion of the Louisville and Portland Canal in 1830 had satisfied Cincinnati's needs for a time, but the construction of larger boats and increasing traffic soon made it an "almost total failure . . . for the purposes for which it was intended."[10] In response, Cincinnatians in 1842 and 1843 mounted a vigorous campaign to convince Congress to enlarge the canal. The failure of this drive apparently stunned the city's sense of initiative, for Cincinnatians in the following years were unable to decide what to do next or how to do it. In 1846, 1851, and 1853, committees resolved on the necessity of a new canal on the north side of the river. In 1856 and 1859, in contrast, natives reiterated their desire for an expansion of the existing facility. Occasionally despairing of more words, Cincinnatians in 1850,

1853, and 1858 backed schemes to build an Indiana canal by private means but were unable to muster adequate financing.[11] At other times the city's entrepreneurs became so bored that the Chamber of Commerce was unwilling even to prepare a petition to support efforts for federal action.[12]

Local capitalists also failed to provide funds for the southern railroad connection, which had been talked about for two decades. Although the depression of the 1840s had killed plans for a single line through Knoxville to Charleston, Cincinnatians were repeatedly reminded in the next decade that the proposed Covington and Lexington and Danville Railroads would link Cincinnati to the Southern rail system. The former line did receive a municipal subscription of $100,000, but its promoters sold only $21,350 of stock to individual Cincinnatians before the crash of 1857.[13] Attempts to raise money for the Danville line were equally futile. A public meeting in 1853 elicited much hot air but little cash, and similar efforts in 1855 fell far short of the modest goal of $100,000. Two years later another committee of leading businessmen was unable to find even $30,000 for the road.[14]

The neglect of both enterprises is easily explained. No matter what benefits they promised the city, neither offered hope of immediate profits. The managers of the Kentucky railroads were of dubious competence and the lines themselves traversed great stretches of unproductive land. Investors in the Danville line could expect heavy responsibilities but no dividends until the company made connections in Tennessee. A new falls canal in Indiana would have required several years to build and would have faced the competition of a fully amortized rival controlled by a hostile city.

Cincinnati businessmen lacked "enlightened public spirit" in other cases as well. Earlier Queen City entrepreneurs had frequently been willing to promote the general growth of their town, anticipating their reward in the effects of increased population and trade on land values and business. Newspapers after mid-century, in contrast, complained that many Cincinnatians concerned themselves with only their most immediate interests and were satisfied so long as their own affairs prospered. In particular, journalists pointed to shortsighted river traders who were uninterested in railroads and to property owners and land speculators who hesitated to risk their capital in uncertain ventures.[15]

The annals of Cincinnati in fact show numerous instances in which natives undermined their future prosperity for immediate profits. The *Cincinnati Gazette,* for example, refused to publish news about local wholesaling and manufacturing because these interests bought insufficient advertising. A plan to bridge the Ohio River met opposition from Cincinnati river traders, from merchants and draymen who wanted to retain the income arising from the transshipment of goods, and from property owners who feared the movement of population and business into Kentucky. The city council even went on record against the bridge because of its possible danger to real estate values. Many Cincinnati capitalists also neglected local investments to buy land in fast growing rivals of the Queen City. An example is William Greene, one of Cincinnati's leading citizens, who not only owned considerable property in Chicago but used his money to promote improvements that might speed its growth.[16]

Complaints about the quality of Cincinnati entrepreneurship were accompanied by indictments of its boosterism. According to one editor,

> every merchant attends to his own trade, and every manufacturer to his own establishment, but he recognizes no policy that would dictate a combined exertion for the general good. He appears to be satisfied within the already established reputation of the Queen City, and reasons that his individual gains must depend only on individual exertions. The result is, a comparatively small number adopt the necessary method [boosterism], and the remainder divide the trade that follows.[17]

This protest was only partly accurate, for a small group of professional publicists remained active up to the Civil War. Charles Cist followed his earlier success with *Cincinnati in 1851* and *Cincinnati in 1859,* while Edward Mansfield wrote numerous pamphlets for Cincinnati railroad promoters and edited the *Railroad Record* after 1853. The chamber of commerce also put out increasingly elaborate annual reports. With the exception of Mansfield's work, however, most of this writing lost its verve after mid-century and assumed an apologetic tone, even though the regional economy continued to hold out a range of opportunities.[18] Nor did Cincinnatians in the

1850s possess Chicagoans' inventiveness in discovering new ways to present their message to the outside world or their inclination to assume individual responsibility for boosting their city.

The liveliest discussion of economic growth appeared not in publicity directed to outsiders but in the literature of controversy and exhortation designed to arouse slumbering capitalists to the importance of railroads. Between 1848 and 1853 a series of local and outside decisions determined Cincinnati's position within the western rail network. During these years the editors of the *Gazette* and the *Commercial* continually pressed for the construction of new lines. Pamphleteers similarly urged that Cincinnati had a brilliant future if it built needed transportation facilities. Though often marred by fierce partisanship on specific questions, these writings contained the most perceptive analysis of Cincinnati's economic position in the prewar decade.

In the later 1850s, however, as Cincinnati showed itself unwilling to expend the necessary energy and money, journalists grew tired of repeating themselves and uncertain of their ability to influence action. Many lost interest in promoting economic growth, and others adopted a defensive stance. The *Gazette* in particular cried out against "the old fogies who imagined that Cincinnati had halted in her progress." Only men fearful of losing current preeminence would have so stridently proclaimed that Cincinnati still had commercial advantages, was still larger than St. Louis, or was still the Ohio Valley's metropolis.[19]

Indeed, the increasingly negative tone of popular economic thought is clearly illustrated by the city's attitude toward its major rivals. As early as the 1840s, Cincinnati editors were touchy about the rapid growth of St. Louis and attempted to belittle that city's accomplishments. By the mid-1850s, many Cincinnatians felt on the defensive and took great pains to refute St. Louis claims to dominance. With a few years, at least some natives admitted that the Queen City had lost its "position as head of the Mississippi Valley. The departed sceptre has gone from Cincinnati to St. Louis, where the census shows a glut of population . . . and a corresponding activity in real estate and commerce."[20]

Because of its faith in the primacy of river trade, Cincinnati was slower to recognize the threat of Chicago. Through the 1840s, editors ridiculed the pretensions of the Lake Michigan city. In the early 1850s, a number thought it possible to make the commerce centering at the Garden City tributary to their own, proposing that railroads to the foot of Lake Michigan would give Cincinnati a vast new market for manufactures and groceries and enable it to tap the grain and provisions of Illinois and Wisconsin. After mid-decade, however, fear replaced unrealistic self-confidence. Even boosters admitted that "the rapid development of some other points" had given Cincinnati "a slight stay in her onward flight to the summit of excellence." By 1857 and 1858, worried Cincinnatians did their best to undercut Chicago's growth by announcing that its economy was based on empty speculation. In 1861, fear of the effects of civil war caused the editor of the *Enquirer* seriously to suggest that Chicago's "heartless, mercenary speculators" had fomented the rebellion specifically to destroy rival cities on the Ohio and Mississippi.[21]

The content of Cincinnati writing about economic development was equally undistinguished. After the early 1840s boosters largely ceased to prescribe suitable strategies of development. Although the neglect may have resulted from the achievement of a diversified economy, it contrasts sharply with other cities. In place of specific recommendations for growth, publicists offered amorphous catalogs of the city's advantages for various activities. Evaluations of its export hinterland were little more than copybook exercises in the use of adjectives. They provided no help to a newly arrived settler or a novice pork merchant. Like pack rats, advocates of local manufacturing treasured every conceivable advantage, from access to markets to the cheapness of food. Seldom, however, did they judge their relative importance.

Indecisiveness concealed an ambivalence in Cincinnati's evaluation of its own position. Two conflicting sets of ideas can be found throughout the two antebellum decades, sometimes in the same essay or article. One was based on the axiom that physiography determined the fate of cities, the other on the premise that human enterprise and artificial lines of communication were the key to urban growth. At best this ambiguity softened the impact of Cincinnati boosterism. At worse the contrasting interpretations damaged the city be calling for contradictory transportation strategies.

Champions of the first idea argued that "the growth of Cincinnati has been the result of natural situation, rather than anything else." Nature, they said, had made no place more central to the richest parts of the Union. Enjoying a position in the very middle of the Ohio Valley, Cincinnati was expected to increase in proportion to the growth of the surrounding territory.[22] It was believed, in addition, that Cincinnati sat squarely athwart *the* natural line of communication between East and West. Neither rival cities nor railroads were expected to divert the flow of trade from its preordained channel along the Ohio.[23]

Discussions of Cincinnati's advantages for manufacturing frequently incorporated this emphasis on centrality. Mixing what were in other cities distinct ideas, local writers asserted that the town's location gave it simultaneously superior access to markets and to raw materials. Although fairly applied to the Queen City, these perennial themes of Western boosterism were developed with less sophistication than in many other towns. Cincinnatians, for example, ignored the several decades of hard work that had been required to develop nearby mineral resources. Similarly, they often failed to recognize that in the pursuit of western markets the city's elaborate apparatus of commercial connections was an invaluable adjunct to its location.

The belief that Cincinnati was the "grand center of the United States" nurtured a desire to reinforce the advantages of its position with a system of transportation lines fanning in all directions. According to one writer, Cincinnati's "commercial power" depended not only on its location but also on "the number and length of its *commercial radii.*" It was precisely this policy that the city pursued in the 1830s and 1840s. The same belief colored perceptions of existing transportation facilities, which were frequently viewed as a set of radials. Some enthusiasts found up to fourteen or twenty such lines "diverging from this central city to every point of the compass."[24]

Cincinnatians less enamored of their town's geography were equally certain that natural advantages were of little value unless exploited by forceful and far-seeing men. Much of the city's success, they argued, came from "the sagacity, labors, zeal, enterprise, and patriotism of its citizens." A key point was the realization that "railroads have diverted trade from natural channels, and this they will continue to do." Prosperity in the 1840s was thus credited to the construction of highways into Ohio and Indiana rather than to the city's central position. In the early 1850s men of this persuasion warned repeatedly that the completion of east-west railroads north of Cincinnati would work "inconceivable and deadly mischief" to the growth of the city.[25]

In response to the contraction of Cincinnati's trade area on the north and east, citizens convinced by these arguments turned to the promotion of trade with the lower Ohio Valley and the South. The slave states were still an open market, they argued, and the height of the Appalachians made it impossible for eastern merchants to reach the region except through the Queen City. An earlier interest in the trade of the "Central West" thus became an obsession after mid-century, promising deliverance from the threats of rivals.[26] This conviction provided much of the rationale for the city's strong interest in Kentucky railroads.

Both interpretations of Cincinnati's situation combined to produce in many inhabitants an almost fanatical belief in the Ohio and Mississippi Railroad. The company was a response to the menacing railroads across northern and middle Ohio and Indiana. By cutting across a number of north-south lines and drawing their traffic to Cincinnati, it was expected to give the city control of southern Indiana, southern Illinois, western Kentucky, and Tennessee. With its connections it would give Cincinnati "iron hooks and grapples stretching through the whole valley of the Mississippi River to the Gulf of Mexico."[27] In combination with the Marietta and Cincinnati across southern Ohio and with the Baltimore and Ohio, it was expected at the same time to form the major rail line between the Mississippi and the Atlantic. By channeling trade through Cincinnati it would reaffirm the city's centrality and prove that the Ohio Valley was indeed the nation's great thoroughfare. As late as 1857, its completion appeared to offer "a fresh start in the race of municipal greatness."[28]

On the whole, the first evaluation of Cincinnati's potential for economic growth was a counsel for inaction, the second a plea for frantic activity. If the former advice now seems in error, it must be remembered that the latter often involved fantasies about the possible effects of one or two railroads, for not even the early completion of the Ohio and Mississippi or the construction of a line into

Tennessee could have overcome all of the city's difficulties. Together the two interpretations of Cincinnati's growth allowed natives to find justification for any action or inaction they wished. In a sense, therefore, the ambivalence of popular economic thought helped to excuse or mask the narrow-minded pursuit of individual interests.

Perhaps the greatest obstacle to collective enterprise was neither the selfishness of its businessmen nor the lack of a coherent strategy, but rather the prevalence of internal strife. Conflicts which had appeared in earlier decades festered unresolved into the 1850s, and Cincinnatians after mid-century seemed almost to enjoy fighting among themselves. Although some of the clashes were tangential to economic issues, other turned directly on questions of developmental policy. All of them diverted the city's energy and reinforced the spirit of self-interest.

Cincinnati's Germans were poorly regarded by the city's antebellum elite. In the early 1840s English-speaking citizens scorned the poverty of the many recent immigrants and disdained their small contribution to the city's growth. By the end of the decade, the success of Germans as businessmen and property owners had reversed the basis for antipathy, causing many native Americans to fear the economic and political aggressiveness of the newcomers.[29] The reaction fed on religious prejudice. Despite early efforts by organizers to play down the movement's specifically xenophobic aspects, Cincinnati Know-Nothings were blatantly anti-German by 1855, and an election-day riot in April of that year killed both Germans and natives. For several days thereafter, the German-speaking tenth ward was a barricaded stronghold reminiscent of Frankfurt or Berlin in 1848.[30] Anti-Semitism surfaced in 1853, when leading businessmen and clergymen applauded a movement for higher wages on the part of the city's seamstresses. Thus unusual support of working-class aspirations appears to have resulted less from moral outrage than from jealousy of the prosperous German Jews who controlled the clothing industry. The debate was filled with references to "extortion," "usurers" and a certain "class of the community" and with direct attacks on "Jew shops."[31]

Outside hostility, however, did little to promote the cohesion of the German community, whose internal divisions in the 1850s reproduced those in the city at large. Many financially successful immigrants abandoned their roots to pass into the English-speaking elite, and middle-class Germans scorned their laboring brethren. German readers supported newspapers ranging from Whig to conservative Democrat to Free Soil to radical socialist, and German voters backed all of the decade's political parties in some strength. Indeed, German radicals and Forty-Eighters helped to arouse much of the anti-Catholic sentiment in the city.[32]

Another source of dissension was the chasm between industrial workers and their employers. The growth of working class consciousness in the city dated at least from the mid-1830s, when the formation of trade associations in a dozen branches of industry had culminated in the creation of a General Trades Union. The preamble to its constitution showed an awareness of the fatuity of calls to let "individuals" regulate wages and advocated unified action on the part of workers. The *Working Man's Friend* similarly agreed on the "necessity and utility" of "Trades Unions and Trades Societies" to prevent the oppression of "hardworkers" by capitalists and speculators.[33]

Depression soon destroyed most of the unions of the 1830s, but 1841 saw the founding of a Working Men's Association, a quasi-political organization that concerned itself with currency reform, tariff legislation, public lands, and education and ran candidates for City Council. A brief parody of boosterism appearing in the sassy, lower-class *Microscope* suggests how meaningful many workers found elaborate discussions of their city's economic growth. Congress would certainly locate a western national armory in Cincinnati, the editor wrote, because "we have better mechanics, better water power, better horses and prettier women than any other city on these waters, and if all these won't draw an *armory*, what will?" Apart from a wave of strikes in 1843, which drew the support of the vehemently locofoco *Sun,* the remainder of the 1840s were largely without direct labor action. The city's elite as a consequence could limit their reaction to homilies on the virtues of hard work.[34]

The years of labor peace ended around 1850. The *Nonpareil,* whose masthead proclaimed "Published by an Association of Journeymen Printers—Association against Monopoly—Labor against Capital," quickly grew into one of the city's largest dailies. Supporting social reforms and "labor emancipation," or the formation of cooperatives, it soon earned the rancor of the powerful *Commercial.* Its editors also advocated labor unions, attacked oppressive capitalists, and dissented from the common goal of economic growth. They feared that the overbuilding of railroads would lead to a monetary crisis and wrote of Cincinnati that "the many *money* making improvements she has made have given a temporary splendor to her name; but these will not always defend her. The people begin to look beneath the pomp of her glorious youth, and discover that the foulest avarice has been her moving spirit."[35]

In 1853 and 1854, rising prices brought a wave of strikes in most branches of Cincinnati manufacturing. The *Nonpareil,* the sensation-mongering *Times,* and occasionally the Democratic *Enquirer* backed the workers. Even the last-named paper, however, joined the *Gazette* and *Commercial* in fierce outrage at a strike for a union shop conducted by journeymen printers. The closing years of the decade saw still another wave of unionization and bitter fights between strikers and scabs. The animosity of many workers toward Cincinnati's business leadership was probably summed up by the worker who said: "The bosses screwed us down to a starving point last winter, and we are now asking for our rights."[36]

Despite their common enmity toward Germans and workingmen, Cincinnati's businessmen were themselves far from united. Both major parties drew their leaders from the same professions, the Democrats in the 1840s and 1850s boasting their share of ambitious lawyers and merchants.[37] Although both parties claimed to favor soundly based economic growth, the ingrained impulse to attack programs advocated by members of the opposition often prevented combined action. Sectional conflicts also split the business community. "Yankees" and "Buckeyes," or natives of Ohio, the South, and the Middle states, moved in different social circles and pursued very different styles of life. The differences carried over into business relations, for the city's domineering and self-satisfied New Englanders aroused resentment among less hard-driving businessmen from the Middle Atlantic or southern states. Though they constituted only 2–3 percent of the labor force, New Englanders accounted for 10–15 percent of the major property owners and over 20 percent of the most active civic leaders. At times the debate over economic projects seems a dialogue between aggressive Yankees and other Cincinnatians less eager to plunge into new undertakings.[38] Differences of opinion about slavery, which carried over into arguments about the importance of southern trade, further divided Cincinnati's New Englanders and New Yorkers from other citizens.[39] The complaints about inadequately energetic entrepreneurship also suggest a submerged division between an older elite satisfied with fortunes made from the pork business and river trade and younger men eager to exploit the city's advantages for railroads and manufacturing. Although rigorous substantiation is impossible, it is interesting to note that the average Cincinnatian worth ten thousand dollars or more in 1860 was four years older than the average Chicagoan of the same wealth.[40]

Following immediate rather than long-range interests and guided by no generally accepted strategy for development, entrepreneurs in the 1850s wasted their own and the city's resources on the duplication of transportation facilities. Before a shotgun marriage of the two lines, rival cliques of editors and businessmen supported the Hillsborough and Cincinnati and the Marietta and Cincinnati Railroads, both of which were designed to connect the Queen City to the upper Ohio.[41] Local entrepreneurs also promoted four different companies that shared the single purpose of providing Cincinnati with access to Chicago independent of the lines centering at Indianapolis. One, the Cincinnati and Fort Wayne, never operated any track. The Cincinnati and Western hoped to build to Marion, Indiana, and there connect with the locally organized Peru, Cincinnati and Chicago. Less than thirty miles to the west its route was paralleled by the Cincinnati and Logansport, which aspired to become part of a through line by tying Richmond to the Wabash and points north. In 1854 it changed its name to the Cincinnati and Chicago and took on some of the officers of the Cincinnati Western, who quickly ruined it. After building two short segments it was unable even to pay the freight on rails ordered for further construction; it completed the entire line only in 1858. Another route to Chicago was finally opened in 1859, when the Cincinnati, Hamilton and Dayton finished an extension that connected it to the Pittsburgh, Fort Wayne, and Chicago. Whether or not a united effort could have succeeded in building a single direct Cincinnati-Chicago railroad, this fragmentation of energy condemned the enterprise to delay and to essential failure.[42]

Some of Cincinnati's more successful railroads were also bitter enemies. The Cincinnati, Hamilton and Dayton, for example, was planned as a direct rival of the Little Miami. Where the latter had aided real estate on the east side of town and in the suburb of Fulton, the former was partly motivated by a desire to increase westside land values. More broadly, the Cincinnati, Hamilton and Dayton competed with the Little Miami for local traffic flowing to Cincinnati from the Northwest. Each line aided western connections, and both attempted to gain control of the line from Dayton to Richmond. The two railroads also battled for through trade by forming shifting alliances with companies in central and eastern Ohio and with trunk lines. Through the 1850s their rivalry was marked by complex campaigns of maneuver and invective interrupted by occasional attempts to still competition with an amicable division of traffic.[43]

Within the city, Cincinnati railroad builders fought over the location of a union terminal. The Little Miami provided the only entrance for the trains of the Marietta and Cincinnati, the Cincinnati, Wilmington and Zanesville, and the Central Ohio. It entered along the river from the east and had its depot at the mouth of Deer Creek on the edge of the downtown. Approaching from the opposite direction, the Cincinnati, Hamilton and Dayton ran parallel to the tracks shared by the Ohio and Mississippi and Indianapolis and Cincinnati. The two lines were connected by a temporary track but maintained separate depots on the west side of the business district. Each northeastern line wanted to enhance its position as a conduit for through trade by making its depot a point of convergence for other railroads. In 1857 the Hamilton Company promoted a scheme by which the Marietta and Zanesville roads were to extend their lines westward and use its tracks to enter Cincinnati from the north. In reply, the Little Miami in 1859 secured permission to build a direct connection to the Ohio and Mississippi along the city's waterfront. Having failed to stop the project in the City Council, the Cincinnati, Hamilton and Dayton halted it with suits filed by protesting property owners.[44]

In pressing these ambitions, both companies had to contend with the Dayton and Cincinnati Short Line as well as each other. Originated by disgruntled property owners in the Miami Valley towns bypassed by the Cincinnati, Hamilton and Dayton, this company was soon taken over by Cincinnati entrepreneurs. Although continuing to claim an interest in supplanting the Hamilton Line, its managers made it clear that the company's principal object was to drill a seventy-nine hundred-foot tunnel through the hills north of the city. As the passage would debouch north of the downtown in the heart of Cincinnati's factory and warehouse district along the Miami Canal, promoters claimed to offer a most suitable and convenient entrance for all railroads converging from the north. At various times in the mid-1840s, the Fort Wayne, Zanesville, and Wilmington companies expressed serious interest in making use of the tunnel.[45] In response, Cincinnati newspapers attacked the entire project as unnecessary and impractical, while the Cincinnati, Hamilton, and Dayton accused its management of being interested chiefly in maintaining the value of real estate holdings near its proposed terminal. The rivalry was made more bitter because the directors of the Hamilton road represented the cream of Cincinnati Whiggery while the promoters of the Short Line included such leading Democrats as George Pendleton and Charles Reemelin. Although digging proceeded slowly, the company remained an active threat to both the Hamilton and Little Miami lines until 1857. Taken together, the conflicts among these three groups of entrepreneurs damaged the Queen City's attempts to become a rail thoroughfare by delaying the union of its railroads until the middle 1860s.[46]

Locofoco hostility to entrepreneurial initiatives also inhibited economic growth in Cincinnati. Through the 1840s and 1850s there was persistent opposition in the city to the official sanctioning of corporations and to the granting of public aid to private projects. Widespread nationally in the early 1840s, this cast of mind survived unchanged in the Queen City years after it had faded in other parts of the Northwest. Appearing most frequently among the city's German and American laborers and expressed most regularly by the *Enquirer,* it made what were questions of economic strategy in other cities issues of partisan politics in Cincinnati.

Unlike the situation in Chicago, where Democratic politicians attacked banks largely out of habit, radical hatred for banks in Cincinnati seriously impeded growth and made banking Ohio's central political issue for twenty-five years. The Bank Riot of January 11,

1841, in which a mob of artisans and mechanics gutted four banking houses resented for their unsound circulation, was merely one expression of a widely shared anger. Scarcely bringing themselves to condemn the violence, Democratic papers in 1841 and 1842 reviled the entire system of banking and note issue as the root of depression and the bastion of privilege. Fighting attempts to renew old charters and pass a General Law in 1842 and again in 1845, assembled Democrats as a group announced their conviction that paper money was "unprofitable, immoral, unsafe and despotic."[47] As the party's extensive working class and German support made Hamilton County Democracy the mainstay of locofocoism within the state, its opposition provided much of the impetus behind the anti-bank clauses of the new state constitution of 1852 and other anti-bank legislation. Spokesmen for Cincinnati business interests—chiefly the Chamber of Commerce, the *Gazette,* and the *Commercial*—could do little but sputter against the short-sighted "war against capital" waged by their political opponents. As late as 1855, State Auditor Charles Reemelin, the unchallenged leader of German Democrats, made political profit by attacking the remnants of Ohio banking, and the party in Cincinnati remained in unqualified opposition to the end of the 1850s.[48] The persistence of the antagonism through two decades gives some indication of the resentment felt by many poorer Cincinnatians toward the commercial manipulations of the entrepreneurial community.

Locofoco attitudes on the narrower issue of public aid to private enterprises were shown in the argument over a municipal loan for the Cincinnati and Whitewater Canal. In 1840, the *Advertiser,* the predecessor of the *Enquirer,* attacked the Canal Company for plundering the city and state treasuries for the profit of a few individuals. A year later it fiercely opposed a $200,000 loan proposed by the Whig majority on the City Council. Though disclaiming opposition to private completion of the waterway, radical editors claimed that most of the city's inhabitants were unhappy that the company had been aided by a forced loan, which it had neither plans nor ability to repay.[49]

The struggle over municipal aid to the Ohio and Mississippi Railroad epitomized both political and entrepreneurial conflict over economic development. In the spring of 1849 the argument over the

Whitewater Canal was repeated in a contest over a million-dollar loan for the railroad. The leaders of the business community organized the advocates of the measure and secured its authorization by the legislature while business newspapers urged its approval on the city's voters. At the same time, however, the city's Democratic representatives in the General Assembly refused to back the authorization bill, and the *Enquirer* warned that a loan would raise taxes without real benefit to the city. Although 77 percent of the voters approved the measure of March 30, the city's heavily German tenth ward came close to rejecting it.[50]

In spite of the overwhelming vote, the City Council for the next eighteen months refused to issue the loan, for members were unable to decide between assisting the Ohio and Mississippi and aiding the Cincinnati and Indianapolis Junction Railroad. The latter company hoped to give Cincinnati an expeditious route to St. Louis by connecting Hamilton to Indianapolis. Not surprisingly, it was supported and aided by the Cincinnati, Hamilton and Dayton and its promoters, among whom was the editor of the *Gazette.* Much of the delay was blamed on the Hamilton line's selfish desire for aggrandizement.[51] After months of public debate and extremely heavy pressure from the city's editors, one of whom called the delay "the inanity of dotage and the sure precursor of decay," the Council on September 20, 1850, decided against subsidizing the Junction line. Instead it proposed to loan three-fifths of the original $1 million to the Ohio and Mississippi, dividing the rest three ways between the Covington and Lexington, the precursor of the Marietta and Cincinnati, and the Eaton and Hamilton, another feeder in which the Cincinnati, Hamilton and Dayton was interested. Three weeks later the electorate overwhelmingly agreed to the changes. Had there been any doubt, the election would have been assured by official attempts to hinder the casting of negative votes.[52]

The loan proved adequate for little more than a start on the Ohio and Mississippi, and mismanagement brought the company near bankruptcy early in 1855. In a rescue attempt, the City Council purchased a wharf property owned by the Ohio and Mississippi for the inflated price of $500,000. The *Enquirer* and the Democratic Party of Cincinnati predictably tried to block "the villanous scheme to swindle the city into a mad and reprehensible extravagance . . . for an extension of river front that is entirely valueless for any purpose whatsoever." A few months later the paper restated the Democratic creed that corporations should rise and fall on their own merits, without special favors from public bodies.[53] The railroad itself was not finished until 1857, after a takeover by eastern financiers. Despite the consensus on the need for a railroad to St. Louis, Cincinnati's own uncertainty about the proper way to pursue the goal helped to postpone its achievement until the pattern of western rail traffic had largely been fixed.

Cincinnati in the 1850s was caught in a trap of its own making. Inert entrepreneurship, tepid boosterism, and internal divisions can be attributed to its success in the previous sixty years. By general agreement, it was the wealthiest of western cities. When Chicago in 1850 had only a few dozen men with twenty thousand dollars or more, Cincinnati counted between six and seven hundred in both 1850 and 1860.[54] Untroubled by the memories of 1837, which haunted Chicagoans, older members of Cincinnati's elite seldom felt that the cessation of growth directly threatened their own fortunes. As a result, no fear of personal poverty compelled the evolution of a clear economic strategy or induced the cooperation of independent businessmen. In fact, Cincinnati's richness meant that many of its citizens were satisfied with things as they were and that groups of such men had the capacity to block or delay new projects.

Cincinnati's size also worked against continued economic expansion. As a settled city with its decades of most rapid growth behind, Cincinnati by mid-century offered fewer opportunities than boom towns like Chicago or Milwaukee for extraordinary returns on investments. Most eastern money drawn westward in the 1850s bypassed the city, and many local capitalists exported their own funds. Conversely, the size of the economy and the extent of its commercial connections presented ambitious businessmen an embarrassing array of choices. The result was the dissipation of money and energy on often contradictory projects. As the largest city in the antebellum Middle West, Cincinnati also offered numerous chances for conflict within and among its constituent groups. The size of the electorate, for one example, made its vote the great prize of Ohio political battles, which were waged more fiercely there than in smaller and more homogeneous cities. Cincinnati in the 1850s, in short, was too fat—both too big and too rich to sustain a unified and vigorous campaign of economic development.

NOTES

1. William M. Corry, *Speech Delivered at the Merchants' Exchange in Favor of the Knoxville Route to the Gulf* (Cincinnati, 1860), pp. 4–5.

2. Wade, *Urban Frontier,* pp. 156–57; Mansfield, *Personal Memories,* p. 200; Cist, *Cincinnati in 1841,* p. vi; *Cincinnati Republican,* April 1, 1841; Rufus King to James G. King, April 17, 1841, King Papers, Cincinnati Historical Society.

3. Flint, *Mississippi Valley;* James Hall, *Statistics of the West, at the Close of the Year 1836* (Cincinnati, 1837); *Western Monthly Review* (1827–30); *Western Monthly Magazine* (1833–36); *Western Literary Journal* (1836); *Cist's Advertiser* (1846–50); Cincinnati *Atlas* (1846–49); *Proceedings . . . on the Subject of a Western National Armory; Memorial of the Citizens of Cincinnati to the Congress of the United States, Relative to the Navigation of the Ohio and Mississippi Rivers* (Cincinnati, 1843).

4. *Railroad Proceedings of Fulton and Vicinity* (Cincinnati, 1835), pp. 20–28; *Liberty Hall and Cincinnati Gazette,* December 24, 1835, September 8, December 29, 1836, January 5, 1837; *Railroad from the Banks of the Ohio to the Tide Waters of the Carolinas and Georgia* (Cincinnati, 1835); *Western Monthly Magazine* 4 (September–December 1835): 186–89, 327–33, 415–19, 5 (April–September 1836): 202–7, 538–48.

5. Hall, *Commerce and Navigation,* pp. 19–20; *Liberty Hall and Cincinnati Gazette,* January 12, 1837; *Cincinnati Enquirer,* May 13, 1841; Cist, *Cincinnati in 1841,* p. 79; *Monthly Chronicle* 1 (May 1839): 243; Schaffer, *Cincinnati Directory for 1840,* p. 507; *Map of Ohio* (St. Clairsville, Ohio, 1846); Scheiber, *Ohio Canal Era,* p. 131; Gallagher, "Ohio in 1838," p. 13; *Hazard's Register* 2 (February 12, 1840): 103.

6. Robert L. Black, *The Little Miami Railroad* (Cincinnati, n.d.), pp. 15–49; O.M. Mitchell, *Survey of the Little Miami Railroad* (Cincinnati, 1837); Little Miami Railroad, Sixth *Annual Report* (1848), p. 6; Timothy Walker to Ellis Gray Loving, May 15 and June 2, 1845, Walker Papers, Cincinnati Historical Society; Cincinnati, Hamilton and Dayton Railroad Company, First *Annual Report* (1850), p. 7; Henry A. Ford and Kate B. Ford, *History of Hamilton County, Ohio* (Cleveland, 1881), p. 210.

7. Jacob Hoffner to Henry Marsden, August 27, 1846, Hoffner Letters, Cincinnati Historical Society. Also see Augustus Roundy to father, May 7, 1845, Roundy Letters, Cincinnati Historical Society.

8. Edward Mansfield, *Memoirs of the Life and Services of Daniel Drake, M.D.* (Cincinnati, 1855), p. 269; *Cincinnati Enquirer,* December 13, 1855. See also: *Cincinnati Atlas,* September 7, 1848; *Cincinnati Commercial,* June 20, 1851; *Cincinnati Gazette,* October 8, 1850, February 24, 1854; *Railroad Record* 2 (September 28, 1854): 517.

9. Glazer, "Cincinnati in 1840," pp. 197, 230–41, 249–50.

10. *Liberty Hall and Cincinnati Gazette,* December 28, 1837; Wade, *Urban Frontier,* pp. 199–200, 327–30.

11. *Memorial . . . Relative to the Navigation of the Ohio and Mississippi Rivers* (1843); *Memorial . . . Relative to the Navigation of the Ohio and Mississippi Rivers* (1844); *Proceedings of a Meeting of the Citizens of Cincinnati . . . on the Subject of Improving the Navigation Around the Falls of the Ohio River* (Cincinnati, 1846); *Improvement of Navigation of the Falls of the Ohio* (Cincinnati, 1851); Cincinnati Chamber of Commerce, "Report on Canal at the Falls of the Ohio," *DeBow's Review* 16 (March–April 1854): 327–31, 416–26; *Cincinnati Commercial,* July 23 and 24, 1856; *Report of the Committee on the Best Mode of Improving Navigation at the Falls of the Ohio* (Cincinnati, 1859); *Charter and Organization of the Indiana Canal Company* (Cincinnati, 1850); Cincinnati Chamber of Commerce, *Report* for 1853, p. 5; *Cincinnati Enquirer,* February 28, 1858.

12. Timothy C. Day to Cincinnati Chamber of Commerce, February 20, 1856, in Sarah J. Day, *The Man on a Hill Top* (1931), pp. 150–51.

13. Cincinnati Chamber of Commerce, *Report* for 1854, p. 5, for 1855, p. 12, for 1857, p. 13; William Bebb, *Cincinnati: Her Position, Duty and Destiny* (1848), p. 26; Taft, *Cincinnati and Her Railroads,* p. 47; H. Goodin, "Cincinnati—Its Destiny," in Cist, *Cincinnati in 1851,* p. 316; *Cincinnati Atlas,* May 13, 1847; *Cincinnati Gazette,* June 3, July 5, 1851; Little Miami Railroad Company, Seventh *Annual Report* (1849), pp. 10–11; Cincinnati, Hamilton and Dayton Railroad Company, Third *Annual Report* (1853), p. 11; *Cincinnati Commercial,* June 6, 1851; Covington and Lexington Railroad, Eighth *Annual Report* (1857), p. 14.

14. *Cincinnati Gazette,* May 31, 1853, April 9, May 5 and 29, November 10, 1855; *Cincinnati Commercial,* May 13, 1857; Leslie Combs to Nathaniel Wright, March 13, 1856, Wright Papers, Cincinnati Historical Society.

15. James Parton, "Cincinnati," *Atlantic* 20 (August 1867): 231–32; *Cincinnati Price Current,* November 17, 1852; *Cincinnati Times,* May 27, 1857; *Cincinnati Commercial,* March 25, 1850, February 21, 1852, December 18, 1855; *Cincinnati Mercury,* June 6, 1849; *Cincinnati Gazette,* June 26, 1852.

16. *Cincinnati Gazette,* June 26, 1852; *Cincinnati Chronicle,* February 17, 1846; Harry R. Stevens, *The Ohio Bridge* (Cincinnati, 1939), pp. 36–37; Charles Anderson to William Greene, March 6, 1854, R.B. Mason to William Greene, December 3, 1855, Greene Papers, Cincinnati Historical Society.

17. *Cincinnati Times,* quoted in *Chicago Magazine* 1 (June 1857): 364.

18. Only in an 1855 essay "On the Commerce of Cincinnati, Including a General View of Her Present Position and Future Prospects: Her Situation, Resources, Growth, Statistics and Advantages, Agricultural, Commercial, Industrial and Financial" did the Chamber of Commerce *Reports* resemble Chicago reviews of trade.

19. *Cincinnati Enquirer,* April 4, 1857; Cincinnati Chamber of Commerce, *Report* for 1857, p. 4; Mayor R.M. Bishop, in *Cincinnati Commercial,* April 12, 1860; *Cincinnati Gazette,* 1856–1860.

20. Corry, *Railroad Speech,* p. 3. See also: *Cincinnati Chronicle,* November 13, 1841; *Cincinnati Gazette,* May 29, June 2, 8 and 15, 1855; *Cincinnati Price Current,* May 30, June 6, 13 and 20, 1855.

21. *Railroad Record* 4 (July 17, 1856): 321; *Cincinnati Enquirer,* January 29, February 5, 1861. Also see: *Western Literary Journal* 1 (September 1836): 246–48; *Cist's Advertiser,* January 4, 1848; Goodin, "Cincinnati—Its Destiny," p. 319; Bebb, *Cincinnati,* pp. 25–26; *Cincinnati Gazette,* May 16, September 1, 1855, January 1, 1858; *Hunt's Merchants' Magazine* 35 (October 1856): 512–13; *Cincinnati Times,* May 27, 1857; *Cincinnati Price Current,* June 29, 1859.

22. *Illinois Monthly Magazine* 2 (July 1832): 465. Also see: Cist, *Cincinnati in 1851,* p. 129; *Western Monthly Review* 3 (April 1830): 512–13; *Railroad Record* 4 (July 17, 1856): 321; *Western Tiller* 2 (March 26, 1830): 241; *Cincinnati Gazette,* November 8, 1850; *Cincinnati Atlas,* September 28, 1848; William Sherwood to Lois Sherwood, November 15, 1848, Sherwood Letters, Cincinnati Historical Society.

23. *Cincinnati Enquirer,* December 16, 1849, June 6, 1855; *Cincinnati Commercial,* September 12, 1851; Mansfield, *Railway Connections of Philadelphia,* pp. 11–16; *Memorial . . . in Relation to a National Armory West of the Alleghenies,* p. 115.

24. *Hunt's Merchants' Magazine* 29 (July 1853): 117; Cincinnati Chamber of Commerce, *Report* for 1855, pp. 5, 10–12. See also: *Cincinnati Price Current,* August 11, 1852; *Cincinnati Commercial,* March 26, 1858; *Cincinnati Gazette,* December 4, 1851; Goodin, "Cincinnati—Its Destiny," p. 320.

25. Mansfield, *Daniel Drake,* p. 129; Cincinnati Chamber of Commerce, *Report* for 1851, p. 4; *Cincinnati Commercial,* December 10, 1849.

26. *Cincinnati Gazette,* February 17, 1851; *Cincinnati Price Current,* August 11, October 6, 1852; *Cincinnati Enquirer,* July 30, 1852; Corry, *Railroad Speech;* Cist, *Cincinnati in 1859,* p. 345; Cincinnati Chamber of Commerce, *Report* for 1851, p. 4, for 1855, p. 13.

27. *Ohio and Mississippi Railroad: Its Vital Importance,* pp. 12–13. See also: Taft, *Cincinnati and Her Railroads,* pp. 31–40; *Cincinnati Gazette,* March 19, 1855; Mansfield, *Railroad Connections of Philadelphia,* pp. 21–32; Cincinnati Chamber of Commerce, *Report* for 1851, pp. 4–5; *Cincinnati Commercial,* November 24, 1849; William P. Smith, *The Book of the Great Railway Celebration of 1857* (New York, 1858), p. 95.

28. *Cincinnati Enquirer,* April 4, 1857.

29. Gerstäcker, *Vereinigten Staaten,* p. 165; Aaron, "Cincinnati," pp. 241–43; Hayes, "Letters from the West," p. 16; Löher, *Deutschen in Amerika,* pp. 331, 333, 475; *Fliegende Blaetter* 1 (Sept. 26, 1846): 99; William A. Baughin, "Development of Nativism in Cincinnati," *Bulletin of the Historical and Philosophical Society of Ohio* 22 (October 1964): 247–51.

30. Charles T. Greve, *Centennial History of Cincinnati* (Chicago, 1904), 1: 732; Eugene Roseboom, *The Civil War Era, 1850–1873,* vol. 4 of *The History of Ohio,* Carl Wittke, ed. (Columbus, 1944), pp. 292–301; William A. Baughlin, "Bullets and Ballots: The Election Day Riots of 1855," *Bulletin of the Historical and Philosophical Society of Ohio* 21 (October 1963): 269–71.

31. *Cincinnati Enquirer,* April 6, 1853; *Cincinnati Commercial,* April 4, 7, 9, and 11, 1853; *Cincinnati Times,* April 11 and 19, 1853.

32. Ziegler, *Skizzen einer Reise,* Reise, 2: 128; Löher, *Deutschen in Amerika,* p. 292; Gerstäcker, *Vereinigten Staaten,* p. 165; *Cincinnati Commercial,* March 4, 1859; Roseboom, *Civil War Era,* p. 254; Baughin, "Development of Nativism," p. 254.

33. *Working Man's Friend,* 1 (July 16, 1836); *Liberty Hall and Cincinnati Gazette,* February 11, 1836; Aaron, "Cincinnati," pp. 89-93.

34. James M. Morris, "The Road to Trade Unionism: Organized Labor in Cincinnati to 1893 (Ph.D. diss., University of Cincinnati, 1969), pp. 43-52; *Cincinnati Microscope,* August 8, 1842; *Cincinnati Sun,* October 26, November 1, December 20, 1843; Charles P. James, *Address Delivered at Camp McRae before the Citizen Guards of Cincinnati* (1842).

35. *Cincinnati Nonpareil,* 1850-52, especially July 31, 1850.

36. *Cincinnati Times,* April 21, 1858. Also see Roseboom, *Civil War Era,* pp. 34-36; Morris, "Trade Unionism," pp. 77-90; *Cincinnati Enquirer,* March 17, 1853; *Cincinnati Times,* February 26, April 5 and 7, 1853; *Cincinnati Gazette,* June 10, 1858; *Cincinnati Press,* March 29, 1859.

37. Glazer, "Cincinnati in 1840," p. 177; Richard T. Farrell, "Cincinnati in the Early Jackson Era, 1816-1834: An Economic and Political Study" (Ph.D. diss., Indiana University, 1967), p. 178-79, 223-24.

38. Glazer, "Cincinnati in 1840," pp. 98-99, 189; Tucker, "Cincinnati—Athens of the West," pp. 17-19; Aaron, "Cincinnati," pp. 210-13; Chevalier, *Society, Manners and Politics,* p. 200; Parton, "Cincinnati," p. 231. The quantitative data come from the census sample described in Appendix A.

39. *Cincinnati Enquirer,* July 23, 1855, January 6, 1857; Aaron, "Cincinnati," pp. 447-49.

40. See census sample. Through the 1850s, the city's most visible elite remained merchants and landowners: Trollope, *North America,* 2: 80; Peyton, *Over the Alleghenies,* p. 80; Charles Lyell, *Travels in North America* (London, 1845), p. 72.

41. *Cincinnati Commercial,* January 30, February 4, 1854; *Cincinnati Enquirer,* 1853; Allan Trimble to Robert Buchanen, November 18, 1854, Buchanen Papers, Cincinnati Historical Society; Benjamin Homans, *The United States Railroad Directory for 1856* (New York, 1856), p. 107.

42. *Exhibit of the Cincinnati and Fort Wayne Railroad Company* (Cincinnati, 1857); *Exhibit . . . of the Conditions and Resources of the Cincinnati, Peru and Chicago Railroad Company* (Cincinnati, 1854); *Exposition of the Business Prospects, and Estimated Profits, of the Cincinnati Western Railroad Company* (Cincinnati, 1854); *Statement of the Conditions and Contracts of the Cincinnati Logansport and Chicago Railway Company* (Cincinnati, 1854); *Condition and Prospects of the Cincinnati and Chicago Rail Road; Cincinnati Enquirer,* January 6, 1854; James Pullan Diary, 1852-52, Ohio Historical Society.

43. Sherry O. Hessler, "Patterns of Transport and Urban Growth in the Miami Valley, Ohio, 1820-1860" (M.A. diss., Johns Hopkins University, 1961), p. 232; Black, *Little Miami Railroad,* pp. 63-137; Cincinnati, Hamilton and Dayton Railroad Company, Second *Annual Report* (1853), pp. 4-5, Third *Annual Report* (1854), pp. 6-9; John Woods, *To the Stockholders of the Eaton and Hamilton Railroad Company* (Hamilton, Ohio, 1853), pp. 5-6.

44. Cincinnati, Hamilton and Dayton Railroad Company, Seventh *Annual Report* (1857), p. 10; *Communication to the Bondholders and Others Interested in the Cincinnati, Wilmington and Zanesville Railroad* (Baltimore, 1858); *Cincinnati*

Commercial, April 10, 1857, April 13, 1858, November 11 and 17, 1859, March 3, April 19, 1860; *Cincinnati Enquirer,* April 4, 1860.

45. Ford and Ford, *Hamilton County,* pp. 212-13; Hessler, "Transport and Urban Growth," p. 149; Homans, *Railroad Directory,* p. 114; Dayton and Cincinnati Short Line Railroad Company, First *Annual Report* (1852), pp. 6-7, 17, Second *Annual Report* (1854), pp. 15-20, 26-27; Cincinnati *Enquirer,* December 19, 1852, December 25, 1856; Marietta and Cincinnati Railroad Company, Third *Annual Report* (1852/53), p. 9; *Exhibit of the Cincinnati and Fort Wayne Railroad,* pp. 11-12; Cincinnati, Wilmington and Zanesville Railroad Company, *Special Report* (January 1857), pp. 20-22.

46. *Cincinnati Gazette,* December 4, 1851; *Cincinnati Price Current,* September 29, 1852; *Cincinnati Enquirer,* January 1, 1857; Cincinnati, Hamilton and Dayton Railroad Company, Second *Annual Report* (1852), p. 9; S.S. L'Hommedieu to English bondholder, September 25, 1855, L'Hommedieu Manuscripts, Ohio Historical Society.

47. *Cincinnati Microscope,* January 11, 1842; *Cincinnati Sun,* November 24, 1843; *Cincinnati Republican,* January 12, 1842; *Cincinnati Enquirer,* January 11 and 17, September 3, December 9, 1842; "Resolution of the Democratic Party of Hamilton County, August 30, 1845," in U.S., Secretary of the Treasury, *Report* for 1845, S. Doc. No. 2, 29th Cong, 1st Sess., 1845, pp. 850-52.

48. *Cincinnati Commercial,* August 27, 1855; *Cincinnati Enquirer,* April 14, 1860; *Bankers' Magazine,* 11 (September 1856): 173; James R. Sharp, *The Jacksonians versus the Banks: Politics in the States after the Panic of 1837* (New York, 1970), pp. 151, 178-83.

49. *Cincinnati Advertiser,* January 29, February 2, 1840, January 19, February 2, 8, and 9, 1841; *Cincinnati Republican,* January 30, February 8 and 17, 1842; *Cincinnati Sun,* December 2, 1843; *Cincinnati Enquirer,* February 15, 1842.

50. *Cincinnati Mercury,* February 8, March 29, 1849; *Cincinnati Enquirer,* March 18, 28 and 30, 1849; *Cincinnati Gazette,* January 11, March 29 and 31, 1849; George Pugh to William Greene, March 10, 1849, Greene Papers, Cincinnati Historical Society.

51. Taft, *Cincinnati and Her Railroads,* pp. 21-31; Little Miami Railroad Company, Eighth *Annual Report* (1850), p. 16; *Cincinnati Atlas,* April 23 and 30, September 6, 1849; *Cincinnati Gazette,* August 30, 1849; *Cincinnati Commercial,* February 16, 1850; Cincinnati and Indianapolis Junction Railroad, First *Annual Report* (n.d.), pp. 5-7, 10.

52. *Cincinnati Commercial,* Special Supplement, March 25, 1850; *Cincinnati Gazette,* September 23, October 14, 1850; *Cincinnati Nonpareil,* October 9, 1850.

53. Smith, *Railroad Celebration,* pp. 96-100; *Report of the Committee . . . Ohio and Mississippi Railroad Company,* pp. 4, 12; *Ohio and Mississippi Railroad: Its Vital Importance,* pp. 19-22; *Cincinnati Enquirer,* March 21, 22 and 27, April 3, 10 and 12, June 3, 1855.

54. *Cincinnati Gazette,* December 3, 1858; Parton, "Cincinnati," pp. 231-32; Andrews, *Report,* p. 56. The census samples showed 3 men in Chicago and 17 in Cincinnati worth twenty thousand dollars. If the same proportions held for the entire labor forces, the totals would have been 27 and 612.

7

INDIANAPOLIS:
THE MIDDLE
OF THE MIDDLE WEST

Indianapolis represented an extreme among western cities in the character of its boosterism and entrepreneurship. Quieter than Chicago, more self-controlled than Cincinnati, it pursued well-measured economic goals. Its citizens agreed on a realistic assessment of its possibilities for growth and united on efforts to achieve common goals. In the later 1840s and 1850s, it epitomized the spirit of public enterprise necessary for successful development. Indeed, the only thing that visitors and residents could find to complain about was that its growth was too calm, too competent, too unexciting.

Indianapolis's evaluation of its position for growth was as coherent and logical as that in any other antebellum city. When the men of the Hoosier capital pored over the map of the Union, they were again and again struck by their central location. Almost precisely in the middle of Indiana and roughly equidistant from the large cities of the lakes and rivers, Indianapolis was the "great central City of the West." Even in the decade after the Civil War, natives continued to believe that its location in the very middle of the Middle West was the "primary influence" on its growth and gave it great advantages over other inland cities.[1]

Indianapolis writers also recognized the reciprocity between their city's geographic position and its centrality within the western transportation system. In the 1830s, the town had been designated as the "grand centre of the various public works in . . . construction by the State of Indiana." By the 1850s westerners noted that its location was a magnet for railroad lines, whose presence in turn added an extra facet to its centrality. Almost automatically boosters and entrepreneurs referred to the city as the "Union Center of Indiana Railroads" or as the "Great Railroad Center of the West" and formulated a railroad strategy intended to increase the nodality of their city.[2] The railroads projected to or from the city in the late 1840s and finished between 1852 and 1854 formed a set of rays. Lines were built south to Lawrenceburg, Madison, and Jeffersonville on the Ohio, west and north to Terre Haute, Lafayette, and Peru on the Wabash, and east to connect with Ohio railways. In the middle of the decade, Indianapolis entrepreneurs attempted to add missing radials by agitating for lines to Fort Wayne, Evansville, Vincennes, and Decatur, Illinois. A map, displaying the various lines built and proposed, published by the board of trade in 1853 shows clearly that the city regarded itself as "the hub of a wheel—the railroads leading from it forming the spokes." The whole system was designed to create a kind of vortex centered on Indianapolis, cutting across Ohio's and Indiana's east-west and north-south railroads and diverting their trade to a single focus.[3]

There was also a strong belief that the interests of Indianapolis required that it become not merely the terminus of diverging lines but rather a point of intersection for major through railroads. Several promoters viewed central Indiana as an isthmus of dry and level land lying between the hills along the Ohio River and the swamps and lakes of the upper Midwest. East-west railroads, they thought, would of necessity pass through this narrow band of suitable terrain and through its pivotal city like sand through the neck of an hourglass.[4] Most entrepreneurs consequently introduced their projects to Indianapolis businessmen as links in the hypothetical "great central Atlantic and Western Railroad," and local writers called for the construction through their town of lines connecting the important peripheral cities of the West.[5] Only the routes to Peru and Jeffersonville were seen solely as outlets to water transportation for middle Indiana.

Indiana businessmen tried several times to promote or put together such a trunk line. In 1847, Marion County interests held a convention to convince outside capitalists that a Cincinnati-St. Louis railroad could most economically be built making use of the tracks of the planned Terre Haute-Indianapolis-Richmond railroad. The proposal received strong support in Indianapolis and was revived two years later when several leading citizens advocated the plan at a railroad convention in Steubenville.[6] In the early 1850s, the Madison and Indianapolis Railroad aspired to become a major link between the Ohio and the lakes. It provided equipment for the Indianapolis and Bellefontaine Railroad, coordinated its operations with those of the Lafayette and Indianapolis, and for a few months in 1854 entirely absorbed the Peru and Indianapolis Railroad, the merger being dissolved only after suit by stockholders of the latter road.[7] John Brough, the enterprising president of the Madison company, shifted his base of operations in 1853. Moving to Indianapolis, he assumed control of the Indianapolis and Bellefontaine Railroad. In the next few years he consolidated that line with the Bellefontaine and Indianapolis in Ohio, gained control of the line to Terre Haute, and tried to build an extension from Terre Haute to St. Louis. When the Illinois legislature frustrated his efforts, he abandoned Indiana to live in Cleveland and tend his Ohio railroad interests.[8] Oliver H. Smith, the ousted president of the Indianapolis and Bellefontaine, took up a new project in the same years. His Evansville, Indianapolis and Cleveland Straight Line Railroad was consistently described as a great highway between Lake Erie and the Ohio River and as a replacement for the Wabash Canal.[9]

The belief in the importance of the city's centrality also underlay discussions of the most suitable economic activities. Because natives were aware that the city's location hindered any extensive grain trade, they wasted no time analyzing its agricultural hinterland or advocating the promotion of commerce in farm commodities. They realized, however, that the same position at the center of Indiana's railroad system gave their town the entire state as its natural hinterland for service activities. Because its railroads placed it within half a day's journey of eighty counties, Indianapolis was the most appropriate site for conventions, for the state university, for the state fair, and for other state functions. Boosters at the same time noted that its position as a transportation node made the city a gateway for travel and emigration to the West. Its railroads simply facilitated a current of travel that had converged on the town with the building of the Indiana road system in the 1830s.[10]

The completion of the city's railroad network also inspired an interest in wholesaling. Newspapers in 1854 and 1855 called for the establishment of wholesale houses and in 1857 backed efforts to publicize Indianapolis's advantages as a jobbing center. Some boosters believed that the "quick, cheap, uninterrupted and abundant communication" supplied by its railroads would soon make Indianapolis a "concentrating wholesale emporium," as the various lines supposedly allowed the supply of "more than two million customers . . . *quicker* and as *cheaply* as from any other point in the country."[11]

Indianapolis publicists spent even more time, discussing their city's need and advantages for manufacturing. Scattered references during the first years of its railroad era gave way in the later 1850s to a flood of agitation, perhaps in response to a diminishing rate of industrial growth. Every important newspaper was crammed with statements about the city's want of industry, and the Board of Trade prepared an elaborate circular on "such additional branches of Manufactures as may be profitably and successfully established in this city." As far as editors were concerned, the city had no hope for the future unless it conserved its energy and resources for manufacturing. "The question whether Indianapolis is to continue to increase in population and wealth," said one, "must depend mainly on whether she becomes a manufacturing city."[12]

Analyses of local advantages for manufacturing stressed the city's central location and its "unrivalled" railroad facilities, which were thought to give it entry to extensive markets.[13] With connections to all parts of the state, the city was considered an excellent site for producing wagons and farm machinery and for processing farm products. Moreover, Indianapolis was not only "the Commercial Metropolis, the largest City and geographical center" of Indiana, but also had easy access to many inhabitants of adjoining states. Natives were convinced, in short, that "the admitted principal [sic] in political economy, that the producer and consumer should be brought as near together as possible, must act with increasing force for years to come, in building up manufactures here in the very center of the great producing interests of the Northwest."[14]

Indianapolis exploited the principle of centrality in its relations with rival Indiana towns. At mid-century one could find more than a dozen independent trading centers with populations of two thousand to eight thousand located in a band between 50 and 150 miles from Indianapolis. On the Ohio River were Lawrenceburg, Madison, New Albany, and Jeffersonville. On the Wabash were Terre Haute, Lafayette, and Logansport. Fort Wayne and Richmond were located in the eastern part of the state, with Evansville, South Bend, and La Porte in its farthest corners. Indianapolis consistently claimed to represent the entire state and to be above petty battles, but in fact took careful measure of the threat posed by various competitors. In particular, its businessmen realized that the completion of direct eastern railroads reduced the city's dependence on both the Ohio River and Wabash River trade routes. The city showed the greatest antipathy toward Madison, an Ohio River town that in the 1840s had dominated Indianapolis trade and envisioned itself a miniature Cincinnati with thronged wharves and smoky factories. As soon as the new railroads opened alternative outlets for Indianapolis and shifted Indiana toward a central route, boosters moved permanently to blacken Madison's reputation, claiming that "its warehouses and stores seemed to be opened solely for ventilation and the clerks are busy in keeping flies from forming permanent colonies on their faces."[15] In relation to Lafayette, in contrast, Indianapolis realized that the agricultural export center posed no serious threat. The capital's spokesmen were roused to attack only when Lafayette tried to upstage Indianapolis at a railroad convention or to undercut its service functions by holding the state fair.[16]

Despite this interest in development and despite the cogent analysis of the city's economic situation, Indianapolis produced little that fell within a narrow definition of "boosterism." Many of its newspapers (the *American, Republican, Free Democrat, Democrat,* and *Statesman)* dealt largely with issues of politics for a statewide audience; they had little concern for the particular needs of the city. Those papers that did serve the interests of the city—the later *Sentinel,* the *Journal,* the *Locomotive,* and at the end of the decade the

Atlas—directed their economic discussions inward, analyzing the bases of growth and urging local action. In the statistically minded West, the City even lacked indigenous statisticians, leaving boosters without a numerical foundation on which to build their forecasts. Occasional correspondents urged greater efforts to advertise the city, arguing that publication of its advantages would cause capital to flow to the city "as the rivers do to the ocean." Most editors, however, remained content that Indianapolis should enjoy a "spontaneous" prosperity rather than a growth "worried out of a victimized Eastern public by systematic advertising and fabulous puffing." Better than such boosterism, they said, was a local and state pride that sought by its own efforts the rapid development of the city.[17]

Indianapolis also lacked a Bross, a Hall, or a Mansfield. Apart from railroad pamphlets designed directly to raise capital, the only publicity directed specifically to an outside audience came from the board of trade. In 1854, the newly formed organization prepared a circular to show "the advantages Indianapolis possesses as a central business point." After two years of dormancy, the organization was revived to issue new pamphlets in 1856 and 1857, the latter being accompanied by a great ado of public meetings and newspaper blurbs. The bustling activity was largely a farce, however, for the board was unable to raise even one thousand dollars to defray its expenses and left stacks of pamphlets undistributed. Three years later, the *Sentinel* remarked sourly: "Spasmodically, our people arouse to the importance of this great interest [manufactures] and talk freely of publishing to the world the advantages we possess; but the fever dies out and nothing is accomplished."[18]

Indianapolis's failure to exhibit the booster spirit paralleled a similar lack in the state as a whole. Many Hoosiers remarked sadly or angrily that the merits of their state were little known abroad.[19] To remedy the situation they advocated measures ranging from the establishment of a new geological survey or a state bureau of statistics to the creation in Indianapolis of a "Central Cabinet" or state museum that would represent "the resources of the State in miniature." On the whole, however, Indianians remained uninterested in publicizing themselves. Small-town papers were distinguished by their lack of boosterism, and writers complained that natives were unwilling even to answer inquiries. As one outside editor said:

"The Hoosiers are in some respects a peculiar people. . . . They certainly do more and say less about it than any other people we have heard of."[20]

Having marked out a coherent set of goals, entrepreneurs pursued them without fanfare. The city's growth came not from a few spectacular enterprises but from the measured operations of numerous small businesses. According to the 1860 federal census, for example, its largest factory employed sixty workers, and its average manufacturing establishment had fewer than ten employees.[21] Residents of Indianapolis were justly proud that wealth was distributed relatively evenly among its citizens. In 1850, 37.9 percent of its employed males twenty years or older owned real property. Ten years later the proportion was 35.7 percent. Both figures were significantly above levels in Cincinnati and Chicago and were slightly higher than the 35 percent average that Lee Soltow has calculated for nonfarm workers in the Middle West.[22] Of major immigrant groups, only the Irish fell below native Americans in percentage of workers holding property, while the British and Germans matched or exceeded the native American level.[23]

A successful Indianapolis entrepreneur was Calvin Fletcher, a lawyer and officer of the State Bank revealed by his diary as a man of intense uprightness and enterprise. Having grown up with the city, Fletcher enjoyed close ties with many of its leaders in manufacturing, commerce, and law. Since the core of Indianapolis's financial community was distinguished by stability over time, many of the leaders he had known in the 1830s wielded influence and held positions of trust into the 1850s.[24] Others in the group resembled Fletcher in character. Contemporary biographies of Indianapolis entrepreneurs show less admiration for the aggressive go-getter than for the steady citizen who pursued his own business and attended to his duty.[25]

Indeed, antebellum Indianapolis possessed only one truly flamboyant entrepreneur. Oliver H. Smith, erstwhile lawyer, Whig politician, and United States Senator, tried to make himself the town's preeminent publicist and promoter in the late 1840s. In speech after speech he boosted railroads, supported the board of trade, and found evidence in the city of wonderful growth. His writings were so enthusiastic that they sometimes parodied the booster style. In practice, however, Smith had difficulty in securing loans from the Indianapolis branch of the State Bank, perhaps the city's central economic institution. The chief fruit of his energetic promotional efforts was the construction of the Bellefontaine Railroad between 1848 and 1852. After he lost control of this line in 1853, however, his further schemes created acrimonious controversy and foundered without broad support.[26]

At the same time, Indianapolis in the 1850s was open to well-mannered newcomers. According to a sample from the manuscript census returns, the average age of employed persons owning five thousand dollars of real estate fell from 46.5 in 1850 to 40.0 in 1860. The proportion of the same group born in the Middle West rose during the decade from 17 percent to 35 percent, indicating that the Indiana capital was a haven for ambitious young Middle Westerners and a center of opportunity for the state. A study by historian James H. Madison has found that a total of eighty-nine businessmen—bankers, merchants, manufacturers, real estate agents, railroad officers, livestock, lumber, and produce dealers—owned at least ten thousand dollars of property in 1860. Fifty-eight had arrived in the city since 1850 and only seven had been present before 1835. Wealth and presumably local influence were held by relatively young men, for only 46 percent of these eighty-nine wealthiest business leaders were over forty.[27]

The absence of divisive issues helped to maintain a calm and measured tone in the economic growth of Indianapolis. The antebellum decades saw little of the labor strife that marred the career of Cincinnati in the 1850s. Similarly, the perennially troublesome issue of banking was treated not as a local problem but as a question of state policy. Although the city's newspapers and businessmen were divided over the free bank system, the recharter of the State Bank, and the incorporation of the new Bank of the State of Indiana, they spent their energy within the framework of political parties, attempting to influence the state legislature rather than fighting with each other.

Also unlike Cincinnati, the city avoided the stressful situation in which it was forced to risk its future on one or two transportation improvements. The success of the Madison and Indianapolis Railroad inspired the organization of railway companies in all parts of

Indiana, many of which were planned by their promoters to pass through Indianapolis. Of the rail lines finished to the capital between 1852 and 1854, only the Bellefontaine and the Indianapolis and Cincinnati required Indianapolis money and enterprise. In the latter case, moreover, local entrepreneurs had the relatively easy job of taking over a line already under construction by downstate interests. The lines from Jeffersonville and Peru were designed chiefly to serve the interests of their namesake towns and were built with almost no Indianapolis participation. Peru promoters, in fact, attacked Indianapolis for its neglect of their company. The remaining lines from Richmond, Lafayette, and Terre Haute were conceived by outsiders and built mainly with funds from their immediate hinterlands or from eastern investors.[28] Indianapolis thus enjoyed the happy circumstances of having much of the entrepreneurial energy and talent in the state devoted to building "its" railroads, a circumstance that must have made the whole problem of economic development less troublesome. Between the completion of the Madison Railroad and the start of the Great Rebellion, the voters of Indianapolis were not once asked to consider the question of public aid to railroads.

In the absence of major controversies about the basic issues of economic growth, public arguments about economic policy in antebellum Indianapolis were relatively calm debates on specific measures. The advocates of manufacturing, for example, sometimes disagreed among themselves about particular projects, scolded the city council for occasional measures inimical to manufacturing, and argued whether real estate speculation hampered the expansion of manufacturing by raising land prices or aided it by attracting capital.[29] The first years of railroad development saw argument whether the several companies should be connected by tracks through the center of town or by an encircling belt line. A single crank letter, however, is the only evidence that anyone wanted to prevent the connection of the railroads, and the decision to construct a union passenger depot south of the business district met nearly unanimous approval.[30]

Emblematic of collective entrepreneurship in Indianapolis were the efforts to free the city of Cincinnati's commercial dominance after the completion of eastern rail connections in the early 1850s. Businessmen were encouraged to invest in local manufacturing "so that we may declare our independence of Cincinnati" and were urged to use the new railroads to bypass Queen City merchants.[31] The desire to build an Indianapolis economy without metropolitan influence came to a head in a controversy over the redemption of Indiana free bank notes. Cincinnati brokers in 1854, 1855, and 1856 gathered the Indiana currency that accumulated in the Queen City and sent it to Indianapolis for conversion into specie. Where Ohioans considered this merely a routine procedure, Indianapolis editors and businessmen thought it a blatant effort to destroy the state's merchants and bankers. While Cincinnati newspapers looked on in sincere puzzlement, Indianapolis prepared to repel the "piratical incursion" of Ohio "rascals" and "bloodsuckers" and called for a boycott of Cincinnati businesses. After two years of verbal salvos, Indiana interests called a commercial convention, which met at Indianapolis in April 1856 and resolved that the state should trade exclusively with Louisville, Toledo, and Cleveland. Two years later, Indianapolis's attitude was summarized in the *Journal:* "All the objection Cincinnati has to Indianapolis and other Indiana towns is that they will not permit themselves to be squeezed, at all times, without resistance."[32]

There was similar clarity of purpose in Indianapolis efforts to further its development as a service center. Citizens pointed out the advantages of its location "for any Institution or business that looks to the patronage of the people of the State," praised its hotels, and recommended its colleges. Newspapers also supported campaigns to remove the state university to Indianapolis and to serve as host for the Republican National Convention of 1860. After several years of discussion on how best to assure the permanent location of the State Fair at Indianapolis, the city's voters approved by a majority of six to one a contribution toward the purchase of new fairgrounds.[33]

The pursuit of economic growth in Indianapolis was thus a coherent and practical process. Residents shared a general agreement on the desirability of economic expansion. The city's German community, for example, seems to have accepted the objectives of growth defined by the native leadership. Henry Ward Beecher, the city's most popular religious leader in the 1840s, also edited an agricultural journal in order to develop the state's "incomparable resources" and to promote "a large-minded, intelligent, settled

PUBLIC SPIRIT." Affirmations of faith in the town's growth were a staple of its newspapers, and few inhabitants doubted that "Indianapolis bids fair to become the largest inland capital in the Union."[34]

At the same time, the city's inhabitants possessed a clear view of their prospects, accepting many of the limitations arising from their location and making the most of the advantages. A kind of Protestant paradise where internal strife failed to surface and the virtues of hard work went unchallenged, the town's steady growth was its own triumph, the result of intelligent operations by dozens of businessmen. Even the scarcity of eastern capital was a blessing that prevented the promotion of quixotic projects and dampened the cycle of boom and bust. An early interest in retrospective articles on the not very historic town indicated the pride citizens took in their city and affirmed their belief that "it is no longer a rugged, scattered village—but a city, young, vigorous and healthful, with a bright future before it."[35]

NOTES

1. *Indiana Sentinel,* May 23, 1844; *Memorial of the Board of Trade and the Common Council of the City of Indianapolis,* H.R. Rep. No. 43, 37th Cong., 2d Sess., 1861; John H.B. Nowland, *Early Reminiscences of Indianapolis, with Short Biographical Sketches* (Indianapolis, 1870), p. vi; *Indianapolis: Its Advantages for Commerce and Manufactures.*

2. Ellsworth, *Upper Wabash,* p. 17; Holloway, *Indianapolis,* p. 316; *Railroad Record* 2 (December 14, 1854): 693; *Indianapolis Journal,* August 30, 1853; Smith, *Trials and Sketches,* p. 286; Lawrenceburg and Upper Mississippi Railroad, *Engineer's Report and Report of the Board of Directors* (1850), p. 14; *Exhibit of the Terre Haute and Richmond Rail Road Company* (New York, 1851), pp. 4–5.

3. *Indianapolis Sentinel,* July 30, 1860; *Indianapolis Journal,* July 23, 1855, June 24, July 14, 1856; Indianapolis Board of Trade, *Indianapolis;* Brown, "History of Indianapolis," p. 55; Board of Trade Map reproduced in Dunn, *Greater Indianapolis,* 1: 355; quote in *Locomotive,* November 20, 1852.

4. *Indianapolis Sentinel,* May 24, 1848; *Indianapolis Journal,* May 29, 1848, April 15, 1857; Indianapolis and Bellefontaine Railroad Company, First *Annual Report* (1849), pp. 12–13; Lafayette and Indianapolis Railroad Company, *Annual Report* for 1851, pp. 7–8; *Lafayette Courier,* November 19, 1850; Smith, *Trials and Sketches,* pp. 422–23.

5. Indianapolis and Bellefontaine Railroad Company, Third *Annual Report* (1851), p. 4.

6. *Proceedings of the St. Louis and Cincinnati Railroad Convention Held at Indianapolis, May 12, 1847* (Terre Haute, Ind., 1847); Calvin Fletcher Diary, May 12, 1847, Indiana Historical Society; *Indianapolis Sentinel,* February 17, April 24, 1847; *Indianapolis Journal,* March 24, 1847, April 20, May 4, 1849.

7. Lafayette and Indianapolis Railroad Company, *Annual Report* for 1851, pp. 6-7; *Indianapolis Journal,* May 17, 1848; John Brough, *A Brief History of the Madison and Indianapolis Railroad* (New York, 1852), p. 13.

8. John H.B. Nowland, *Sketches of the Prominent Citizens of 1876* (Indianapolis, 1877), p. 413; Smith, *Trials and Sketches,* p. 588; Kohlmeier, *Old Northwest,* p. 221; Alvin F. Harlow, *The Road of the Century: The Story of the New York Central* (New York, 1947), pp. 353-67.

9. *Western Democratic Review* 2 (November 1854): 325; Evansville, Indianapolis and Cleveland Straight Line Railroad, *Address of the President* (Indianapolis, 1853), pp. 10-14; Evansville, Indianapolis and Cleveland Straight Line Railroad, First *Annual Report* (1855), p. 13, Second *Annual Report* (1856), pp. 8-9.

10. *Indiana State Gazeteer . . . for 1860 and 1861,* p. 177; *Indianapolis Atlas,* November 22, 1859; *Indianapolis Sentinel,* January 11, 1851; *Locomotive,* January 22, 1853, July 25, 1857; Smith, *Trials and Sketches,* p. 425.

11. *Locomotive,* April 1, September 9, 1854; *Indianapolis Journal,* October 4, 1855, August 3, 1857; *Indianapolis Sentinel,* April 11, 1854; *Indiana Statesman,* October 1, 1851; Dunn, *Greater Indianapolis,* 1: 346; Indianapolis Board of Trade, *Indianapolis;* Evansville, Indianapolis and Cleveland Straight Line Railroad Company, Second *Annual Report* (1856), p. 12.

12. Indianapolis Board of Trade, *Indianapolis; Indianapolis Journal,* June 24, 1856. See also: *Indianapolis Atlas,* August 24, September 7, 1859; *Freie Presse von Indiana,* August 14, 1856; *Indianapolis Sentinel,* August 26, 1857, May 2, 1860; *Locomotive,* August 29, 1857, July 16, 1859.

13. Indianapolis Board of Trade, *Circular and Map,* printed in *Indianapolis Journal,* September 10, 1856; Smith, *Trials and Sketches,* p. 114; Perkins, "Address," pp. 388-89; *Indianapolis Sentinel,* August 28, 1851, April 11, 1854; *Indiana Statesman,* October 1, 1851; *Indianapolis Journal,* October 12, 1849, June 10, 1859; *Memorial of the Board of Trade,* pp. 162-64.

14. *Indianapolis Atlas,* August 26, 1856; *Indianapolis Journal,* August 4, 1856; *Locomotive,* April 3, 1853; Indianapolis Board of Trade, *Indianapolis.*

15. *Indianapolis Journal,* September 15, 1851, January 19, 1852, August 4, 1854; *Indianapolis Sentinel,* September 25, 1851; *Indiana Statesman,* September 17, 1851; *Madison Courier,* April 5, 1855, February 19, 1857, April 18, 1858; *Cincinnati Enquirer,* April 10, 1856; "Report of the Secretary, Superintendent and President of the Madison and Indianapolis Railroad Company . . . April 10, 1855," in Indiana, *Documentary Journal* (1856/57), pp. 351-52.

16. *Indianapolis Journal,* July 13, August 2, September 19, 1853, April 17, 1860; *Indianapolis Sentinel,* December 15, 1853.

17. *Indianapolis Journal,* August 3, 1857. Also see: Perkins, "Address," p. 388; *Indianapolis Sentinel,* December 25, 1852, August 5, September 10, 1857.

18. *Indianapolis Sentinel,* August 10 and 24, 1857, May 2, 1860; *Locomotive,* August 29, 1857; *Freie Presse von Indiana,* September 10, 1857; *Indianapolis Journal,* October 12, 1853, June 14, 1856; Brown, "History of Indianapolis," p. 59; Nowland, *Early Reminiscences,* p. 416.

19. Power, *Planting Corn Belt Culture,* pp. 78–79; *Indianapolis Sentinel,* February 27, 1856; Evansville, Indianapolis and Cleveland Straight Line Railroad Company, First *Annual Report* (1855), p. 10.

20. Indiana, Governor Joseph Wright, Message to the Indiana General Assembly, 1851, *Documentary Journal* (1851/52), p. 172, Message to the Indiana General Assembly, 1857, *Documentary Journal* (1856/57), p. 303; Indiana, State Board of Agriculture, *Report* for 1859, pp. xl–xlii; *Indiana Farmer,* 1 (October 1840): 146; *Indianapolis Journal,* February 10, 1857; *Indianapolis Sentinel,* May 7, 1859; *Indiana Gazetteer* (1849), pp. vii–viii; Walter R. Houf, "A Rural Indiana Weekly as Promoter: Editorials from the Peru Gazette of 1839," *Indiana Magazine of History* 65 (March 1969): 46; *Western Journal and Civilian,* 3 (January 1850): 248–49.

21. The 1860 census reported one hundred manufacturing firms in Marion County, with a total of 713 employees, of whom 477 were in Indianapolis. Eighth Census, *Mortality and Miscellaneous Statistics,* xviii, *Manufactures,* p. 128. The *Indianapolis City Directory 1860–61,* pp. 287–88, lists 200 manufacturing enterprises for Indianapolis. The sample of employed persons from the 1860 census returns indicates that manufacturing employment totaled 1600.

22. Indianapolis Board of Trade, *Indianapolis; Indiana State Gazetteer . . . for 1858–59,* p. 125; Lee Soltow, *Men and Wealth in the United States, 1850–1870* (New Haven, 1975), p. 41. The figures for individual cities are computed from the census sample. For 1850 the precise comparative figures from these sources are: Chicago, 14.9 percent; Cincinnati, 13.6 percent; Ohio, 36.0 percent; Indiana-Illinois-Michigan, 35.0 percent.

23. The following table, based on the census sample, shows the percentages of all workers in Indianapolis owning real property:

	1850	1860
All workers	36.2%	27.6%
Workers Born in U.S.	36.3	25.1
Workers Born in Great Britain	37.0	23.8
Workers Born in Germany	43.2	39.1
Workers Born in Ireland	15.3	17.7

24. See James H. Madison, "Businessmen and the Business Community in Indianapolis, 1820–1860" (Ph.D. diss., Indiana University, 1972), p. 222, and lists of leading businessmen and citizens in the following: D.T. Kimball to Augustus Kimball, February 12, 1837, Kimball Manuscripts, Indiana State Library; *The Indiana Annual Register and Pocket Manual,* pp. 123–24; Daniels, *Village,* p. 93. Out of a group of fifty-five business leaders of the antebellum years who received biographical sketches in Sulgrove, *Indianapolis,* or Nowland, *Reminiscences,* forty-three had arrived in the city by 1837.

25. Nowland, *Reminiscences;* Samuel Smith, Autobiography, Indiana Historical Society Library.

26. Smith, *Trials and Sketches;* Smith, "Address"; Smith, "Railroads of Indiana"; Oliver H. Smith, letter in *Indianapolis Journal,* July 21, 1856; Holloway, *Indianapolis,* p. 326; *Indianapolis Sentinel,* November 17, 1853; Calvin Fletcher Diary, March 23, 1846, Indiana Historical Society.

27. Data from the census sample and from Madison, "Business Community in Indianapolis," pp. 215-37.

28. Homans, *Railroad Directory,* pp. 125, 127-28, 132; Ared Murphy, "The Big Four Railroad in Indiana," *Indiana Magazine of History* 21 (June 1925): 113-71; *Indianapolis Journal,* January 30, 1850, July 18, 1851; *Locomotive,* September 22, 1849, January 26, 1850; *Indianapolis Sentinel,* July 14, 1849, September 11, 1851; *Indiana Statesman,* October 1, 1851; Nowland, *Reminiscences,* pp. 252-53; *Indiana Gazetteer* (1849), p. 30; Jeffersonville Railroad Company, First *Annual Report* (1848/49), pp. 13-14; *Letter from Capt. E.G. Barney, Chief Engineer of the Peru and Indianapolis Railroad* (Indianapolis, 1852), pp. 6-9.

29. *Freie Presse von Indiana,* August 14, December 18, 1856, March 5, 1857; *Indianapolis Journal,* September 29, 1853; *Indianapolis Sentinel,* June 10, 1853, February 9, 1858; *Indianapolis Atlas,* August 29, 1859.

30. *Locomotive,* January 20, February 24, March 3 and 10, 1849, February 16, 1850, June 19, 1852; *Indianapolis Journal,* July 26, 1851; *Freie Presse von Indiana,* October 2, 1856; Daniels, *Village,* p. 99.

31. *Locomotive,* January 1, April 2 and 30, July 23, 1853; *Indianapolis Journal,* July 30, December 7, 1857; *Indianapolis Sentinel,* May 6, 1848, August 29, 1850, August 28, 1857; *Indiana Statesman,* October 1, 1851; Indianapolis and Bellefontaine Railroad, First *Annual Report* (1849), pp. 12-14.

32. *Indianapolis Journal,* April 5, August 18 and 30, 1854, March 21, April 11, 1856, February 25, 1858; *Indianapolis Sentinel,* October 21, 1854, February 22, March 15, 1855; *Locomotive,* March 22, 1856; *Cincinnati Times,* March 24, 1856; *Cincinnati Price Current,* April 26, May 10, 1854; *Cincinnati Commercial,* March 24, April 4, 1856; *Cincinnati Enquirer,* March 23 and 30, 1856.

33. *Indianapolis Journal,* August 12, 1851, April 17, 1852, November 16, 1859; *Indianapolis Sentinel,* October 8, 1857; *Indianapolis Atlas,* November 22, 1859; *Freie Presse von Indiana,* July 23, 1857; *Locomotive,* January 22, 1853, July 25, 1857, October 15, November 5, 1859, February 4 and 18, 1860; Indiana, State Board of Agriculture, *Report* for 1859, pp. lxxvi-lxxviii.

34. Henry Ward Beecher, in *Indiana Farmer and Gardener* 1 (November 15, 1845): 370; Lafayette and Indianapolis Railroad Company, *Annual Report* for 1851, p. 6.

35. *Indianapolis Sentinel,* March 28, 1853. See also *Indianapolis Journal,* October 29, 1847, and a series of articles, November 4 and 24, December 1, 1846, March 10 and 17, 1847; "Historical Sketch," in *Directory of the City of Indianapolis* (1857).

GALENA:
THE FAILURE
OF COLLECTIVE ACTION

Galena was a failure among the cities of the antebellum West. Entering the 1840s with commercial prominence and influence, it ended the 1850s with its hopes in ruins. Its problems included the decline of lead production, the energy of its rivals, and its peripheral location. The most basic cause of its stagnation, however, was the absence of effective collective entrepreneurship. Galena's few boosters developed no clear program for growth; its small elite refused the cooperation required to carry out needed improvements in transportation. As a contemporary critic summarized its difficulties, the town by the later 1850s lacked the capacity for a "combined and concerted effort of the popular will."[1]

Unlike the situation in Chicago or Cincinnati, it is not possible in antebellum Galena to distinguish between talkers and doers. The city's fate was controlled by a single elite, which took responsibility for all aspected of economic growth. The same men conceived plans, publicized projects, raised funds, and enjoyed the fruits of success or failure. To their occasional perspicacity can be attributed some of the city's early prosperity and to their purblindness, much of its later failure.

The Galena elite in the 1840s was small and self-contained. At its core were export merchants. Many had arrived in the city with capital from previous ventures, and others had compiled fortunes in smelting before the collapse of the permit and lease system in the early 1830s had ended their monopoly. In Galena's golden decade, the expansion and diversification of its economy also made it a lodestone for aspiring lawyers and had opened its business community to a number of newly arrived wholesalers and a scattering of manufacturers. By the later 1840s, further expansion of the business elite largely ceased. Of a group of sixty prominent citizens of the period listed in local histories, 88 percent arrived before 1850. As a traveler reported, "a great secret of the success of the merchants here lies in their fewness, they have a regular monopoly, and they make very determined opposition to anyone who attempts to invade it." Mid-century businessmen could usually finance ventures from their own resources or through the partnerships and family alliances that connected many of the city's important businessmen. As a small and intimately linked group, these few families maintained a "good deal of good society" to stand apart from the rudeness of the mining region. As the same elite aged, 83 percent of the men owning five thousand dollars of real or personal property in 1860 were older than thirty-five years.[2]

Into the early 1850s, this compact elite of a few-score businessmen held an iron grip on the Galena economy. Although nominally partisan, city elections usually placed in office manufacturers, merchants, and lawyers who could be expected to represent the city's business interests. The same names appeared time and again as organizers of this or that worthy project. The same community leaders led a short-lived movement for annexation to Wisconsin, served as bank and insurance company directors, built a large hotel, and incorporated plank roads and railroads.[3]

The same businessmen also controlled Galena's agencies of publicity. In 1836, for example, leading merchants organized a chamber of commerce, in part to mediate local mercantile disputes and in part to promote the improvement of navigation at the Rock Island rapids on the Mississippi. In pursuit of the latter goal, the chamber in 1840 and 1841 submitted memorials to Congress showing the volume of river trade done by the town and the exorbi-

tant cost of carrying goods across the rapids at low water. Galena's
newspapers always stood ready to break out trumpets and drums
for the pet project of an important entrepreneur. At the most
blatant, an editor might discourse at length on the need for a new
hotel or a new railroad only to announce at the end of the article or
in the next issue that ground had just been broken.[4]

Apart from such day-to-day boosting, Galena's newspapers contained little that merits the name economic thought. Their editors
apparently treated economic development only when they found
politics dull. Galena boosters, moreover, wrote with neither imagination nor style. Even the arrival of dozens of eastern dignitaries
on the Rock Island Railroad Excursion of 1854 merely inspired
editors to drag forth from their trays of type a few weary adjectives and standardized statistics.[5] Both the *Jeffersonian* and the
Gazette often reprinted articles about the lead region published in
eastern papers rather than bothering to write their own publicity.

When newspapers did chart Galena's economic future, they dis-
played a striking vacillation. As the city's economy changed during
the late 1840s and early 1850s, they hesitated to choose among
alternate courses of development. Editors simultaneously urged the
city to make itself the great importer for the upper Mississippi, advocated the development of its grain business, and argued that its
lead trade was either actually or potentially on the rise. In the midst
of this hullabaloo, only two themes were consistently pressed.
From the early 1840s Galenians maintained that the city's location
gave it an incomparable and unshakable position for wholesaling.
In the next decade, they also reiterated that the city should expand
its manufacturing sector in order to reduce the reliance on imports
and to increase the supply of goods readily available to local wholesalers.[6]

The uncertainty about economic strategies was symptomatic of a
larger ambiguity. Through the antebellum decades, Galenians were
unable to decide whether they lived in a Mississippi River town
whose fate was tied to the development of Iowa and Minnesota or
in a local center identified with northern Illinois and southern Wisconsin. In the former case, efforts should go to the development of
the town's import and grain trades. In the latter, capital and entrepreneurship might better be applied to the revitalization of mining

and the building of local roads and railroads. Much of the city's unwillingness to choose a path for development was a function of its inability to decide on its most secure or suitable hinterland.[7]

The choice was made even more difficult by a lack of confidence in the city's continued prosperity. At times in the 1850s, the city's editors warned that the town was in serious trouble unless improvements were quickly made in its commercial facilities. At other times, Galenians made a virtue of slow growth, describing the city's progress as "gradual and healthy." More belligerent editors cried out against this attitude, shouting: "Why then this whining and doubting? Why this want of confidence?"[8] Whether worried or hopeful, such discussion showed that Galena was far from self-assured.

Galena residents were equally uncertain about relations with its most immediate rival of Dubuque, Iowa. Local papers in the early 1850s were unable to decide whether the Iowa town should be treated with condescension, ridiculed, or attacked. At times editors vilified Dubuque for claiming to be the equal of Galena, calling it "a place of inferior importance, whether we regard its business or its location." At other times they declared that the economic expansion of Dubuque would merely serve to build up the business of their own town. In still other instances they mocked their competitor, asserting that it compiled its commercial statistics with a new system of arithmetic and planned a "Dubuque, Pacific, Japan and Shanghai Railroad." In the second half of the decade, as the competition proved more and more troublesome, any sense of play disappeared and Dubuque was described only as a town known for "bankruptcy, hotel runners and fleecing of travelers."[9]

Dubuque was indeed Galena's oldest enemy, a town that had tried to usurp the lead trade since the early 1840s and that observers sometimes described as one of the twin cities of the mining region. After mid-century, however, it ceased to be Galena's sole rival. Though the latter city was only half-conscious of the fact, it was increasingly engaged in a losing contest with every other Mississippi town from Rock Island to St. Paul. Galena enthusiasts anticipated that the fast-growing import and export trade of the upper valley would make their town a great city, but the completion of railroads to half a dozen points on the upper river jeopardized this hope by making each terminal town an equal commercial competitor. Narrowly fearful of Dubuque, however, Galenians were scarcely aware of this larger danger. The same sort of befuddlement that pervaded other facets of their economic thought prevented effective steps to reassert Galena's primacy.

The confusion in attitudes contributed to errors of policy as Galena leaders faced the mid-century revolution in transportation. Many residents were uncertain whether the Galena and Chicago Union Railroad would assist or interfere with their city's growth. Early enthusiasts believed that it would make Galena the channel for imports and emigrants bound for the upper Mississippi and would give their city commercial advantages that could "hardly be appreciated by the most sanguine." Other Galenians, however, feared that the line would reverse the pattern of trade east of the Mississippi.[10]

After Chicago promoters temporarily allayed their fears and construction commenced, many Galenians generously supported the road. Although the town rejected a proposal to tax itself for the benefit of the company, its businessmen dug into their pockets time and again to defray the expenses of survey and building.[11] However, ill-feeling toward the company mounted as the majority of Chicago directors revealed no great desire to hurry the tracks westward. Galena jealously watched the company use funds raised in Jo Daviess County to improve the line's eastern division and to build a new Chicago depot. In response to newspaper agitation, public meetings, and the complaints of the stockholders, the management thrice gave assurance that it intended speedy completion of the entire line. Galena fears proved well-founded, however, for the Chicago directors in 1851 voted down a resolution specifically commiting the company to lay tracks west of Rockford. They instead agreed with the Illinois Central that the latter company, in which Galena had no influence or voice, should provide the railway between the Rock and Mississippi rivers. In retaliation many Galenians in 1853 gave strong support to the St. Charles Air Line, an abortive company organized specifically to compete with or blackmail the Galena and Chicago Union. The new line had several Galena directors and the backing of the city's newspapers. One citizen openly informed the *Chicago Democratic Press* that the St. Charles line was intended to revenge his city's betrayal.[12]

Galena was also jealous of the Illinois Central, the only railroad actually built through the city before the Civil War. Most business leaders were deeply offended when the nation's lawmakers and the company's promoters ignored their mass meetings, petitions, and strenuous lobbying and made Dunleith rather than Galena the line's terminus. The next two years saw a mixed reaction as the municipal government bargained with the company over the terms of its entrance to the city. Anticipating the benefits of the railroad, some citizens wanted to ease its entry by providing valuable waterfront property. Others maintained that the town could at least exact concessions from the company. At times a single individual held clashing ideas. The editor of the *Jeffersonian,* for instance, argued that the city should stand up to the Illinois Central's extortionate demands but should be willing to compromise to secure the railroad.[13]

In specific, the issue turned on whether the Illinois Central should be allowed to bridge the Fever River at the center of town, impeding access to and from the Mississippi. The rationale developed by the anti-railroad forces was succinctly stated by the City Council in its reply to an Illinois Central proposal:

> While the importance of your road is fully recognized, the waters of this Port are of yet greater consequence to the city. By these natural channels of trade, this city has reached its present position, its tonnage and its commerce outstripping any Port on the Mississippi above St. Louis . . . the freedom of the Port must forever be guarded by the city as its greatest advantage.

In the minds of many citizens the city's river trade gave it such a secure commercial position that it could bargain with the railroad as an equal. The importance of the city would, in their opinion, force the company to come to terms. Instead, the Illinois Central bypassed the city by building its depot on the south bank of the river and bridging it below town.[14]

Galena merchants also showed their interest in the town's river trade by investing heavily in steamboats. In 1848 two sets of local businessmen started packet lines serving the upper river. When the lines were consolidated four years later, Galenians owned at least a dozen large boats. The newly unified Galena and Minnesota Company continued to prosper as the arrival of railroads at the Mississippi increased passenger travel. The firm employed six hundred men and returned large profits from the business of Galena, Dunleith, Dubuque, and Prairie du Chien. At the same time, other Galena entrepreneurs controlled a large share of the St. Louis–St. Paul packet line. Together the city's inhabitants owned about five thousand tons of shipping in the years just before the Civil War.[15]

By the mid-1850s, unfortunately, few of these boats were able to visit Galena except at highest water. The Fever River was a backwater of the Mississippi, and no current cleared the silt which washed from the hills north and east of town. As early as 1839 a traveler described the problem during a period of low water: "Had some difficulty in getting out of Fever River—so crooked—and water low—six miles to Mississippi took us nearly two hours—twisting and turning getting on and off sand or rather mud bars." By the late 1840s, business leaders agreed that it was necessary to combat the rapid filling of the river with a "Mud Machine." Despite the agitation of more far-reaching measures in the next few years, however, the city government took no action other than sporadic dredging. Steamboats were soon unable even to turn around in Galena's vaunted harbor.[16]

In the middle and later 1850s, Galena's business leadership failed to halt the weakening and collapse of the city's economy. At the root of its problems during these years was a drain of energy and talent that had begun with the rush to California in 1849. The early 1850s had seen the departure not only of hundreds of skilled miners but also of lawyers seeking more fruitful fields for litigation. Through the later years of the decade, the stream of emigrants was swelled by merchants ruined in 1857 or attracted by superior opportunities in Chicago. The exodus was reflected in the age composition of Galena's labor force and of its elite. Where 72 percent of the city's workers were between twenty and thirty-nine years old in 1850, only 58 percent fell in the same age group ten years later. The slack was taken up by teenagers and older persons both.[17] The median age of five thousand dollar real estate holders also rose from forty to forty-five. Another startling figure is the place of origin of five thousand dollar wealth holders in 1860 (a larger group than the holders of five thousand dollars in real estate). Forty percent were foreign born, and only 5 percent born in the Middle West. Apparently the men born within Galena's hinterland in the 1820s and 1830s moved away rather than try their fortunes in a declining town. Those businessmen who remained, moreover, were increasingly compelled to scramble for an adequate share of the available business. In the middle 1850s, for example, the larger of the city's two bankers suddenly ended a dozen years of peaceful coexistence by organizing a run on his rival's currency. A few years later the business community was bitterly divided by a conflict over the relative importance of local railroad and harbor improvements.[18]

Those entrepreneurs who remained interested in Galena's growth were largely unable to carry out projects of benefit to the city. An expansion of the local franchise in 1853 had allowed the control of the city government to pass out of the hands of the elite. Elections for city offices became partisan contests between Republican mercantile interests and the usually victorious Democrats representing mechanics and laborers. The Democratic leaders were more concerned with building a party organization than in promoting urban growth. Their followers had similarly shown their lack of interest in economic development, when the town voted 294 to 137 against the Illinois free bank law. In response to the new circumstances, the *Gazette* in 1856 found it necessary to urge explicitly the election of a ticket pledged to promote the city.[19]

As a result of these changes, Galena failed to take practical steps to solve its growing commercial problems in the years after 1855. A Galena and Southern Wisconsin Railroad into the lead region, a Galena and Northwestern Railroad into Iowa, and a proposal to raise the level of water in the Fever River by placing a lock at its mouth all generated loud support from the *Courier* and the *Gazette* and backing from municipal officials. The city's only action to aid the railroads, however, was to issue $100,000 of bonds for the first line and $500,000 for the second. Given the state of the market for western municipal securities by 1857, this was an idle gesture. Any hope of raising money for harbor improvement vanished in 1859, when the promoters of the defunct Galena and Northwestern refused to surrender their unsold bonds, thereby preventing the city from issuing others for the new project.[20]

Worried by the failure to act effectively to secure commercial goals, editors in 1856 and 1857 attempted to rouse the somnolent spirit of civic action. Galenians of "means and influence" were scolded for their "want of earnestness," a lack that supposedly damped the fires of enthusiasm in other citizens. Inhabitants who substituted "oft-repeated disquisitions upon its advantages" for hard work were warned that "the future of Galena depends upon the actions of her citizens now. Too long have these projects been delayed already. Further procrastination will be ruinous to the business of the city." On a more positive note, the city was assured that with a little exertion it could make itself one of the great cities of the West. Its citizens were offered the inspiring motto "We Can Do So If We Will."[21]

The tone of Galena's newspapers deteriorated after the disastrous financial panic of 1857. No longer civic cheerleaders, its editors asserted that their city was suited for any and every economic activity they might imagine. They suddenly discovered that the pockmarked hills of the lead region bloomed with new opportunities for mining and farming. Indiscriminantly they strove to convince their readers that the town's merchants were prepared to redeem its commercial position, that its agricultural trade was certain to increase, that its exporters were paying top prices for lead, and that the time was ripe for laying the foundations for extensive manufacturing. Even the bankruptcy of many of its businessmen was treated as proof that the town was in a position to start afresh free of debt and unencumbered by impractical fancies.[22]

The severity of economic crisis in Galena in the later 1850s can be judged from the rising population and trade of the other towns along the upper Mississippi. With the completion of the Illinois Central Railroad to the east bank of the Mississippi opposite Dubuque, for example, the total commerce of that city shot from $2 million in 1852 to an estimated $15 million in 1853. Its population rose from three thousand to thirteen thousand over the course of the decade. Rock Island and Davenport experienced similar booms. After the arrival of the Rock Island Railroad, produce merchants swarmed in the towns "as thick as potato-bugs," and their combined populations reached sixteen thousand by 1860. To the north, railroads transformed La Crosse and Prairie du Chien from sleepy villages into ambitious commercial centers, while St. Paul merchants moved to declare their independence. Where Galena's six thousand inhabitants in 1850 had almost equalled the combined population of these other towns, its 1860 population of eight thousand was barely a seventh of the total urban population along the upper Mississippi.[23]

In a sense, Galena had been too richly blessed. Prosperity in its first decades had come effortlessly from the lead trade and then from wholesale commerce. Few of the town's leading citizens were forced to resolve their ideas about the most promising strategies of development or to learn to work together in times of adversity. In the 1840s, the unified and cooperative elite had been more interested in preserving openings for private gain than in attending the general growth of the city. By the 1850s, the city suffered from the control of established and aging leaders who were unwilling to accept or develop new ideas. One editor summed up the problem in 1856:

Galenians have lacked enterprise hertofore, and they can scarcely be blamed for it. They have mostly grown old and rich with the place, and until within the past few years, their enterprise did not require precisely the same scope of commercial foresight that is now absolutely essential to maintain Galena in its proper position of importance in the race with other western towns.[24]

NOTES

1. *Galena Gazette,* April 26, 1859.

2. The quote comes from Alexander Leslie Diary, 1857–58, Chicago Historical Society, p. 24. The names were taken from *History of Jo Daviess County* and from Chetlain, *Recollections.* Also see: Wright, *Lead District,* pp. 15, 20, 23–28; Owens, *Galena,* pp. 8–9, 23–26; McMaster, *Upper Mississippi,* pp. 23, 114, 131; *Galena Courier,* February 1, 1856; *Galena Gazette,* November 21, 1854; Rodolph, "Lead Region," p. 344; Cadwallader Washburn to family, July 11, 1839, in Hunt. *Israel, Elihu and Cadwallader Washburn,* p. 306.

3. *History of Jo Daviess County,* pp. 478–82, 534; Owens, *Galena,* pp. 23–26; Chetlain, *Recollections,* pp. 23–26; *Galena Jeffersonian,* October 22, 1851; *Galena Gazette,* April 13, 1852, April 5, 1853.

4. *History of Jo Daviess County,* p. 478; *Documents Showing the Statistics of the City of Galena, April 1, 1840,* S. Doc. No. 349, 26th Cong., 1st Sess., 1840; Galena Chamber of Commerce, *Memorial . . . Relative to Obstructions of the Navigation on the Rapids of the Mississippi River,* H.R. Doc. No. 68, 26th Cong., 1st Sess., 1840; "Letter of Thomas Melville;" *Galena Jeffersonian,* June 22, 1853; *Galena Gazette,* August 2 and 9, 1853.

5. *Chicago Democratic Press,* June 8, 1854; *Galena Gazette,* June 13, 1854.

6. H.H. Gear in *Galena Gazette,* July 6, 1841; Mayor A.T. Crow, Inaugural Address, ibid., March 19, 1842; Mayor Charles Hempstead, ibid., January 13, 1843; Mayor Nicholas Dowling, Inaugural Address, *Galena Jeffersonian,* March 6, 1852; *Gem of the Prairie,* November 27, 1852; *Galena Gazette,* 1849-57.

7. For examples of orientation to the upper Mississippi, see *Galena Gazette,* May 7, 1850, June 22, 1852. For orientation to northern Illinois and southern Wisconsin, see *Galena Jeffersonian,* August 22, 1851, *Galena City Directory 1858-59,* pp. 135-36. For an ambiguous orientation, see *Galena Gazette,* March 25, 1837; *Galena Jeffersonian,* January 8, 1846.

8. *Galena Jeffersonian,* August 22, 1851. See also: *Galena Courier,* June 20, August 28, December 16, 1856, March 23, 1858; *Western Journal and Civilian,* 7 (March 1852): 399; *Galena Directory 1848-49,* p. 33.

9. *Galena Courier,* October 3, 1859; *Galena Gazette,* April 22, 1851, January 24, 1854; *Galena Jeffersonian,* August 24, September 6, November 26, 1851, May 30, June 2, September 1, 1853.

10. *Galena Gazette,* April 2, 1836, February 26, 1847, September 4, 1850; *Galena Jeffersonian,* November 26, 1846; *Galena Directory 1847-48,* p. 7; Scammon, *William B. Ogden,* p. 64.

11. *Galena Gazette,* February 14, 1849, February 8, 15 and 22, 1850; Isaac N. Arnold, *William B. Ogden and Early Days in Chicago,* Fergus Historical Series no. 17 (Chicago, 1882), p. 39; Owens, *Galena,* p. 14; Galena subscription lists for first survey of the Galena and Chicago Union Railroad and for the construction of the "third division," both in Charles Hempstead Collection, Chicago Historical Society.

12. Galena stockholders, memorial to the board of directors of the Galena and Chicago Union Railroad, December 20, 1850, and proposed resolution, June 8, 1851, both in Charles Hempstead Collection, Chicago Historical Society; *Galena Gazette,* January 14, 1851, June 21, July 12, October 11, 1853, June 24, November 7, 1854; *Galena Jeffersonian,* June 4, July 9 and 20, 1853; *Chicago Journal,* August 12, 1850; *Chicago Democrat,* December 11, 1850; *Chicago Democratic Press,* March 15, 1853.

13. Clarissa Emily Gear Hobbs, "Autobiography," *Journal of the Illinois State Historical Society* 17 (January 1925): 647; Brownson, *Illinois Central,* p. 56; Ferguson, *River and Rail,* pp. 399-400; Owens, *Galena,* pp. 14-16; *Galena Jeffersonian,* December 29, 1852.

14. Owens, *Galena,* p. 15. Also see: *Chicago Democratic Press,* February 25, 1853; *Galena Gazette,* April 15, 1851, February 25, 1853.

15. Robert C. Toole, "Competition and Consolidation: The Galena Packet Company, 1847-63," *Journal of the Illinois State Historical Society,* 57 (Autumn 1964): 229-33; Merrick, *Upper Mississippi,* pp. 172-73; McMaster, *Upper Mississippi,* p. 205; *Galena City Directory 1858-59,* p. 133; *Galena Jeffersonian,* September 6, 1851.

16. Anonymous diary, 1839, Chicago Historical Society; *Galena Directory 1848-49,* p. 36; Report of City Council Committee on Harbor Improvement, in *Galena Gazette,* October 26, 1847; *History of Jo Daviess County,* p. 536; U.S., Chief of Engineers, *Report* for 1874, H.R. Doc. No. 1, 43d Cong., 2d Sess., 1874, pp. 290-91; Owens, *Galena,* p. 19; *Galena Gazette,* April 20, July 27, 1852, October 25, November 29, 1853.

17. Chetlain, *Recollections,* pp. 27-47; *Chicago Democratic Press,* September 19, 1854. Quantitative data from census sample.

18. McMaster, *Upper Mississippi,* pp. 103-4; *Bankers' Magazine* 9 (July and August 1854): 20, 112; Alexander Leslie Diary, 1857-58, Chicago Historical Society, p. 24; *Galena Courier,* March 15, 1859.

19. Owens, *Galena,* pp. 26-32; *Galena Jeffersonian,* November 15, 1851; *Galena Gazette,* February 12, 1856.

20. Mayor Robert Brand, in *Galena Gazette,* March 16, 1858; Mayor Stockert, in *Galena Courier,* March 9, 1857; *Galena Gazette,* May 5, 1857, March 16, 1858; *Galena Courier,* March 9, April 21, 1857, March 15, 1859.

21. *Galena Courier,* August 28, 1856, August 27, 1857; *Galena Gazette,* January 15, 1856, January 26, 1857.

22. *Galena Gazette* and *Galena Courier,* 1858-59.

23. *Hunt's Merchants' Magazine,* 38 (October 1857): 439-43; *Edwards' Descriptive Gazetteer and Commercial Directory of the Mississippi River* (St. Louis, 1866), p. 342; Nathan H. Parker, *Iowa As It Is* (Chicago, 1855), pp. 170-73; J.M.D. Burrows, "Fifty Years in Iowa," in Milo M. Quaife, ed., *The Early Days of Rock Island and Davenport* (Chicago, 1942), p. 270; Rufus King, "Milwaukee to St. Paul in 1855," *Wisconsin Magazine of History,* 11 (Decemberr 1927): 178, 182; *Galena Gazette,* November 28, 1854.

24. *Galena Courier,* December 22, 1856.

THE FINAL HOME
OF EMPIRE

City dwellers in the antebellum Middle West lived in the midst of sustained excitement about urban growth. The large majority of commercial magnates, political leaders, and aspiring immigrants were delighted to be carried by the cresting wave of regional and urban development that followed the opening of the Great Lakes and Mississippi Valley frontiers. For the men at the top, there was little distinction between urban growth and personal success in banking, trade, transportation, and land speculation. Further down the social ladder, the chance for "participation in the thriving cities gave even the losers in the free-for-all a vicarious victory."[1] In a region and an era that viewed cities primarily as series of economic possibilities, every new warehouse and every new citizen was simultaneously a confirmation of achievement and a promise for the future. The opportunities for urban growth were clear and imperative. Cincinnati, said one orator, should "seize upon all the mighty instrumentalities which the inventive genius of the age has laid at her feet to make the gifts of God, so bountifully strewn around her, minister to her coming greatness."[2]

In the environment of local enthusiasm, the promotion of urban growth was a civic duty. Urban promotion in the specialized twentieth century has become its own specialty, with sophisticated advertising strategies and financial incentives administered by professionals employed in chambers of commerce, state economic development departments, and redevelopment authorities. A century and a quarter ago, any and every resident might be an amateur promoter who voluntarily shared the same responsibilities. Civic leaders had little embarrassment about indulging in undignified advertisement of themselves and their cities. Businessmen cited trade statistics on their letterheads and printed their own pamphlets on growth strategies. New settlers became boosters within a week. Other residents worked diligently to define their communities as economic units by writing local chronicles, publishing city directories, and collecting commercial data. Commercial organizations did begin to take on promotional functions in the 1850s in Chicago and Cincinnati, but the open mass meeting with a memorial and petition was equally common as a technique.

Antebellum journalism showed the pervasiveness of urban and regional boosterism. Editors of western magazines saw themselves as regional spokesmen, symbolizing their interest by titling their journal with a western state or city or a regional term such as "prairie." One editor expected to devote his magazine to the promotion of the western states, "the collection of their early history, the depicting of their social condition, the recording of their physical progress, and the advocacy of what we conceive to be their true interests." Another wrote that "we propose to fill these pages with such matter in the aggregate as will make this publication a Chicago-Western Magazine. . . . We shall aim to make it a vademecum between the West and the East—a go-between, carrying to the men of the East, a true picture of the West." As we have seen, even agricultural and religious magazines caught the excitement and offered their analyses of the benefits of urbanization.[3]

The boosters of Chicago and Cincinnati and Detroit and Dayton were participants as much as observers. Their enthusiasm was based on the specific experience of each city and referred very practically to the development of growth strategies. Boosters in each

city formulated a set of priorities appropriate to local circumstances. Chicago stressed its suitability for commerce arising from
its location. Indianapolis chose to elaborate the theme of centrality
and to stress its advantages for manufacturing and service activities. Galena, which was outstandingly fitted for no single activity,
claimed to be at least partly suited for all. Cincinnati concerned itself with the means by which it might augment all sectors of an
already diversified economy.

There were also differences in the attitudes that each city dis-
played toward its rivals. Those towns which had sampled the
pleasures of commercial importance reacted with confusion to the
appearance of new competitors. They floundered for want of a
clear program of development, wasted money on contradictory
projects, and substituted invective for ideas. These tendencies can
be seen in the response of Galena to Dubuque and of Cincinnati to
Chicago. An alternative reaction in Indianapolis and especially in
Chicago was to take the offensive, to probe for weaknesses in other
cities, and to act on the revealed opportunities. Even the position
and extent of a town's hinterland, in short, was partly a result of its
own response to commercial circumstance.

The evaluation of the danger posed by rival cities was as much a
part of the entrepreneurial process as was the accurate description
of the current economic environment in city and hinterland. A
broad understanding of the situation facing each city was important in the evolution and implementation of a successful growth
strategy. Indeed, attitudes toward urban adversaries faithfully mir-
rored the economic imagination and confidence which each city
brought to the analysis of its own position. Indianapolis and Chicago, clearly the more successful of the four cities in the 1850s, accepted
single coherent analyses of their economic growth. In Cincinnati,
where growth slowed by prosperity was maintained, economic thought
was rational but contradictory. Galena's decline was accompanied
by increasingly incoherent discussion of its economic future.

In all four towns, finally, the character of collective action matched
that of boosterism. The vigor of entrepreneurship in Chicago and
Indianapolis was in part a result of the clarity of their strategies
of growth, while its weakness in Cincinnati was partially a function

of that town's ambivalent attitudes. The failure of urban entrepreneurship in Galena reflected the nature of its economic thought. Although not even the successful towns acted in entire harmony or passed the maze of economic choices without doubts and wrong turns, the rationality and cogency of their economic thought influenced their success in carrying out programs of development.

Although popular economic thought was rooted in the circumstances of individual cities, antebellum boosters shared common patterns in approach and rhetoric. In particular, the magnitude of urban and regional growth often persuaded them to seek concrete measures and analogs. Behind the festoons of adjectives with which they dressed their pieces, many boosters were amateur statisticians. Time and again, they found that numbers offered the most convenient standard of comparison when everything was new and changing. Other urban advocates wrote what amounted to gazetteers of the future, describing urban ambitions in terms of natural resources and trade zones.

Most editors and boosters were fluent with quantitative data on both the characteristics of their city and the dimensions and products of its hinterland. It was customary throughout the West for writers of railroad prospectuses or similar documents to present elaborate tables showing the agricultural surplus in the region trading over a certain line or with a certain city. Although historian Alfred Chandler has argued that western railroad builders confined their dry statistics about finances and earning capacity to promotional literature intended for easterners and regaled local residents with bombastic prose, westerners in fact seem to have been just as interested in studying the numbers. The procedure was so common that one Cincinnatian complained as follows:

"Of the General Business and Probable Revenue of the Road"—It is customary under this head of a Railroad Report, to display a mass of statistical information, gleaned from the County Auditors, or the Census Bureau of the United States, and then adopt a hypothesis of movement, which shall apparently cause the great mass of men and things, upon or near the line of the proposed route, to use it periodically at suppository rates and times, and thus contribute to the revenue of the road, a previously determined amount.[4]

This western interest in quantitative boosterism developed at a time of increasingly sophisticated attention to the compilation of statistics on the national level. One of the first actions of the American Statistical Association after its organization in 1839 was to criticize the Sixth Census. ASA founder Lemuel Shattuck's city census of Boston in 1845 became a model for more scientific data-gathering in the federal census of 1850. A census board created by Congress in 1849 gathered ideas for the 1850 enumeration from European and American experts, and Joseph C.G. Kennedy and J.D.B. DeBow as directors made it the first modern census. In the *Compendium* of this Seventh Census, DeBow remarked the growing "public zest" for statistical information and urged the creation of permanent statistical bureaus in every state and city. In the same years, DeBow's monthly review assiduously published economic statistics, and DeBow himself served as director of the pioneering Louisiana state office of statistics.[5]

The difference between DeBow's New Orleans and the cities north of the Ohio lay in the number of westerners interested in statistical boosterism. In Cincinnati, for example, the Merchants' Exchange in 1847 set the collection of commercial statistics as its primary goal. James Hall in the same year urged his friend Robert Buchanen to attend the upcoming River-and-Harbor Convention and to "bring all the statistics you can." Edward Mansfield practiced statistical analysis in a series of railroad reports in the 1850s and assumed the tailor-made post of state Commissioner of Statistics in 1857. Charles Cist in the same decade served the city both as census taker and as compiler of booster publications, while astronomer O. M. Mitchel applied his mathematics to railroad promotion.[6]

Boosters in other cities matched Cist's work with their own "historical and statistical sketches." The *Sketch Book of St. Louis* in 1858 was a guide to the city's economy as well as its sights. Edward Deering described *Louisville: Her Commercial, Manufacturing and Social Advantages* in 1852, Robert Roberts provided *Sketches of the City of Detroit, State of Michigan, Past and Present* in 1855, and Charles Spalding published his *Annals of the City of Kansas* in 1858. *Pittsburgh As It Is, or Facts and Figures Exhibiting the Past and Present of Pittsburgh, Its Advantages, Resources, Manufactures, and Commerce* (1857) offered statistics on coal mining, railroads, population, climate, real estate, boat building, banks, and "progressional ratio" of growth compared to that of the entire West. Author George Thurston explicitly stated his intention to make up for the lack of a "yearly balance sheet of prosperity" with a general statistical outline of his city. Immediately after the Civil War, the genre continued with William Holloway's *Indianapolis: A Historical and Statistical Sketch of the Railroad City* and the *Historical and Statistical Sketch of the Garden City* by Elias Colbert, the commercial editor of the *Chicago Tribune*. His subtitle summarized the contents of the typical urban profile of the 1850s and 1860s: "A Chronicle of Its Social, Municipal, Commercial and Manufacturing Progress from the Beginning until Now, Containing Also Names of the Early Settlers and Office Holders, with Full Statistical Tables."

The antebellum passion for statistics had already been carried to its extreme in Chicago. It is hard to imagine a description of Illinois agriculture that quantified more factors than J.L. Peyton's *Statistical View of the State of Illinois* or a railroad prospectus with more tables showing potential trade than George Baldwin's 1847 *Report Showing the Cost and Income of a Railroad as Surveyed from Toledo, Ohio, to Chicago, Illinois.* At the same time, its citizens delighted in printing statements of the city's commerce in city directories, gazetteers, and newspapers. In a word, many Chicagoans had the conviction that the propagation of statistics "better enabled the public everywhere to appreciate its advantages than anything else which has ever been done." The editor of the *Democratic Press* wrote that "facts and figures . . . if carefully pondered, become more interesting and . . . astonishing than the wildest visions of the most vagrant imagination" and asserted that "figures are themselves more eloquent and absorbing than any language at our command." His counterpart at the *Journal* agreed that "the West is emphatically a world of facts and figures. Its history cannot be made the theme of embellished and well-turned periods—the *digits,* rather than the muses, give it utterance."[7]

A geographical consciousness also suffused western boosterism, for urban economic growth seemed most real when described in terms of commercial territory. Antebellum westerners were constantly aware of spatial relationships and the effects of topography on human activity. They thought of transportation developments as the unfolding of a visible system on a map, and they were intensely interested in the definition of hinterlands and the commercial conquest of territory. Many boosters would have found it hard to analyze urban development in abstract terms as the assembly at low cost of different factors of production. Instead, they considered it analogous to the development of political empires, with its essential characteristic being the extension of control over the earth's surface. In a sense, they were more interested in the goal to be attained than in the processes by which it was achieved.

More specifically, every city in the antebellum West boasted its counterparts of those enthusiasts who believed in the 1840s and 1850s that the manifest destiny of the United States could be read directly from a map. Editors in every town could tick off the particular natural advantages which assured its prosperity. Other boosters of urban growth focused on the geographic destiny of the West as a whole, believing that "the Valley of the Mississippi seems to have been designed by nature for the final home of empire." In the growth of the great central valley, boosters argued, western cities could not fail to find prosperity. As the *Chicago Journal* wrote, that city "reflects and indicates the rising glory of the region, amidst which it is set."[8]

It was in this context that John S. Wright and William Gilpin and Jesup W. Scott constructed their elaborate semi-scientific theories of American growth. As has been described, their writings were familiar to every local booster and provided a framework that made less systematic discussion intellectually respectable. They also extrapolated statistical trends and used the latest geographical theories to relate urbanization to national growth. According to their analysis, the center of population and wealth was moving inexorably into what Gilpin called the Great Central Plain, "the amphitheatre of the world." The Atlantic coast would soon be an appendage, foreign trade irrelevant. "The west is no longer the west," wrote Scott, "nor even the great west. It is the great center. It is the body of the American eagle whose wings are on the two oceans." The result of this westward movement would be magnificent cities in the American interior. Their growth could only be beneficial, for cities were one of the "remarkable phenomena of human progress." As Scott said, "all people take pride in their cities. In them naturally concentrate the great minds and great wealth of the nation. There the arts that adorn life are cultivated, and from them flows out knowledge that gives its current of thought to the national mind."[9]

Practicing politicians also analyzed the meaning of western growth from a geographical perspective. It was not just that westerners were section-conscious in dealing with the East and South. To some of the region's statesmen, development of the West promised to transform national politics. Most notably, Stephen Douglas argued that it could reunify the quarreling country by making the petty disputes of North and South insignificant. His ideas drew directly on the imagery of urban boosters:

> There is a power in this nation greater than either the North or the South—a growing, increasing, swelling power, that will be able to speak the law to the nation. . . . That power is the country known as the great West—the Valley of the Mississippi. . . . There, sir, is the hope of this nation—the resting place of the power that is not only to control, but to save, the Union. . . . This is the mission of the great Mississippi Valley, the heart and soul of the nation and the continent.[10]

Western boosterism thus embraced more than a discussion of the possibilities of growth in particular towns. One Cincinnati merchant expressed a common sentiment when he remarked that "it was always a pleasure to me to discuss the growth of the west." It was not unusual to assert that the Northwest presented "the most remarkable instance of growth and prosperity recorded in History," and publicists were as willing to apply extravagant adjectives to the entire section as to its urban components.[11] Directly or indirectly, popular economic writing of the 1840s and 1850s indicated how westerners expected the occupation of the continent to affect the United States and fit into world history. Indeed, boosterism contained a grand vision of the future in which regional development was the true realization of national destiny. When a native assured outsiders that "you must have confidence in the west," he meant just that, for many believed that the section and its cities were intended for a "grand and noble purpose."[12]

Boosters in Indianapolis or Chicago would have felt little in common with the eastern writers and reformers whose antipathy toward urban growth has been well documented by Morton and Lucia White and Thomas Bender.[13] In part, there was a contrast of styles and temperaments between entrepreneurs who kept their eyes on the main chance and intellectuals who delighted in exploring the moral and political ambiguities of urbanization. Even more, the divergence of viewpoints was rooted in attention to different sets of experiences. Anti-urban essayists and philosophers looked eastward to Europe. Their reaction was not so much to Boston or New York as to the Paris of 1789 and 1848 and the Manchester of the 1830s. Middle-western boosters looked westward to the American future. Like the secular and religious utopians who located their experiments in the western forests and prairies, they saw the West as a series of possibilities.

The nearest parallel to the urban and regional boosterism of the antebellum Middle West was found in the new cities of the Far West between 1850 and 1880. The founders of American California held a vision of creating a new society in a new land much like the hopes of antebellum middle-westerners. When Hubert Howe Bancroft found on the Pacific coast "the ringing up of universal intelligence for a final display of what man can do at his best . . . surrounded by conditions such as had never before befallen the lot of man to enjoy," he was speaking the language of the booster. In more detail, Gunther Barth has examined urban patriotism in the "instant cities" of Denver and San Francisco, whose first settlers viewed the cities as "depositories of wealth, to be mined as rigorously as placers and veins." Denverites and San Franciscans shared dreams of economic success, overweening confidence in their towns, and faith that urbanization made a direct contribution to the national purpose. At the same time that they scrambled for immediate gain, they lived with one foot firmly in the future. "Men and women carried in their heads a set of accomplishments that they hoped to see in their lifetime, the firsts of practically everything . . . all fused into their image of new cities."[14]

Whether they were Chicagoans or Denverites, there seems little doubt that westerners took their vision seriously in the decades around mid-century, accepting the future that it sketched not as a rhetorical extravagance but as a real opportunity. Much of the popular economic writing in the early Middle West was a worldly sermon, stiff with conviction of high purpose. Boosters delighted in bold and bombastic predictions because they believed that "vainglorious boasting" expressed an inner conviction about the growth of the section that was both "prophetic and true."[15] Some professed to believe that the West would produce men "endowed with superior courage, energy, eloquence, ambitions, boldness, and business zeal." New ways of life and thought would require a "new Practical Philosophy, social, moral, political, religious, and literary." Tradition-bound easterners could scarcely comprehend the western man who was "independent of antecedents" and who saw "the momentous question of the future . . . upon him, its opening grandeur all around him." More broadly than the advocates of manifest destiny, boosters asserted that the west stood "on the eve of a great, permanent, and propitious social advancement."[16]

Antebellum boosterism was an embodiment of a deep American optimism about the effects of economic expansion. In the same decades, the "ardent, evangelical nationalism" of the Young America movement provided a political complement. With Stephen Douglas as its premier representative, Young America stirred desires for achievement of national greatness through territorial expansion and the full use of "the energies of this great and progressive people."[17] Urban boosterism expressed the same sense of national mission. Although some Americans have considered the republican experiment to be the country's chief contribution to a reformed world, many others have expected the new order of the ages to be built on a foundation of economic power and trade. The popular economic writers of Cincinnati and Chicago bore a basic resemblance to Frederick Jackson Turner's pioneer and to the nineteenth-century American described by foreign travelers. Confident, assertive, hustling, and materialistic, they all believed in the rapid exploitation of the continent as a national duty. To the urban booster, successful development would bring the "most remarkable instance of growth and prosperity recorded in History" and hold up an example of the possibilities for human happiness.[18] The booster pamphlet in this context was the twin of the Fourth of July oration. Independence Day rhetoric reiterated the republican virtues of the nation. Urban boosters reaffirmed the commercial mission of its people. "We owe it to the new home we have all of us chosen," wrote the *Chicago Journal,* "to our posterity, and to the general good of the human race, that we do not sit idly by and see others grasp the improvements . . . which an advancing age has placed within our reach."[19]

NOTES

1. Gunther Barth, *Instant Cities: Urbanization and the Rise of San Francisco and Denver* (New York, 1975), p. 129.

2. Zane Miller, "Scarcity, Abundance and American Urban History," *Journal of Urban History* 4 (February 1978): 137-40; Wohl, "Urbanism," pp. 53-54; Bebb, *Cincinnati,* pp. 23-24; Stephen A. Douglas in *Railroad Record* 7 (June 23, 1859): 205; Anselm Strauss, *Images of the American City* (New York, 1961), pp. 155-61, 200-205.

3. *Hesperian,* preface to vol. 4; *Chicago Magazine* 1 (March 1857): 9-10; Herbert E. Fleming, "The Literary Interests of Chicago," *American Journal of Sociology* 11 (November 1905): 380-84; Daniel J. Boorstin, *The Americans: The National Experience* (New York, 1965), pp. 113-34, 161-68.

4. Alfred Chandler, *Henry Varnum Poor: Business Editor, Analyst and Reformer* (Cambridge, Mass., 1956), p. 92; Elwood Morris, *Report on the Preliminary Surveys Made for the Cincinnati, Hillsborough and Parkersburg Railway* (Cincinnati, 1852), p. 28.

5. Ottis Clark Skipper, *J.B.D. DeBow: Magazinist of the Old South* (Athens, Ga., 1958), pp. 29, 31, 36-38, 69-80; U.S., Seventh Census of the United States: 1850, *Statistical View of the United States* (Washington, 1854), pp. 10, 18-19.

6. James Hall to Robert Buchanen, June 22, 1847, Buchanen Papers, Cincinnati Historical Society; *DeBow's Review,* 3 (May 1847): 446-47; Edward D. Mansfield, *Geographical, Geological and Statistical Relations* of the Ohio and Mississippi Railroad (n.p., n.d.), pp. 9-10; *Exhibit of the Conditions and Resources of the Cincinnati and Chicago Railroad* (Cincinnati, 1854), pp. 10-12; O.M. Mitchel, *Conditions and Prospects of the Ohio and Mississippi Railroad* (Cincinnati, 1852), p. 32.

7. Norris, *Business Advertiser . . . 1845-46,* p. 3; *Chicago Democratic Press, Review of Commerce* for 1853, pp. 1, 3; *Chicago Journal,* January 5, 1852.

8. *Cincinnati Times,* May 7, 1859; *Chicago Journal,* January 5, 1852; *Chicago Democratic Press, Review of Commerce* for 1857, p. 6; Indianapolis Board of Trade, *Map and Circular.*

9. William Gilpin, *The Central Gold Region: The Grain, Pastoral and Gold Regions of North America* (Philadelphia, 1860); Jesup W. Scott, "The Great West," *DeBow's Review* 15 (July 1853): 50-53; Jesup W. Scott, "Commercial Cities and Towns of the United States—Our Cities, Atlantic and Interior," *Hunt's Merchants' Magazine* 19 (October 1848): 383-86; Jesup W. Scott, "Progress of the West," *Hunt's Merchants' Magazine* 14 (February 1846): 163-65; Scott, "Westward the Star of Empire," pp. 125-36.

10. Robert W. Johannsen, *Stephen A. Douglas* (New York, 1973), p. 280.

11. James Pullan Diary, June, 1857, Pullan Manuscripts, Ohio Historical Society; *Cincinnati Gazette,* March 18, 1851.

12. Luther Bixby to John C. Bixby, April 4, 1850, Bixby Manuscripts, Chicago Historical Society.

13. Morton and Lucia White, *The Intellectual versus the City* (Cambridge, Mass., 1962); Thomas Bender, *Toward an Urban Vision: Ideas and Institutions in Nineteenth Century America* (Lexington, Ky., 1975).

14. Kevin Starr, *Americans and the California Dream* (New York, 1973), p. 125; Barth, *Instant Cities,* pp. 129-31.

15. James, *Address Delivered at Camp McRae,* quoted in Aaron, "Cincinnati," p. 227; Lyle Dorsett and Mary Dorsett, "Rhetoric versus Realism: 150 Years of Missouri Boosterism," *Bulletin of the Missouri Historical Society* 28 (January 1972): 77-84.

16. *Cincinnati Chronicle,* October 29, 1845; William H. Channing (ed.), *The Memoirs and Writings of James Handasyd Perkins* (Cincinnati, 1852), pp. 154, 254; John Wilstach, *The Imperial Period of National Greatness: A Lecture on the Destiny of the West* (Lafayette, Ind., 1855), p. 9; *Chicago Democratic Press, Review of Commerce* for 1857, p. 47.

17. Merle Curti, "Young America," *American Historical Review* 21 (October 1926): 34-55; Johannsen, *Douglas,* pp. 344-45.

18. *Cincinnati Gazette,* March 18, 1851; *Railroad Record* 2 (August 24, 1854): 401.

19. *Chicago Journal,* January 19, 1846.

APPENDIX A: SAMPLING PROCEDURE

The original manuscript returns for the 1850 federal census record the occupation of all employed males fifteen years and older; the manuscript schedules for the 1860 census record the occupation of all employed persons fifteen years or older. For all persons enumerated, the census marshals in both years also listed sex, age, and state or country of birth. Where applicable, they recorded the value of real property owned (in 1850 and 1860) and of personal property (in 1860 only). In those cities large enough to be so divided, each census was taken by wards.[1] Within a ward, all members of a single family were listed together, starting with the head of the household and proceeding through wife and children. All inmates of such institutions as convents, orphanages, hospitals, or jails were listed together.

For the present study, a systematic sample was taken for each city in both years of all persons for whom either a specific occupation or the word "unknown" was entered in the column for employment. For each of the eight samples, a starting point between 1 and K was picked randomly; every K^{th} person with an occupation was then included in the sample. Such a procedure is normally assumed to produce a random sample from populations whose elements are arranged randomly.[2]

The following table gives the value of K and the size of each sample.

CITY	YEAR	SAMPLE SIZE	K
Chicago	1850	956	every 9th occ., starting with # 3
Chicago	1860	1078	every 35th occ., starting with #25
Cincinnati	1850	1041	every 36th occ., starting with #25
Cincinnati	1860	1026	every 60th occ., starting with #27
Galena	1850	863	every 2nd occ., starting with # 1
Galena	1860	917	every 3rd occ., starting with # 2
Indianapolis	1850	762	every 3rd occ., starting with # 1
Indianapolis	1860	1052	every 6th occ., starting with # 5

For every person in each sample, information was recorded on ward, sex, age in calendar years, and value of real and personal property in dollars. The place of birth was recorded in one of the following categories: New England, Middle Atlantic, South, other Midwest, state in which city located, Ireland, Great Britain, Germany, other foreign, illegible or unknown (see Table 2, Chapter 3). Occupation was recorded in one of these categories: transportation and communications (draymen, carter, wagoner, teamster, boatman, railroad employee, pilot, expressman, steamboat worker); personal service (servants, housekeeper, barber, laundress, musician, innkeeper, restaurant keeper, coffee house keeper, prostitute, nurse, bartender, saloonkeeper); professional service and government (lawyer, doctor, minister, teacher, civil engineer, architect, employee of state or charitable institutions, elected official, constable, watchman, editor, postman); retailing (grocer, butcher, bookseller, druggist, huckster, peddler, merchant tailor, fruiterer, "dealer" or "seller"); commerce and finance (banker, insurance or real estate broker, collector, agent, merchant, auctioneer, gentleman); building trades (carpenter, bricklayer, mason, painter, plasterer, paver, gasfitter, house mover); laborers; clerks and bookkeepers; metal goods manufacturing (machinist, mechanic, engineer, moulder, finisher, blacksmith, tinsmith, coppersmith, foundry and machine shop workers); other basic manufacturing (printer, brickmaker, sashmaker, stonecutter, sawyer, glassmaker, wagon and carriage makers, chemical and paint workers, cooper, textile worker, paper and box makers, turner, ship carpenter); food and consumer goods manufacturing (brewer, distiller, soap and candle makers, tanner, tailor, seamstress, baker, jeweler, cabinet maker, gunsmith, "___maker"); farming and gardening; mining and smelting; illegible or unknown.

Any set of occupational categories is in some ways unsatisfactory. This set was formulated in order to obtain a rough division of employment by functional type rather than by industry. For this reason, the large number of persons listed only as "clerks" or "laborers," any of whom might have worked for any enterprise in the city, are placed in separate categories. Although hardly satisfactory, this procedure seemed superior to excluding such workers from the sample. In addition, the boundaries of the "retailing" category are unavoidably ambiguous. Some of the importers listed as merchants, for example, may also have retailed goods. More importantly, some of the mechanics and artisans included in the category "food and consumer goods manufacturing" undoubtedly sold directly to many consumers. One can guess that the figures presented in the category somewhat underestimate the retailing sector in the several cities.[3]

[1]Cincinnati and Chicago were divided into wards in both years; Galena and Indianapolis were so divided only in 1860.

[2]In those cities divided into wards, the technique described gives the equivalent of a stratified random sample with proportional allocation. Because the differences in the distribution of employment from ward to ward are small, however, the variance of the results when the samples are treated as such is little different from the variance obtained by treating it as a simple random sample. For discussion of systematic sampling and its problems, and for formulas for computing the variance of different types of samples, see Leslie Kish, *Survey Sampling* (New York: John Wiley and Sons, Inc., 1965), pp. 86–89, 112–22, 139–42.

[3]If census enumerators had followed guidelines, they would have assigned all "clerks" and "laborers" to a place of employment and would have distinguished between artisans and retailers and among different types of merchants. Unfortunately, the enumerators in the four cities ignored their instructions completely.

APPENDIX B:
CINCINNATI AND CHICAGO
TRADE DATA

Numerical data available in printed sources can be used to supplement verbal descriptions of the Cincinnati and Chicago trade areas. In both cities, reviews of trade issued by newspapers and commercial organizations not only reported their cities' volume of imports and exports but also listed the amounts received and shipped by the various agencies of transportation. Such information gives a rough indication of the relative importance of the different sectors of a city's hinterland. It can be used in conjunction with data contained in annual reports of railroads and canals, which sometimes allow a crude estimation of the distance a city's trading area extended in a particular direction.

The chief problem facing the user of both types of information is the incompatibility of data drawn from different sources. No two reviews of trade organized their information on quite the same principles, making comparisons from city to city hazardous. Even more annoyingly, every transportation line had an idiosyncratic system for reporting the volume of traffic it carried, making the preparation of an internally consistent map of a city's trade area impossible. As they were drawn from three different sources, the following tables should therefore be considered as three independent approximations of hinterland position and size.

Tables 8 and 9 are taken from the annual *Reports* of the Cincinnati Chamber of Commerce. Although the categories are crude, they allow a rough description of the relative importance of the different segments of Cincinnati's import hinterland—the areas buying merchandise, groceries, and manufactured goods from the Queen City. Most of the shipments by canal and railroad were destined for the interior of Indiana and Ohio; most shipments upriver for northeastern Kentucky, southeastern Ohio, western Virginia, and western Pennsylvania; and most consignments downriver for eastern Kentucky, the Wabash Valley, and areas along the Mississippi.

The next three tables, numbered 10, 11 and 12, are compiled from figures in the annual reports of the Galena and Chicago Union and the Chicago, Burlington and Quincy Railroads. To estimate values for the Rock Island, the total volume of freight carried eastward on the Fulton Branch of the Galena and on the main line of the Burlington was calculated from the reports of these companies. The percentage of the total carried on the Burlington through Mendota and the Galena east of Dixon was taken as the value for the eastern segment of the Rock Island. The percentage of the total carried on the Burlington between Mendota and Burlington and on the Galena from Dixon to Fulton was taken for the western segment of the Rock Island. For the town of Rock Island itself, the percentage of the total received at Fulton and Burlington was used.

Together, the three tables indicate how far Chicago's hinterland reached toward the West. As discussed in the text, they show that most Chicago trade was confined to the area east of the Mississippi but that Iowa was of increasing importance. Indeed, as the Rock Island east of La Salle had to share freight with the Canal, these values may overestimate the portion of its freight from the eastern part of its line. At the same time, the line enjoyed a bridge across the Mississippi and good connections in Iowa. It therefore probably received a higher percentage of its freight from Iowa than the values indicate. For a confirmaton of this suspicion, see *Chicago Tribune, Review of Trade* for 1860. p. 4.

Table 13 comes from the annual reviews of trade published by the *Chicago Democratic Press* starting in 1853. Put out in pamphlet form, these reviews of the previous year's commerce were more elaborate and detailed than similar summaries published during the early 1850s in late December or January issues of the *Chicago Journal* and the *Chicago Tribune.* After the merger of the *Democratic Press* and the *Tribune,* the newspaper continued to issue the reviews as the *Chicago Press and Tribune* (reviews for 1858 and 1859) or the *Chicago Tribune* (reviews for 1860 and after).

Among the information included was a breakdown of Chicago's total receipts and shipments of certain commodities by the twelve major routes of transportation terminating in the city: Lake Michigan, the Illinois and Michigan Canal, and the city's ten trunk railroads. The figures were supposedly compiled from the books of the various railroad companies and for the years after 1857 agreed closely, though not exactly, with those published in the annual reports of the Chicago Board of Trade. Except for crude estimates, neither the reviews nor the Board of Trade reports included figures on the city's wagon trade.

Table 13 gives Chicago's receipts of corn, wheat, flour, live cattle, and live and dressed hogs and its shipments of lumber as given in the two sources. To show more clearly the spatial pattern of the city's trade, the data for the several transportation lines have been grouped geographically. Category 1 includes the city's receipts and shipments by the Lake. Category 2 includes its trade by the three eastward railways—the Michigan Central, the Michigan Southern and Northern Indiana, and the Pittsburgh, Fort Wayne, and Chicago. Category 3 includes the two railroads running south from the city—the Illinois Central and the Chicago and Alton. Category 4 includes the Illinois and Michigan Canal and the Chicago, Burlington, and Quincy, Rock Island, and Galena and Chicago Union railroads, all of which ran between the Illinois River and the Wisconsin border. Category 5 includes the city's northern railroads—the Chicago and North Western and the Chicago and Milwaukee. Category 6 includes flour manufactured in the city, grain arriving by wagon, and livestock arriving on foot.

Through 1856, the freight of the Burlington was delivered to Chicago by the Galena Railroad. As both lines tapped the same sector of Illinois, this connection had no effect on the pattern shown. In addition, the western branch of the Illinois Central delivered its freight to the Galena line before 1856, when the company finally finished its Chicago branch. For these years, therefore, the figures may overstate the share of Chicago's trade done with Sector 4 and understate the share done with Sector 3. After 1856, in contrast, some of the freight carried to Chicago on the Illinois Central came from its Galena branch; the figures may thus overstate the contribution of Sector 3.

TABLE 8
Destination of Cincinnati Shipments of Manufactured Goods

	1850/51	1851/52	1852/53	1853/54	1854/55	1855/56	1856/57	1857/58	1858/59	1859/60
Candles:										
% to South	60	77	67	82	75	66	60	81	57	77
% to North	40	23	33	18	25	34	40	19	43	23
Soap:										
% to South	72	70	61	63	43	24	22	23	26	32
% to North	28	30	39	37	57	76	78	77	74	68
Iron (pieces):										
% to South	56	53	46	49	46	38	30	35	40	42
% to North	44	47	54	51	54	62	70	65	60	58
Castings (pcs.):										
% to South	78	85	83	64	63	61	66	41	49	49
% to North	22	15	17	36	37	39	34	59	51	51

Sundry Mfgs.:										
% to South	91	91	88	89	90	93	95	36	63	67
% to North	9	9	12	11	10	7	5	64	37	33
Boots & Shoes:										
% to South	—	—	—	—	—	—	—	23	12	11
% to North	—	—	—	—	—	—	—	77	88	89
Furniture:										
% to South	—	—	—	—	—	—	—	71	81	86
% to North	—	—	—	—	—	—	—	29	19	14

"South" includes shipments to New Orleans and other downriver points.
"North" includes shipments by canal and railroad and to upriver points.

SOURCE:
Annual Reports of the Cincinnati Chamber of Commerce.

TABLE 9
Destination of Cincinnati Shipments of Merchandise and Groceries

	1850/51	1851/52	1852/53	1853/54	1854/55	1855/56	1856/57	1857/58	1858/59	1959/60
Merchandise-pkgs:										
% by Canal & Rr.	34	34	55	65	70	64	60	66	68	73
% upriver	20	22	13	10	8	7	15	12	12	11
% downriver	39	40	30	21	20	26	22	19	18	13
% to New Orleans	7	4	1	4	2	3	3	3	2	3
Coffee:										
% by Canal & Rr.	47	48	55	55	55	74	68	72	78	79
% upriver	21	20	15	16	9	5	8	6	3	2
% downriver	32	32	30	29	36	21	24	22	19	19
Molasses:										
% by Canal & Rr.	40	39	36	46	56	68	71	67	70	67
% upriver	52	51	51	46	40	30	25	30	27	29
% downriver	8	10	13	8	4	2	4	3	3	4

SOURCE: Annual Reports of the Cincinnati Chamber of Commerce.

TABLE 10

Chicago Export Hinterland: Percentage of Total Eastward Freight Received from Different Segments of Chicago's Western Railroads

	1855	1857	1858	1859
Galena and Chicago Union:				
Wisconsin Branches	15.3	6.1	8.5	11.2
Freeport Line	56.8	56.0	45.0	38.2
(from Illinois Central)	(11.5)	(18.5)	(8.9)	(7.4)
Fulton Line	26.5	29.0	37.9	35.7
Fulton	1.0	7.9	6.8	14.5
Chicago, Burlington and Quincy:				
Mendota and East		44.1	37.9	24.6
Burlington Line		40.7	39.0	40.6
Burlington		5.5	7.0	13.9
Quincy Line		8.7	9.6	11.8
Quincy		1.2	5.7	8.0
Rock Island:				
La Salle and East		48.0	46.5	36.0
Western Illinois		43.0	44.0	45.0
Rock Island		9.0	9.5	19.0

SOURCES: pp. 31; *Report* for 1859, p. 28. Galena and Chicago Union data from *Report* for 1855-56, p. 24; *Report* for 1858, Chicago, Burlington and Quincy data from *Reports* for 1858, 1859, and 1860.

TABLE 11
Chicago Import Hinterland: Percentage of Total
Westward Freight Delivered to Different Segments
of Chicago's Western Railroads

	1855	1857	1858	1859
Galena and Chicago Union:				
Wisconsin Branches	11.5	6.2	8.5	9.5
Freeport Line	58.3	49.6	53.9	53.0
(to Illinois Central)	(17.5)	(17.8)	(13.8)	(10.5)
Fulton Line	29.9	44.4	35.8	38.1
Fulton		3.5	5.1	8.8
Chicago, Burlington and Quincy:				
Mendota and East		44.7	42.8	30.7
Burlington Line		34.5	29.6	33.8
Burlington		6.9	8.6	7.6
Quincy Line		10.2	11.4	10.4
Quincy		2.8	7.6	19.6
Rock Island:				
La Salle and East		55.0	55.0	45.0
Western Illinois		39.0	37.0	43.0
Rock Island		6.0	8.0	12.0

SOURCES:
Galena and Chicago Union data from *Report* for 1855-56, p. 24; *Report* for 1858,
    pp. 31; *Report* for 1859, p. 28.
Chicago, Burlington and Quincy data from *Reports* for 1858, 1859, and 1860.

TABLE 12

Volume of Freight on Galena and Chicago Union and Chicago, Burlington and Quincy Railroads (millions of pounds)

		Eastward					
Originating in		1857		1858		1859	
River towns:	GCU	32		46		100	
	CBQ	32		28		51	
	Total	**64**	(7%)	**74**	(10%)	**151**	(19%)
Western Illinois	GCU	237		178		238	
	CBQ	160		125		100	
	Total	**397**	(44%)	**303**	(40%)	**338**	(42%)
Eastern Illinois:	GCU	212		146		112	
	CBQ	218		233		197	
	Total	**430**	(49%)	**379**	(50%)	**309**	(39%)

		Westward					
Originating in		1857		1858		1859	
River towns:	GCU	44		57		97	
	CBQ	12		13		22	
	Total	**56**	(7%)	**70**	(12%)	**119**	(19%)
West Illinois:	GCU	205		145		157	
	CBQ	100		79		81	
	Total	**305**	(39%)	**224**	(37%)	**239**	(39%)
East Illinois:	GCU	204		151		110	
	CBQ	215		149		147	
	Total	**419**	(54%)	**300**	(51%)	**257**	(42%)

East Illinois includes stations on the GCU east of Freeport and Dixon and on the CBQ from Chicago through Mendota; the river towns are Fulton, Burlington, and Quincy; West Illinois includes the remaining stations. For sources see Table 3.

TABLE 13
Receipts and Shipments of Major Commodities at Chicago, by Sectors

| | Chicago Corn Receipts, by Sectors (in 1,000 bus.) | | | | | |
	Sector 1	Sector 2	Sector 3	Sector 4	Sector 5	Sector 6
1852	—	—	—	2,483	—	508
1853	—	—	4	2,788	—	138
1854	—	—	232	7,001	57	200
1855	—	—	473	14,926	38	200
1856	—	—	520	10,079	—	200
1857	—	145	275	6,777	7	200
1858	—	42	1,389	6,727	71	3
1859	—	30	954	4,388	31	—
1860	—	102	3,937	11,162	34	250
1861	—	20	7,120	19,081	49	100
1862	—	20	5,702	23,260	467	125

| | Chicago Flour Receipts, by Sectors (in 1,000 bbls.) | | | | | |
	Sector 1	Sector 2	Sector 3	Sector 4	Sector 5	Sector 6
1852	—	4	—	46	—	—
1853	—	7	—	38	—	83
1854	—	3	—	149	—	67
1855	—	3	11	221	—	80
1856	—	9	13	244	54	86
1857	—	9	17	319	43	96
1858	—	24	76	355	57	140
1859	—	28	166	481	58	166
1860	—	28	59	330	239	232
1861	—	16	243	398	398	292
1862	—	12	366	321	321	261

| | Chicago Wheat Receipts, by Sectors (in 1,000 bus.) | | | | | |
	Sector 1	Sector 2	Sector 3	Sector 4	Sector 5	Sector 6
1852	—	14	—	614	—	181
1853	—	15	15	1,297	—	298
1854	—	8	30	2,750	36	200
1855	—	7	772	6,427	124	200
1856	—	59	627	6,310	—	200
1857	—	25	1,129	8,805	280	200
1858	—	65	1,898	6,981	343	200

	Sector 1	Sector 2	Sector 3	Sector 4	Sector 5	Sector 6
1859	—	78	1,830	5,584	485	200
1860	—	169	2,938	9,196	1,971	200
1861	—	54	2,573	11,956	2,454	200
1862	—	200	3,265	7,774	2,450	250

Chicago Cattle Receipts, by Sectors (in 1,000's)						
	Sector 1	Sector 2	Sector 3	Sector 4	Sector 5	Sector 6
1857	—	1	27	20	1	—
1858	—	—	50	68	3	21
1859	—	2	25	57	3	25
1860	—	1	36	111	8	20
1861	—	1	45	114	4	40
1862	—	1	51	113	15	25

Chicago Hog Receipts, by Sectors (in 1,000's)						
	Sector 1	Sector 2	Sector 3	Sector 4	Sector 5	Sector 6
1858	—	6	217	303	14	—
1859	—	10	94	157	9	—
1860	—	33	118	216	25	—
1861	—	9	218	394	23	30
1862	—	14	353	847	104	30

Chicago Lumber Shipments, by Sectors (in 1,000,000 ft.)						
	Sector 1	Sector 2	Sector 3	Sector 4	Sector 5	Sector 6
1852	—	—	—	71	—	—
1853	—	—	—	88	—	—
1854	—	—	7	123	—	—
1855	—	—	—	210	—	—
1856	—	—	—	234	19	—
1857	—	—	50	251	8	—
1858	—	—	66	165	8	—
1859	—	4	66	151	6	—
1860	—	6	71	142	5	—
1861	—	5	60	119	6	—
1862	—	4	65	117	4	—

SOURCES:

Corn, flour, wheat, and lumber 1852-60, and cattle, 1857, from Reviews of Trade.

Corn, flour, wheat, and lumber, 1861-62, and cattle and hogs, 1858-62, from Board of Trade Reports.

BIBLIOGRAPHY

CONTEMPORARY SOURCES

Gazetteers, Geological Surveys, Guidebooks, and Other Regional Descriptions

Andrews, Israel D. *Report . . . on the Trade and Commerce of the British North American Colonies and upon the Trade of the Great Lakes and Rivers.* S. Exec. Doc. No. 112, 32nd Cong., 1st Sess., 1853.

Atwater, Caleb. *A History of the State of Ohio.* Cincinnati: Glezen and Shepard, 1838.

Bross, William. "The State of Illinois." In *Illinois State Gazetteer and Business Directory for 1858 and 1859.* Chicago: George W. Hawes, 1857.

Buttner, J.G. *Der Staat Ohio.* Bayreuth: Verlag der Buchnerscher Buchhandlung, 1839.

Campbell, A. *A Glance at Illinois: Her Lands, and Their Commercial Value: Her Coal Fields, Rail Roads, and General Resources and Advantages.* LaSalle, Illinois: C. Boynton and Co., 1856.

Conclin, George. *Conclin's New River Guide, or a Gazetteer of All the Towns on the Western Waters.* Cincinnati: J.A. and U.P. James, 1854.

Cumings, Samuel. *The Western Pilot.* Cincinnati: George Conclin, 1839.

Curtiss, Daniel S. *Western Portraiture and Emigrant's Guide.* New York: J.H. Colton, 1852.

Daniels, Edward. *Geological Survey of the State of Wisconsin.* Annual Reports for 1854, 1857.

Edwards' Descriptive Gazetteer and Commercial Directory of the Mississippi River. St. Louis: Edwards, Greenough and Deved, 1866.

Ellsworth, Henry W. *Valley of the Upper Wabash, Indiana, with Hints on Its Agricultural Advantages.* New York: Pratt, Robinson and Co., 1838.

Fisher, Richard S. *Indiana: In Relation to Its Geography, Statistics, Institutions, County Topography, Etc.* New York: J.H. Colton, 1852.

Fleischmann, C.L. *Erwerbszweige, Fabrikwesen und Handel der Vereinigten Staaten von Nordamerika.* Stuttgart: Verlag von Franz Köhler, 1852.

Flint, Timothy. *The History and Geography of the Mississippi Valley.* Cincinnati: L.H. Flint and L.R. Lincoln, 1832.

Ford, Thomas. *History of Illinois.* Edited by Milo M. Quaife. 2 vols. Chicago: The Lakeside Press, 1945.

Foster, John W. *Report upon the Mineral Resources of the Illinois Central Railroad.* New York: George Scott Roe, 1856.

Gallagher, William D. "Ohio in Eighteen Hundred Thirty-Eight." *Hesperian* 1 (May–July 1838): 7–17, 95–103, 183–91.

Gerhard, Fred. *Illinois as It Is.* Chicago: Keen and Lee, 1857.

Gilpin, William. *The Central Gold Region.* Philadelphia: Sower and Co., 1860.

Guide to the Illinois Central Railroad Lands. Chicago: Illinois Central Railroad Office, 1859.

Hall, James. *Statistics of the West, at the Close of the Year 1836.* Cincinnati: J.A. James and Co., 1837.

———. *The West: Its Commerce and Navigation.* Cincinnati: H.W. Derby and Co., 1848.

———. *The West: Its Soil, Surface and Productions.* Cincinnati: Derby, Bradley and Co., 1848.

Homans, Benjamin. *The United States Railroad Directory for 1856.* New York: B. Homans, 1856.

Howe, Henry. *Historical Collections of Ohio.* Cincinnati: Derby, Bradley and Co., 1847.

Illinois State Gazetteer and Business Directory for 1858 and 1859. Chicago: George W. Hawes, 1857.

The Indiana Annual Register and Pocket Manual, Revised and Corrected for the Year 1846. Indianapolis: Samuel Turner, 1846.

The Indiana Gazetteer or Topographical Dictionary. Indianapolis: Douglas and Maguire, 1833.

The Indiana Gazetteer, or Topographical Dictionary of the State of Indiana. Indianapolis: E. Chamberlain, 1849.

Indiana State Gazetteer and Business Directory for 1858–59. Indianapolis: G.W. Hawes, 1858.

Indiana State Gazetteer and Business Directory for 1860 and 1861. Indianapolis: George W. Hawes, 1860.

Jones, A.D. *Illinois and the West.* Boston: Weeks, Jordan and Co., 1838.

Lapham, Increase A. *Wisconsin: Its Geography and Topography, History, Geology and Mineralogy.* Milwaukee: I.A. Hopkins, 1846.

Lloyd, James T. *Lloyd's Steamboat Directory and Disasters on the Western Waters.* Cincinnati: James T. Lloyd and Co., 1856.

Lyford, William G. *The Western Address Directory.* Baltimore: Joseph Robinson, 1837.

Newhall, John B. *A Glimpse of Iowa in 1846.* Iowa City: State Historical Society of Iowa, 1857.

The Northern Counties Gazetteer and Directory for 1855–56: A Complete and Perfect Guide to Northern Illinois. Chicago: Robert Fergus, 1855.

Norwood, J.G. *Abstract of a Report on Illinois Coals.* Illinois Geological Survey. Chicago, 1858.

The Ohio Railroad Guide Illustrated: Cincinnati to Erie via Columbus and Cleveland. Columbus: Ohio State Journal Co., 1854.

Owen, David Dale. *Report of a Geological Exploration of Part of Iowa, Wisconsin, and Illinois.* S. Doc. No. 407, 28th Cong., 1st Sess., 1839.

———. *Report of a Geological Reconnaissance of the State of Indiana: Part First, 1837; Part Second, 1838.* Indianapolis: John C. Walker, State Printer, 1859.

Parker, Nathan H. *Iowa as It Is.* Chicago: Keen and Lee, 1855.

Peck, John Mason. *A Gazetteer of Illinois.* Jacksonville, Ill.: R. Goudy, 1834.

———. *A New Guide for Emigrants to the West.* Boston: Gould, Kendall and Lincoln, 1837.

Percival, James G. *Geological Survey of the State of Wisconsin.* Annual Reports for 1855, 1856.

Scott, Jesup W. "Commercial Cities and Towns of the United States—Our Cities, Atlantic and Interior." *Hunt's Merchants' Magazine* 19 (October 1848): 383–86.

———. "The Great West." *DeBow's Review* 15 (July 1853): 50–53.

———. "Internal Trade." *Hesperian* 1 (June 1838): 115–19, 2 (November 1838, March 1839): 42–49, 347–51; 3 (October 1839): 355–61.

———. "Internal Trade of the United States." *Hunt's Merchants' Magazine* 9 (July 1843): 31–46.

———. "Progress of the West." *Hunt's Merchants' Magazine* 14 (February 1846): 163–65.

———. "Westward the Star of Empire." *DeBow's Review* 27 (August 1859): 125–36.

Smith, William R. *Observations on Wisconsin Territory.* Philadelphia: E.L. Carey and A. Hart, 1838.

The State of Indiana Delineated. New York: J.H. Colton, 1838.

Whitney, J.D. "Geology of the Lead Region," in A.H. Worthen (ed.). *Geological Survey of Illinois.* Vol. I: *Geology.* Published by Authority of the Legislature of Illinois, 1866.

———. *The Metallic Wealth of the United States.* Philadelphia: Lippincott, Grambo and Co., 1854.

Whitney, J.D., and Hall, James. *Report on the Geological Survey of the State of Wisconsin.* Printed by Authority of the Legislature of Wisconsin, 1862.

Travel Reports

Atwater, Caleb. *Remarks Made on a Tour to Prairie du Chien.* Columbus: Isaac N. Whiting, 1831.

Beste, Richard. *The Wabash, or Adventures of an English Gentleman's Family in the Interior of America.* 2 vols. London: Hurst and Blackett, 1855.

Buckingham, James Silk. *The Eastern and Western States of America.* 3 vols. London: Fisher, Son and Co., 1842.

Caird, James. *Prairie Farming in America.* London: Longman, Brown, Green, Longmans and Roberts, 1859.

Chevalier, Michel. *Society, Manners and Politics in the United States.* Boston: Weeks, Jordan and Co., 1839.

Cunynghame, Arthur. *A Glimpse of the Great Western Republic.* London: Richard Bentley, 1851.

Dicey, Edmund. *Six Months in the Federal States.* 2 vols. London: Macmillan and Co., 1863.

Ferguson, William. *America by River and Rail.* London: James Nisbet and Co., 1856.

Gerstäcker, Freidrich. *Streif- und Jagdzüge durch die Vereinigten Staaten Nordamerikas.* Jena: Verlagsbuchhandlung von Herman Costenoble, 1901.

Hancock, William. *An Emigrant's Five Years in the Free States of America.* London: T. Cautley Newby, 1860.

Hoffman, Charles F. *A Winter in the West.* 2 vols. New York: Harper and Brothers, 1835.

Kohl, J. G. *Reisen im Nordwesten der Vereinigten Staaten.* New York: D. Appleton and Co., 1857.

Lanman, Charles. *A Summer in the Wilderness.* New York: D. Appleton and Co., 1847.

Löher, Franz. *Geschichte und Zustände der Deutschen in Amerika.* Cincinnati: Verlag von Eggers und Wulkop, 1847.

Lyell, Charles. *Travels in North America.* 2 vols. London: John Murray, 1845.

Mackey, Charles. *Life and Liberty in America.* 2 vols. London: Smith Elder and Co., 1859.

Martineau, Harriet. *Society in America.* 3 vols. New York: Saunders and Otley, 1837.

Peyton, John Lewis. *Over the Alleghenies and across the Prairies.* London: Simpkin, Marshall and Co., 1870.

A Pioneer in Northwest America, 1841–58: The Memoirs of Gustaf Unonius. Edited by Nils William Olsson. 2 vols. Minneapolis: University of Minnesota Press, 1960.

Schoolcraft, Henry R. *Summary Narrative of an Exploratory Expedition to the Sources of the Mississippi River in 1820; Resumed and Completed by the Discovery of its Origin in Itasca Lake, in 1832.* Philadelphia: Lippincott, Grambo and Co., 1855.

Trollope, Anthony. *North America.* Philadelphia: J.B. Lippincott and Co., 1863.

Wagner, Mortiz, and Scherzer, Carl. *Reisen in Nordamerika in den Jahren 1852 und 1853.* 3 vols. Leipzig: Arnoldische Buchhandlung, 1857.

Weld, Charles Richard. *A Vacation Tour in the United States and Canada.* London:

Longman, Brown, Green, and Longmans, 1855.

Ziegler, Alexander. *Skizzen einer Reise durch Nordamerika und Westindien.* Dresden und Leipzig: Arnoldische Buchhandlung, 1848.

Monthly and Bi-Weekly Periodicals

Bankers Magazine. 1–14 (July 1846–June 1860).

Chicago Magazine: The West as It Is. 1 (1857).

The Chicago Record, Devoted to Religion, Literature and the Fine Arts. 1–3 (April 1857–March 1860).

The Cincinnati Miscellany and Antiquities of the West. 1–2 (October 1844–April 1846).

The Cincinnatus: Devoted to Scientific Agriculture, Horticulture, Education, and Improvement of Rural Taste. 1–5 (1856–1860).

DeBow's Review. 1–29 (1846–1860).

The Elevator. 1 (1841–42).

Fliegende Blaetter. 1 (August 1846–September 1847).

Hazard's Register. 1–6 (July 1839–July 1842).

Herald of Truth, a Monthly Periodical Devoted to the Interests of Religion, Philosophy, Literature, Science, and Art. 1–3 (1847–1848).

Hesperian, or Western Monthly Magazine. 1–3 (May 1838–October 1839).

Hunt's Merchants' Magazine. 1–43 (1839–1860).

Illinois Monthly Magazine. 1–2 (1830–1832).

Indiana Farmer. 1 (1840–41).

Indiana Farmer and Gardener (continued as *Western Farmer and Gardener).* 1–3 (1845–1848).

Monthly Chronicle of Interesting and Useful Knowledge. 1 (December 1838–November 1839).

Prairie Farmer. 1–20 (1841–1859).

Railroad Record, or Journal of Commerce, Banking, Manufactures, and Statistics. 1–7 (1853–1860).

Scientific American. 1–14 (October 1848–June 1859). New Series, 1–3 (July 1859–December 1860).

Western Cultivator. 1–2 (January 1844–August 1845).

Western Democratic Review. 1–2 (1854).

Western Journal and Civilian. 1–15 (1848–1856).

The Western Literary Journal and Monthly Review. 1 (1836).

Western Monthly Magazine. 1–5 (1833–1836).

The Western Monthly Review. 1–3 (May 1827–June 1830).

Western Quarterly Review. 1 (1849).

Western Railroad Gazette. 1–3 (November 1856–April 1860).

Western Tiller. 1–4 (September 1828–November 1831).

Daily and Weekly Newspapers

Chicago American (weekly). June 1835–October 1837.

Chicago American (daily). April 1840–October 1842.

Chicago Commercial Advertiser. 1849–50.

Chicago Democrat. December 1833–November 1836, 1837–1843 (incomplete), 1844–1845, 1847–1852.

Chicago Democratic Press. September 1852–March 1858.

Chicago *Gem of the Prairie and Temperance Advocate.* June 1844–May 1845.

Chicago *Gem of the Prairie.* December 1847–December 1852.

Chicago Herald. March–October 1859.

Chicago Journal (weekly). May 1844–1848, 1850, 1852–53.

Chicago Journal (daily). April–June 1849.

Chicago Times (weekly). April 1855–August 1857.

Chicago Times (daily). September 1857–March 1860.

Chicago Tribune. April 1840–August 1841.

Chicago Tribune. December 1852–March 1861.

Chicago *Watchman of the Prairies.* August 1847–August 1852.

Chicago *Western Citizen.* July 1842–October 1853.

Cincinnati Advertiser and Ohio Phoenix. January 1833–April 1837.

Cincinnati Advertiser and Journal. January 1839–March 1841.

Cincinnati Atlas. May 1846–November 1849.

Cincinnati *Catholic Telegraph and Advocate.* 1849–1850.

Cincinnati Chronicle. 1841–1846.

Cincinnati *Cist's Weekly Advertiser.* March 1847–February 1850.

Cincinnati Commercial. October 1843–September 1844; October 1849–April 1850; April 1851–November 1854; June 1855–April 1860.

Cincinnati Enquirer. April 1841–March 1861.

Cincinnati Gazette. 1849–1860.

Cincinnati Herald. August 1843–August 1845; January 1846–May 1847; November 1847–September 1848.

Liberty Hall and Cincinnati Gazette. December 1835–July 1845.

Cincinnati Evening Mercury. February–July 1849.

Cincinnati Microscope. 1842.

Cincinnati Nonpareil. May 1850–January 1853.

Cincinnati Press. February 1859–June 1860.

Cincinnati Price-Current. September 1851–August 1859.

Cincinnati Republican. October 1840–April 1842.

Cincinnati Republikaner. 1859.

Cincinnati Sun. September–December 1843.

Cincinnati Sunbeam. November 1848–February 1849.

Cincinnati Times. 1841, 1853, 1856–1859.

Cincinnati Volksblatt (daily). 1843–1846.

Cincinnati Volksblatt (weekly). 1847–1852.

Cincinnati Volksfreund. 1856.

Cincinnati *Western Christian Advocate.* 1837–1855.

Cincinnati *Western General Advertiser.* January–June 1846.

Cincinnati *The Working Man's Friend.* July–August 1836.

Galena Advertiser. July 1829–May 1830.

Galena Courier. 1856–1860.

Galena *Galenian.* May 1832–January 1833.

Galena Jeffersonian (semi-weekly). October 1845–December 1846.

Galena Jeffersonian (daily). August 1851–April 1852; September–December 1852; May–September 1853.

Galena *Miners' Journal.* July 1828–September 1829.

Galena Northwestern Gazette and Weekly Advertiser. November 1834–June 1860.

Indianapolis Citizen. April 1858–May 1859.

Indianapolis Evening Atlas. August 1859–March 1860.

Indianapolis *Freie Presse von Indiana.* January–July 1856–1859.

Indianapolis *Indiana American.* September 1858–December 1860.

Indianapolis *Indiana Democrat* (precursor of Indiana Sentinel). 1837–June 1841.

Indianapolis *Indiana Democrat.* November 1845–September 1846.

Indianapolis *Indiana Free Democrat.* January 1853–September 1854.

Indianapolis *Indiana Republican and Chapman's Chanticleer.* November 1854–September 1855.

Indianapolis *Indiana State Journal* (weekly or tri-weekly). 1834–1850.

Indianapolis *Indiana State Journal* (daily, some editions called *Indianapolis Journal).* 1851–1860.

Indianapolis *Indiana State Sentinel* (weekly or semi-weekly). July 1841–May 1853.

Indianapolis *Indiana State Sentinel* (daily, some editions called *Indianapolis Sentinel).* June 1853–1860.

Indianapolis *Indiana Statesman.* September 1850–August 1852.

Indianapolis *Locomotive.* 1848–1860.

State and Federal Documents

Illinois. Board of Trustees of the Illinois and Michigan Canal. Reports. 2d–16th (1846–1860). In *Illinois Reports,* 1846/47–1861.

Illinois. Governor. Biennial Messages and Inaugural Addresses. 1839–1861. In *Illinois Reports,* 1839/40–1861.

Illinois. House of Representatives. Report of the Committee on Finance. In *Illinois Reports,* 1842/43, pp. 165–74.

Illinois. Report to Messrs. Baring, Brother and Co. and Messrs. Magniac, Jardine and Co., March 1, 1844 (by John Davis and William H. Swift). In *Illinois Reports,* 1844/45.

Illinois. State Census, 1835. 9th General Assembly, 2d Sess., 1835/36. *House Journal,* facing p. 372.

Illinois. State Census, 1840. In *Illinois Reports,* 1840/41, pp. 403–414.

Illinois. State Census, 1845. In *Illinois Reports,* 1846/47, pp. 65–71.

Indiana. Bank of the State of Indiana. Annual Reports. 1856–1860. In *Documentary Journals.*

Indiana. Board of Internal Improvements. Annual Reports. 1836–41. In *Documentary Journals.*

Indiana. Governor. Annual Messages and Inaugural Addresses. 1837–61. In documentary Journals.

Indiana. *Messages and Papers relating to the Administration of David Wallace, Governor of Indiana, 1837–1840*. Edited by Dorothy Riker. Indiana Historical Collections, vol. 43. Indianapolis: Indiana Historical Bureau, 1963.

Indiana. *Messages and Papers relating to the Administration of Samuel Bigger, Governor of Indiana, 1840–43*. Edited by Gayle Thornbrough. Indiana Historical Collections, vol. 44. Indianapolis: Indiana Historical Bureau, 1964.

Indiana. Senate. Bank Investigating Committee. *Bank Frauds: Journal, Testimony and Reports*. Indianapolis: Joseph J. Bingham, 1857.

Indiana. State Bank of Indiana. Annual Reports. 1836–1858. In *Documentary Journals*.

Indiana. State Board of Agriculture. Reports. 1852–1859.

Indiana. Wabash and Erie Canal Superintendent. Annual Reports. 1847–1860. In *Documentary Journals*.

Ohio. Auditor of State. Annual Reports. 1840–1860.

Ohio. Board of Public Works. Annual Reports. 1836–1858.

Ohio. Commissioner of Statistics. Annual Reports. 1857–1861.

Ohio. Governor. Messages. 1835–1860.

Ohio. State Board of Agriculture. Annual Reports. 1st–15th (1846–60).

U.S. Chief of Engineers. Report for 1874. H.R. Exec. Doc. No. 1, pt. 2, 43d Cong., 2d Sess., 1874.

U.S. Secretary of the Treasury. *Report Communicating Statistical Information in Relation to the Condition of the Agriculture, Manufactures, Domestic Trade, Currency, and Banks of the United States*. S. Doc. No. 21, 28th cong., 2d Sess., 1845.

U.S. Secretary of the Treasury. Report for 1845. S. Doc. No. 2, 29th Cong., 1st Sess., 1845.

U.S. Sixth Census of the United States: 1840. *Compendium of the Enumeration of the Inhabitants and Statistics of the United States*. Washington: Thomas Allen, 1841.

U.S. Sixth Census of the United States, 1840. *Sixth Census or Enumeration of the Inhabitants of the United States*. Washington: Blair and Rives, 1841.

U.S. Sixth Census of the United States: 1840. *Statistics of the United States of America*. Washington: Blair and Rives, 1841.

U.S. Seventh Census of the United States: 1850. *Seventh Census of the United States*. Washington: Robert Armstrong, Public Printer, 1853.

U.S. Seventh Census of the United States: 1850. *Statistical View of the United States . . . being a Compendium of the Seventh Census*. Washington: Beverly Tucker, Senate Printer, 1854.

U.S. Eighth Census of the United States: 1860. *Preliminary Report*. Washington: Government Printing Office, 1862.

U.S. Eighth Census of the United States: 1860. Vol. I: *Population of the United States in 1860*. Vol. II: *Agriculture of the United States in 1860*. Vol. III: *Manufactures of the United States in 1860*. Vol. IV: *Statistics of the United States (including Mortality, Property, etc.) in 1860*. Washington: Government Printing Office, 1864–66.

Railroad Reports and Pamphlets

Baldwin, George R. *Report Showing the Cost and Income of a Rail-Road as Surveyed from Toledo, Ohio, to Chicago, Illinois, Incorporated as the Buffalo and Mississippi Rail-Road.* Toledo: Scott and Fairbanks, 1847.

Brough, John. *A Brief History of the Madison and Indianapolis Railroad.* New York: Van Norden and Amerman, 1852.

Chicago and North Western Railway Company. *Annual Reports.* 1st–4th (1859/60–1862/63).

Chicago and Rock Island Railroad Company. *Annual Reports.* 1854, 1857/58, 1860/61.

_____. *Statement of the Condition and Prospects of the Chicago and Rock Island Railroad Company.* New York: William C. Bryant and Co., 1852.

Chicago, Burlington and Quincy Railroad Company. *Annual Reports.* 1st–8th (1856/57–1863/64).

Chicago, St. Paul and Fond du Lac Rail-Road Company. *Annual Reports.* 1st–2d (1855–1856/57).

_____. *Exhibit, March 1, 1856.* New York, 1856.

Cincinnati, Hamilton and Dayton Railroad Company. *Annual Reports.* 1st–14th (1850–1864).

Cincinnati, Wilmington and Zanesville Railroad Company. *Annual Reports.* 3d, 6th, 7th (1854, 1856/57, 1857/58).

_____. *Special Report.* January 1857.

Circular of the Cincinnati, Harrison and Indianapolis Straight Line Railroad Company. Cincinnati: Cincinnati Gazette Co., 1854.

Columbus, Piqua and Indiana Railroad. *Report and Estimates to the Receivers.* Columbus: Ohio Statesman Steam Press, 1856.

Communication to the Bondholders and Others Interested in the Cincinnati, Wilmington and Zanesville Railroad. Baltimore: John Murphy and Co., 1858.

Correspondence between a Committee of the Citizens of Cincinnati and the President of the Marietta, Hillsboro and Cincinnati Railroad. Cincinnati: Moore, Wilstach, Keys and Co., n.d.

Covington and Lexington Railroad Company. *Annual Reports.* 1st, 2d, 5th, 6th, 8th (1850, 1851, 1854, 1855, 1857).

_____. *Exhibit of the Condition, Progress and Business of the Covington and Lexington Rail Road Company.* New York: Curran Dunsmore and Co., 1852.

Dayton and Cincinnati (Short Line) Rail Road. *Annual Reports.* 1st, 2d (1852, 1854).

Documents Submitted to the Stockholders of the Galena and Chicago Union Railroad Company. Chicago, 1858.

Drake, Daniel; Bakewell T.W.; and Williams, Jonathan S. "Report in Relation to a Proposed Railroad from the River Ohio to the Tide Waters of the Carolinas, August 15, 1835." *Journal of the Franklin Institute* 21 (February 1836): 101–6.

Dunn, George H. *Open Letter to Nicholas Longworth, in Relation to the Lawrence-burg and Indianapolis Railroad.* 1851.

Eaton and Hamilton Railroad. *Annual Reports.* 1st–3d (1853–55).

Exhibit of the Cincinnati and Fort Wayne Railroad Company. Cincinnati, 1857.

Exhibit . . . of the Conditions and Resources of the Cincinnati, Peru and Chicago Railroad Company. Cincinnati, 1854.

Evansville, Indianapolis and Cleveland Straight Line Railroad. *Address of the President.* Indianapolis: Austin H. Brown, Printer, 1853.

_____. *Annual Reports.* 1st–2d (1855–56).

_____. *Exhibit.* New York, 1854.

_____. *Organization of the Evansville, Indianapolis and Cleveland Straight Line Railroad.* Indianapolis, 1853.

Exposition of the Cincinnati and Western Railroad Company. Cincinnati, 1854.

Exposition of the Plan, Prospects, Character and Advantages of the Cincinnati and Mackinaw Railroad. Cincinnati: Achilles Pugh, 1854.

Fernon, Thomas S. *Report to J. Edgar Thompson on the Trade of the West.* n.p. 1852.

Fort Wayne and Chicago Rail-Road Company. *Report of the President and Chief Engineer.* n.p., 1854.

Galena and Chicago Union Railroad Company. *Annual Reports.* 1st–13th (1847/48–1859).

Gest, Erasmus. *Receiver's Report on the Cincinnati, Wilmington and Zanesville Railroad.* n.p., 1859.

_____. "Report of Preliminary Surveys of the Western Division of the Ohio and Mississippi Railroad." *Western Journal and Civilian* 7 (October 1851): 12–22.

Illinois Central Railroad Company. *Annual Reports.* 3d–11th (1852/53–1860/61).

Indiana and Illinois Central Railway Company. *Organization . . . with the Report of the Engineer.* Indianapolis: Ellis and Spann, 1853.

_____. *Statement of Affairs.* Indianapolis, 1854.

Indiana Central Railroad Company. *Annual Reports.* 1st–9th (1851–60).

Indianapolis and Bellefontaine Railroad Company. *Annual Reports.* 1st–4th (1849–1851/52).

_____. *Exhibit of the Affairs of the Indianapolis and Bellefontaine Railroad Company.* n.p., 1850.

Indianapolis and Cincinnati Junction Railroad Company. *Annual Reports.* 1st (n.d.), 3d (1855/56).

Indianapolis and Cincinnati Railroad Company. *Annual Reports* (1856–59).

Indianapolis, Pittsburgh and Cleveland Railroad Company. *Annual Report.* 10th (1858).

Jeffersonville Railroad Company. *Annual Reports.* 1st–3d (1848/49–1851/52).

_____. *Exhibit of the Affairs of the Jeffersonville Rail Road Company.* Louisville: Morton and Griswold, 1850.

_____. *Statement of Conditions and Prospects.* New York, 1851.

Jervis, John. *Report on the Michigan Southern and Northern Indiana Rail-Roads.* New York: Van Norden and Amerman, 1850.

Lafayette and Indianapolis Railroad. *Annual Report* (1851).

_____. *Exhibit of the Lafayette and Indianapolis Railroad Company.* New York: Oliver and Brother, 1851.

Lawrenceburg and Upper Mississippi Railroad. *Engineer's Report and Report of the Board of Directors* (1850).

_____. *Exhibit.* New York, Oliver and Brother, 1851.

Letter from Capt. E.G. Barney, Chief Engineer of the Peru and Indianapolis Rail Road, July, 1852. Indianapolis: Ellis and Spann, 1852.

Little Miami Railroad Company. *Annual Reports.* 1st–18th (1843–60).

Madison and Indianapolis Railroad Company. *Annual Reports.* 2d–14th (1844–1856).

_____. *Railroad Map of the State of Indiana.* New York, 1850.

_____. *Reports of the Secretary, Superintendent and President of the Madison and Indianapolis Railroad Company . . . April 10, 1855.* Indiana. *Documentary Journal, 1856/57.*

Mansfield, Edward D. *Exposition of the Business Prospects and Estimated Profits of the Cincinnati Western Railroad Company.* Cincinnati: John D. Thorpe, 1854.

_____. *Geographical, Geological and Statistical Relations of the Ohio and Mississippi Railroad.* n.p., n.d.

_____. *Ohio and Mississippi Railroad: Estimate of Value of Stock.* n.p., 1852.

_____. *On the Railway Connections of Philadelphia with the Great West.* Philadelphia: John C. Clarke, Printer, 1853.

_____. *Statistical Documents of the Ohio and Mississippi Railroad, No. 2.* n.p., n.d.

Marietta and Cincinnati Railroad Company. *Annual Reports,* 1st–6th (1850/51–1855/56).

_____. *Statement to the Council of the City of Cincinnati.* 1854.

_____. *Special Report* (February 1858).

_____. *Exhibit of the Affairs of the Marietta and Cincinnati Railroad Company.* New York: George E. Leefe, 1852.

Memorial of the Hillsborough and Cincinnati Railroad Company, to the Committee on Roads and Canals and the Honorable Council of Cincinnati. Cincinnati: Cincinnati Gazette Co., 1852.

Michigan Central Railroad Company. *Annual Reports.* 1st–14th (1846/47–1859/60).

_____. *Circular of the Treasurer.* Boston, 1855.

Michigan Southern and Northern Indiana Rail-Road Companies. *Report of the Boards of Directors.* New York: Van Norden and Amerman, 1853.

_____. *Circular Statement of the Condition and Prospects of the Michigan Southern Rail-Road.* New York: Van Norden and Amerman, 1849.

Mitchell, O.M. *Report of Preliminary Reconnaissance of the Country between Cincinnati and St. Louis.* Cincinnati: Wright, Ferris and Co., 1850.

_____. *Report of the Present Conditions and Prospects of the Ohio and Mississippi Railroad.* Cincinnati: John D. Thorpe, 1852.

_____. *Survey of the Little Miami Railroad.* Cincinnati: Pugh and Dodd, 1837.

Morgan, Richard P. *Report of the Survey of the Route of the Galena and Chicago Union Rail Road.* Chicago: Daily Tribune Plant, 1847.

Morris, Elwood. *Report of the Final Location and Probable Cost of the Cincinnati, Hillsborough and Parkersburg Railroad.* Cincinnati, 1853.

_____. *Report on the Preliminary Surveys Made for the Cincinnati, Hillsborough and Parkersburg Railway.* Cincinnati: Cincinnati Gazette Co., 1852.

Ohio and Mississippi Railroad Company. *Annual Reports* (1857/58–1859/60).

The Ohio and Mississippi Railroad: Its Vital Importance to the Prosperity of Cincinnati. Cincinnati, 1855.

Pittsburgh, Fort Wayne and Chicago Rail Road Company. *Annual Reports.* 1st–5th (1857–1861).

_____. *Exhibit of the Pittsburgh, Fort Wayne and Chicago Rail Road Company with Relation to their General Mortgage of $1,000,000.* New York: H. Anstice and Co., 1857.

Proceedings of the St. Louis and Cincinnati Railroad Convention Held at Indianapolis, May 12, 1847. Terre Haute: Wabash Express Plant, 1847.

Railroad from the Banks of the Ohio River to the Tide Waters of the Carolinas and Georgia. Cincinnati: James and Gazlay, 1835.

A Report Exhibiting Some Statistical Facts and Arguments, Favorable to the Construction of the Belpre and Cincinnati Railroad. Chillicothe: Ely and Allen, 1848.

Report of the Conditions and Prospects of Cincinnati and Chicago Rail Road. Cincinnati: John D. Thorpe, 1854.

Report upon the Preliminary Surveys of the Mississippi and Wabash Railroad. Lafayette, 1853.

Statement of the Conditions and Contracts of the Cincinnati, Logansport and Chicago Railway Company. Cincinnati: T. Wrightson, Printer, 1854.

Terre Haute and Richmond Railroad Company. *Annual Reports.* 1st, 3d, 8th, 9th, 12th (1849, 1851, 1856–57, 1860).

_____. *Exhibit of the Terre Haute and Richmond Rail-Road Company.* New York: C.C. Childs, 1851.

Woods, John. *To the Stockholders of the Eaton and Hamilton Railroad Company.* Hamilton, 1853.

Yungmeyer, D.W., ed. "Selected Items from the Minute Book of the Galena and Chicago Union Railroad Company." *Bulletin of the Railroad and Locomotive Historical Society,* no. 65 (1944), pp. 27–42.

Books, Articles, Pamphlets, Memoirs, and Other Local Documents

Chicago

Arnold, Isaac N. *William B. Ogden and Early Days in Chicago.* Fergus Historical Series, no. 17. Chicago: Fergus Printing Co., 1882.

Balestier, Joseph N. *The Annals of Chicago: A Lecture Delivered before the Chicago Lyceum, January 21, 1840.* Fergus Historical Series, no. 1. Chicago: Fergus Printing Co., 1876.

[Barry, Patrick]. *Inquiry into the Practicability, Benefit and Means of Establishing Direct Western Trans-Atlantic Trade, by a Chicago Broker.* Chicago: P.L. and J.H. Wells, 1857.

_____. *The Theory and Practice of International Trade of the United States and England.* Chicago: D.B. Cooke and Co., 1858.

Bross, William. *Address before the Mechanics' Institute.* Chicago, 1853.

_____. *The Northwest—Growth of Its Commerce and Necessity for New Outlets.* Published by R.K. Swift and Co., Bankers, n.d.

[Brown, Henry]. *A Letter to the People of the State of Illinois, on the Subject of Public Credit . . . and the Illinois and Michigan Canal, by a Citizen of Chicago.* Chicago, 1841.

_____. *The Present and Future Prospects of Chicago: An Address Delivered before the Chicago Lyceum, Jan. 20, 1846.* Fergus Historical Series, no. 9. Chicago: Fergus Printing Co., 1876.

Case and Company's Chicago City Directory for the Year ending June 1, 1857. Chicago: John Gager and Co., 1856.

Chamberlin, Everett. *Chicago and Its Suburbs.* Chicago: T.A. Hungerford and Co., 1874.

Chicago Almanac and Advertiser for 1855. Chicago, 1855.

Chicago Board of Trade. *Annual Statement of the Trade and Commerce of Chicago.* 1st–5th (1858–1862).

Chicago City Directory and Annual Advertiser for 1849–50. Compiled by O.P. Hatheway and J.H. Taylor. Chicago: James K. Langdon, 1849.

Chicago City Directory for 1851. Chicago: W.W. Danenhower, 1851.

Chicago City Directory for the Year 1860–61. Chicago: D.B. Cooke and Co., 1860.

Chicago Democratic Press. Annual Review of the Commerce of Chicago (title varies). Issues for 1852–1857, published 1853–1858.

"Chicago in 1856." *Putnam's Monthly Magazine* 7 (June 1856): 606–613.

Chicago in 1860: A Glance at Its Business Houses. Chicago: W. Thorn and Co., 1860.

Chicago Press and Tribune. Annual Review of the Trade and Commerce of Chicago. Issues for 1858–59 (published 1859–60).

Chicago Tribune. Annual Review of Commerce. 1850–1852. Issue for 1851 printed in *Hunt's Merchants' Magazine* 26 (April 1852): 426–43, 509–10. Issue for 1852 printed in *Hunt's Merchants' Magazine* 28 (May 1853): 558–74.

Chicago Tribune, Annual Review of the Trade, Business and Growth of Chicago. Issues for 1860, 1863–65, published 1861, 1864–66.

Cleaver, Charles. *Early-Chicago Reminiscences.* Fergus Historical Series, no. 19. Chicago: Fergus Printing Co., 1882.

Colbert, Elias. *Historical and Statistical Sketch of the Garden City.* Chicago: P.T. Sherlock, 1868.

Farwell, John V. *Some Recollections.* Chicago: R.R. Donnelley and Sons Co., 1911.

Flint, Henry M. "The Commerce and Banking System of Chicago." *Hunt's Merchants' Magazine* 35 (August 1856): 173–78.

The Georgian Bay Canal: Reports of Col. R.B. Mason, Consulting Engineer, and Kivas Tully, Chief Engineer. Chicago, 1858.

Graham, James D. *Report on Harbors in Wisconsin, Illinois, Indiana and Michigan.* S. Exec. Doc. No. 16, 34th Cong., 3d Sess., 1857.

Griswold, David D. *Statistics of Chicago, Illinois, Together with a Business Advertiser and Mercantile Directory for July, 1843.* Chicago, 1843.

Guyer, I.D. *History of Chicago: Its Commercial and Manufacturing Interests and Industry*. Chicago, 1862.

Hall's Business Directory of Chicago. Chicago: Hall and Co., 1856.

Memorial to the Government of the United States from the Citizens of Chicago, Illinois, Setting Forth the Advantages of that City as the Site for a National Armory and Foundry. H.R. Rep. No. 43, 37th Cong., 2d Sess., 1861.

Norris, J.W. *General Directory and Business Advertiser of the City of Chicago for the Year 1844*. Chicago: Ellis and Fergus, 1844.

_____. *Business Advertiser and General Directory of the City of Chicago for the Year 1845-46*. Chicago: J. Campbell and Co., 1845.

_____. *Norris' Business Directory and Statistics of the City of Chicago for 1846*. Chicago, 1846.

Parton, James. "Chicago." *Atlantic Monthly* 19 (March 1867): 325-45.

Peyton, John Lewis. *A Statistical View of the State of Illinois, to Which Is Appended an Article upon the City of Chicago*. Chicago, 1855.

Scammon, J.Y. *William B. Ogden*. Fergus Historical Series, no. 17. Chicago: Fergus Printing Co., 1882.

Scripps, John Locke. *The Undeveloped Northern Portion of the American Continent*. Chicago, 1856.

Statistics of the City of Chicago, Illinois, for 1856, Showing Its Growth and Improvement. Chicago, S.H. Kerfoot and Co., n.d.

The Stranger's Guide and Hand Book to Chicago. Chicago: Hall and Co., 1857.

Thomas, Jesse B. "Statistics Concerning the City of Chicago, 1847." In *Chicago River-and-Harbor Convention*. Fergus Historical Series, no. 18. Chicago: Fergus Printing Co., 1882.

Wright, John S. *Chicago Investments*. Chicago, 1860.

_____. *Chicago: Past, Present, Future*. Chicago, 1868. 2d Edition, 1870.

_____. *Investments in Chicago*. Chicago, 1858.

Cincinnati

Bebb, William. *Cincinnati: Her Position, Duty and Destiny: An Address before the Young Men's Mercantile Library Association of Cincinnati, April 18, 1848*.

Channing, William H., ed. *The Memoirs and Writings of James Handasyd Perkins*. Cincinnati: Tuneman and Spofford, 1852.

Charter and Organization of the Indiana Canal Company. Cincinnati, 1850.

Cincinnati Almanac for 1840. Cincinnati: Glazen and Shepard, 1840.

Cincinnati Board of Trade. *Annual Reports*. 1st-3d (1869-71).

Cincinnati Chamber of Commerce. *Review of the Trade and Commerce of Cincinnati*. 1850-1854.

_____. *Annual Statement of the Trade and Commerce of Cincinnati*. 1855-1861.

Cincinnati Directory Advertiser for 1831. Cincinnati: Robinson and Fairbank, 1831.

The Cincinnati Directory for the Year 1843. Compiled by Charles Cist. Cincinnati: R.P. Brooks, Printer, 1843.

Cincinnati Guide and Business Directory for 1857-58. Compiled by F.W. Hurtt. Cincinnati: Rickey, Mallory and Webb, 1857.

Cincinnati Wholesale Business Directory for 1853. W.H. Fagan, Publisher. Cincinnati: T. Wrightson, 1853.

Cist, Charles. *Cincinnati in 1841: Its Early Annals and Future Prospects.* Cincinnati, 1841.

_____. *Sketches and Statistics of Cincinnati in 1851.* Cincinnati: William H. Moore and Co., 1851.

_____. *Sketches and Statistics of Cincinnati in 1859.* n.p., n.d.

The Coal River Mining and Manufacturing Company, Kanawha County, Virginia. Cincinnati, 1854.

Corry, William M. *The Railroad Speech Delivered at the Merchants' Exchange in Favor of the Knoxville Route to the Gulf.* Cincinnati: Railroad Record Office, 1860.

Description of the Sycamore Coal Mines: Plan of a Company Now Forming in Cincinnati. Cincinnati, 1850.

Drake, Benjamin. "Cincinnati at the Close of 1835." *Western Monthly Magazine* 5 (January 1836): 26-31.

Drake, Benjamin, and Mansfield, Edward D. *Cincinnati in 1826.* Cincinnati: Morgan, Lodge and Fisher, 1827.

Drake, Daniel. *Discourse on the History, Character and Prospects of the West.* Cincinnati: Truman and Smith, 1834.

Goodin, S.H. "Cincinnati—Its Destiny." In Charles Cist. *Sketches and Statistics of Cincinnati in 1851.*

Gray and Company's Cincinnati Business Mirror and City Advertiser. Cincinnati: A. Gray and Co., 1851.

Hall, James. *Address before the Young Men's Mercantile Library Association of Cincinnati.* Cincinnati, 1846.

Improvement of Navigation at the Falls of the Ohio, May, 1851. Cincinnati, 1851.

James, Charles P. *Address Delivered at Camp McRae before the Citizen Guards of Cincinnati.* n.p., 1842.

Mansfield, Edward D. "Cincinnati and Its Future: Its Growth, Industry, Commerce and Education." In George E. Stevens. *The City of Cincinnati.* Cincinnati: George S. Blanchard and Co., 1869.

_____. *Memoirs of the Life and Services of Daniel Drake, M.D.* Cincinnati: Applegate and Co., 1855.

_____. *Personal Memories: Social, Political and Literary.* Cincinnati: Robert Clarke and Co., 1879.

Memorial of the Chamber of Commerce in the City of Cincinnati, to the Congress of the United States, in Relation to a National Armory West of the Alleghenies. H.R. Rep. No. 43, 37th Cong., 2d Sess., 1861.

Memorial of the Citizens of Cincinnati to the Congress of the United States, Relative to the Navigation of the Ohio and Mississippi Rivers. Cincinnati: L'Hommedieu and Co., 1843.

Memorial of the Citizens of Cincinnati, to the Congress of the United States, Relative to the Navigation of the Ohio and Mississippi Rivers. Cincinnati: Daily Atlas Office, 1844.

The Mill Creek Cannel Coal Field and the Manufacture of Coal Oil. Cincinnati, 1859.

Neville, Morgan. "Returns from the State of Ohio." In U.S., Secretary of the Treasury. *Documents Relative to the Manufactures in the United States.* H.R. Exec. Doc. No. 308, 22nd Cong., 1st Sess., 1832.

Parton, James. "Cincinnati." *Atlantic Monthly* 20 (August 1867): 229–46.

Proceedings of a Meeting of the Citizens of Cincinnati . . . Expressing the Sense of the Citizens on the Subject of Improving the Navigation around the Falls of the Ohio River. Cincinnati: Daily Atlas, 1846.

Proceedings of a Public Meeting of the Citizens of Cincinnati, on the Subject of a Western National Armory, Sept. 30, 1841. H.R. Doc. No. 149, 27th Cong., 2d Sess., 1841.

Railroad Proceedings of Fulton and Vicinity; of Cincinnati and Vicinity; and Address to the People of Ohio, with the Proceedings of a Board of Internal Improvement. Cincinnati: Kendall and Henry, 1835.

Report of a Special Committee Appointed to Examine into the Necessity and Cost of the Purchase of Additional Ground for Public Wharves in the City of Cincinnati. January 12, 1853.

Report of a Committee on the Best Mode of Improving Navigation at the Falls of the Ohio. Cincinnati, 1859.

Report of the Committee Appointed by the City Council of the City of Cincinnati . . . at the Request of the Ohio and Mississippi Railroad Company. Cincinnati: Enquirer Office, 1855.

Report of the President to the Stock-Holders in the Cincinnati and Whitewater Canal Company. Cincinnati: Gazette Printers, 1840.

Schaffer, David H. *The Cincinnati, Covington, Newport and Fulton Directory for 1840.* Cincinnati: J.B. and R.P. Donogh, 1839.

Smith, William Prescott. *The Book of the Great Railway Celebrations of 1857.* New York: D. Appleton and Co., 1858.

Storer, Bellamy. *Address Delivered before the Hamilton County Agricultural Society.* Cincinnati: Office of the Farmer and Mechanic, 1835.

Taft, Alphonso. *A Lecture on Cincinnati and Her Rail-Roads.* Cincinnati: D. Anderson, 1850.

Walker, Timothy. *Annual Discourse, Delivered before the Ohio Historical and Philosophical Society, at Columbus, on the 23rd of December, 1837. Transactions of the Historical and Philosophical Society of Ohio* 1 (1839).

Galena

Chetlain, Augustus L. *Recollections of Seventy Years.* Galena: The Gazette Publishing Co., 1899.

Documents Showing the Statistics of the City of Galena, April 1, 1840. S. Doc. No. 349, 26th Cong., 1st Sess., 1840.

Documents Relating to the Sale of the Mineral Lands in the State of Illinois and Territories of Iowa and Wisconsin, June 22, 1842. S. Doc. No. 331, 27th Cong., 2d Sess., 1842.

"Galena and Its Lead Mines." *Harper's New Monthly Magazine* 32 (May 1866): 681–96.

Galena Chamber of Commerce. *Memorial . . . Relative to the Obstructions of the Navigation on the Rapids of the Mississippi River, Feb. 6, 1840.* H.R. Doc. No. 68, 26th Cong., 1st Sess., 1840.

The Galena Directory and Miners' Annual Register, for 1847–48. Galena: E.S. Seymour, 1847.

The Galena Directory and Miners' Annual Register, for 1848–49. Galena: E.S. Seymour, 1848.

The Galena City Directory. Galena: H.H. Houghton and Co., 1854.

Galena City Directory, 1855–56. Galena: H.H. Houghton and Co., 1855.

Galena City Directory, 1858–59. Galena: W.W. Huntington, 1858.

Grant, Ulysses S. *Personal Memoirs.* New York: Charles L. Webster and Co., 1885.

Hayes, Stephen H. "Letters from the West in 1845." *Iowa Journal of History and Politics* 20 (January 1922): 3–69.

Hobbs, Clarissa E.G. "Autobiography." *Journal of the Illinois State Historical Society* 17 (January 1925): 612–714.

Hodge, James T. "On the Wisconsin and Missouri Lead Region." *American Journal of Science* 43 (1842): 35–72.

"Journal of William Rudolph Smith." *Wisconsin Magazine of History* 12 (December 1928, March 1929): 192–220, 300–321.

"Letter from Thomas Melville, Secretary of the Galena Chamber of Commerce, 27 Feb., 1844." In *Documents Showing the Annual Amount of the Trade and Commerce on the Upper Mississippi River, March 29, 1844.* S. Doc. No. 242, 28th Cong., 1st Sess., 1845.

McMaster, S.W. *Sixty Years on the Upper Mississippi: My Life and Experiences.* Rock Island, 1893.

Map of the United States Lead Mines on the Upper Mississippi River. Galena: R.W. Chandler, 1829. Reproduced in *Wisconsin Historical Society Collections* 11 (1888): 400.

Meeker, Moses. "Early History of Lead Region in Wisconsin." *Wisconsin State Historical Society Collections* 6 (1872): 271–96.

Merrick, George B. *Old Times on the Upper Mississippi.* Cleveland: The Arthur H. Clarke Co., 1909.

"Narrative of Morgan L. Martin." *Wisconsin State Historical Society Collections* 11 (1888): 385–415.

Report of Walter Cunningham, Late Mineral Agent on Lake Superior. S. Doc. No. 98, 28th Cong., 2d Sess., 1845.

Rodolph, Theodore. "Pioneering in the Wisconsin Lead Region." *Wisconsin State Historical Society Collections* 15 (1900): 338–89.

Indianapolis

Bolton, Nathaniel. *Lecture . . . on the Early History of Indianapolis and Central Indiana, 1853.* Indiana Historical Society Publications, vol. 1, no. 5. Indianapolis: Bobbs-Merrill Co., 1897.

Brown, Ignatius. "History of Indianapolis from 1818 to 1868." In *Logan's Indianapolis Directory.* Indianapolis: Logan and Co., 1868.

Directory of the City of Indianapolis. Indianapolis: A.C. Howard, 1857.

Grooms and Smith's Indianapolis Directory, City Guide, and Business Mirror, 1858-59. Indianapolis: Grooms and Smith, 1855.

Holloway, William R. *Indianapolis: A Historical and Statistical Sketch of the Railroad City.* Indianapolis, 1870.

Indianapolis Board of Trade. *Circular and Map, 1856.* Printed in *Indianapolis Journal,* September 10, 1856.

———. *Indianapolis: Its Manufacturing Interests, Wants, Facilities.* Printed in *Indianapolis Journal,* March 25-26, 1857.

Indianapolis: Its Advantages for Commerce and Manufactures, Published and Compiled by the Manufacturers and Real Estate Exchange. Indianapolis, 1874.

McCulloch, Hugh. *Men and Measures of Half a Century.* New York: Charles Scribner's Sons, 1900.

Memorial of the Board of Trade and Common Council of the City of Indianapolis [in regard to a Western National Armory]. H.R. Rep. No. 43, 37th Cong., 2d Sess., 1861.

Nowland, John H.B. *Early Reminiscences of Indianapolis.* Indianapolis: Sentinel Printing House, 1870.

Perkins, Samuel E. "Address Delivered before the Marion County Agricultural Society." In Indiana State Board of Agriculture. *Report* (1854/55).

Sloan, George W. *Fifty Years in Pharmacy.* Indiana Historical Society Publications, vol. 3, no. 5. Indianapolis: Bobbs-Merrill Co., 1903.

Smith, Oliver H. "Address Delivered before the Agricultural Society of Marion County." In Indiana State Board of Agriculture. *Report* (1855/56).

———. *Early Indiana Trials and Sketches.* Cincinnati: Moore, Wilstach, Keys and Co., 1858.

———. "The Railroads of Indiana," in Indiana State Board of Agriculture. *Report* (1855/56).

Sutherland and McEvoy's Indianapolis City Directory and Business Mirror for 1860-61. Indianapolis: Sutherland and McEvoy, 1860.

Thornbrough, Gayle; Riker, Dorothy; and Corpuz, Paula, eds. *The Diary of Calvin Fletcher.* Vols. 1-6, 1837-1860. Indianapolis: Indiana Historical Society, 1972-78.

Personal and Business Manuscripts

Chicago

Anonymous Diary, 1849-50: Account of a Trip from Boston, Massachusetts up the Mississippi River. Chicago Historical Society.

A.E. Austin Collection. Chicago Historical Society.

Benjamin F. Barker Collection. Chicago Historical Society.

Luther Bixby Collection. Chicago Historical Society.

Arthur Bronson Collection. Chicago Historical Society.

George Brown Collection. Chicago Historical Society.

Chicago Democratic Press Account Book, 1852–54. Scripps and Bross Volumes. Chicago Historical Society.

L.C.P. Freer Collection. Chicago Historical Society.

Jacob Gross Collection. Chicago Historical Society.

D.C. Hall Collection. Chicago Historical Society.

Gurdon S. Hubbard Collection and Volumes. Chicago Historical Society.

Bemsley Huntoon Collection. Chicago Historical Society.

John Kirk Volumes. Chicago Historical Society.

James Lawrence Collection. Chicago Historical Society.

Charles Mears Volumes. Chicago Historical Society.

William B. Ogden Collection and Volumes. Chicago Historical Society.

J.M. Peck Collection. Chicago Historical Society.

Benjamin W. Raymond Collection and Volumes. Chicago Historical Society.

Henry S. Spaulding Collection. Chicago Historical Society.

Edward B. Talcott Collection. Chicago Historical Society.

H.H. Warden Collection. Chicago Historical Society.

James Warnock Collection. Chicago Historical Society.

Tolman Wheeler Collection. Chicago Historical Society.

Cincinnati

H.A. Amelung Letters. Cincinnati Historical Society.

Robert Buchanan Papers. Cincinnati Historical Society.

Caledonia Freight Book, 1859. Cincinnati Public Library.

Calvin Carpenter Letterbook, 1844–47. Ohio Historical Society.

Erasmus Gest Papers. Ohio Historical Society.

William Greene Papers. Cincinnati Historical Society.

E. Harwood Diary, 1850. Cincinnati Historical Society.

Heffner and Chappell Account Book, 1852. Cincinnati Historical Society.

Jacob Hoffner Letters. Cincinnati Historical Society.

S.S. L'Hommedieu Letters. Ohio Historical Society.

Phillip Hunkle Letters. Ohio Historical Society.

King Family Papers. Cincinnati Historical Society.

E. Levassor and Son: Bill of Lading Book, 1845–46. Cincinnati Public Library.

Lytle Family Papers. Cincinnati Historical Society.

James Pullan Diaries, 1850–60. Ohio Historical Society.

Augustus Roundy Letters. Cincinnati Historical Society.

William Sherwood Letters. Cincinnati Historical Society.

Timothy Walker Papers. Cincinnati Historical Society.

Robert Williams Papers. Cincinnati Public Library.

Nathaniel Wright Papers. Cincinnati Historical Society.

Galena

Galena, Illinois, Steamboat Register, 1838. Illinois State Historical Library.

Galena, Illinois, Steamboat Register, 1855–56. Galena Public Library.

Charles Hempstead Collection. Chicago Historical Society.

William Hempstead Papers. Illinois State Historical Library.

Journey by Steamboat, Railroad and Stagecoach from New York to Michigan, Indiana, Illinois, Wisconsin, Missouri, and Kentucky, 1839. Anonymous Diary. Chicago Historical Society.

Alexander Leslie Diary, 1857–58. Chicago Historical Society.

C.W. Mappa Letters, Galena, Illinois, Collection. Chicago Historical Society.

Indiana and Indianapolis

Hervey Bates Letters. Samuel Moore Collection. Indiana State Library.

Burr Bradley Letters. Indiana State Library.

Theodore V. Denny Letters. Denny Collection. Indiana State Library.

Calvin Fletcher Diary. Indiana Historical Society.

William H. Gray Letters. Indiana State Library.

Elijah Hackleman Reminiscences. Hackleman Scrapbook no. 2. Indiana Historical Society.

John Hewitt Jones Reminiscences. Indiana State Library.

D.T. Kimball Letters. Indiana State Library.

John M. Legg Diary, 1851–54. Indiana Historical Society.

Sawyer and Co. Account Book, 1862–63. Indiana State Library.

Business Papers of William and Thomas Silver Store. Indiana State Library.

Samuel Smith Autobiography. Indiana Historical Society.

Milton Stapp Memoirs. Lilly Library, Indiana University.

SOURCES PUBLISHED SINCE 1875

American Nineteenth-Century Ideas about Urban and Regional Growth

Atherton, Lewis. *Main Street on the Middle Border.* Bloomington: Indiana University Press, 1954.

Barth, Gunther. *Instant Cities: Urbanization and the Rise of San Francisco and Denver.* New York: Oxford University Press, 1976.

Bender, Thomas. *Toward an Urban Vision: Ideas and Institutions in Nineteenth Century America.* Lexington: University Press of Kentucky, 1975.

Boorstin, Daniel. *The Americans: The National Experience.* New York: Random House, 1965.

Brownell, Blaine. *The Urban Ethos in the New South.* Baton Rouge: Louisiana State University Press, 1975.

Cole, Arthur H. *Business Enterprise in Its Social Setting.* Cambridge: Harvard University Press, 1959.

Curti, Merle. *The Growth of American Thought.* New York: Harper and Brothers, 1943.

Davenport, Francis G. *Cultural Life in Nashville on the Eve of the Civil War.* Chapel Hill: University of North Carolina Press, 1941.

Donald, David, and Ralmer, Frederick A. "Toward a Western Literature, 1820–1860." *Mississippi Valley Historical Review* 35 (December 1948): 413–28.

Dorsett, Lyle, and Dorsett, Mary. "Rhetoric versus Realism: 150 Years of Missouri Boosterism." *Bulletin of the Missouri Historical Society* 38 (January 1972): 77–84.

_____, and Schafer, Arthur. "Was the Antebellum South Antiurban? A Suggestion." *Journal of Southern History* 38 (February 1972): 93–100.

Dykstra, Robert. *The Cattle Towns.* New York: Alfred A Knopf, 1968.

Glaab, Charles. "Jesup W. Scott and a West of Cities." *Ohio History* 73 (Winter 1964): 3–12.

_____. "Vision of Metropolis: William Gilpin and Theories of City Growth in the West." *Wisconsin Magazine of History* 45 (Autumn 1961): 21–31.

_____. "Historical Perspectives on Urban Development Schemes," in Leo Schnore, ed. *Social Science and the City.* New York: Praeger, 1968.

Goldfield, David. *Urban Growth in the Age of Sectionalism: Virginia, 1847–61.* Baton Rouge: Louisiana State University Press, 1977.

Jakle, John. *Images of the Ohio Valley: A Historical Geography of Travel, 1790–1860.* New York: Oxford University Press, 1977.

Karnes, Thomas L. *William Gilpin: Western Nationalist.* Austin: University of Texas Press, 1970.

Meyers, Marvin. *The Jacksonian Persuasion: Politics and Belief.* New York: Vintage Books, 1960.

Rubin, Julius. *Canal or Railroad? Imitation and Innovation in the Response to the Erie Canal in Philadelphia, Baltimore and Boston. Transactions of the American Philosophical Society,* n.s. 51, p. 7 (1961).

Smith, Henry Nash. *Virgin Land: The American West as Symbol and Myth.* New York: Vintage Books, 1957.

Starr, Kevin. *Americans and the California Dream.* New York: Oxford University Press, 1973.

Schnell, J. Christopher. "William Gilpin: Advocate of Expansion." *Montana: The Magazine of Western History* 19 (July 1969): 30–37.

Schnell, J. Cristopher, and Clinton, Katherine B. "The New West: Themes in Nineteenth Century Urban Promotion." *Bulletin of the Missouri Historical Society* 30 (January 1974): 75–88.

Strauss, Anselm L. *Images of the American City.* New York: Free Press, 1961.

Turner, Frederick Jackson. *Frontier and Section: Selected Essays.* Edited by Ray A. Billington. Englewood Cliffs, New Jersey: Prentice-Hall, 1961.

White, Morton, and White, Lucia. *The Intellectual Versus the City.* Cambridge: Harvard University Press, 1962.

Wohl, R. Richard. "Urbanism, Urbanity and the Historian," *University of Kansas City Review* 22 (October 1955): 53–61.

Wohl, R. Richard, and Brown, A.T. "The Usable Past: A Study of Historical Tradition in Kansas City." *Huntington Library Quarterly* 23 (May 1960): 237–59.

Regional and National Economic Development

Atherton, Lewis. *The Pioneer Merchant in Mid-America.* "University of Missouri Studies, vol. 14, no. 2. Columbia: University of Missouri, 1939.

Bidwell, Percy W., and Falconer, John I. *History of Agriculture in the Northern United States, 1620–1860.* New York: Peter Smith, 1941.

Borchert, John A. "American Metropolitan Evolution." *Geographical Review* 57 (1967): 301–32.

Buck, Norman S. *The Development of the Organization of Anglo-American Trade, 1800–1850.* New Haven: Yale University Press, 1925.

Burgess, George H., and Kennedy, Miles C. *Centennial History of the Pennsylvania Railroad Company.* Philadelphia: Pennsylvania Railroad Co., 1949.

Callender, Guy S., ed. *Selections from the Economic History of the United States, 1765–1860.* New York: Ginn and Co., 1909.

Chandler, Alfred D. *Henry Varnum Poor: Business Editor, Analyst, and Reformer.* Cambridge: Harvard University Press, 1956.

———. "The Organization of Manufacturing and Transportation." In David T. Gilchrist and W. David Lewis, eds. *Economic Change in the Civil War Era.* Greenville, Delaware: Eleutherian Mills-Hagley Foundation, 1965.

Clark, John G. *The Grain Trade in the Old Northwest.* Urbana: University of Illinois Press, 1966.

Clark, Victor S. *History of Manufactures in the United States.* 3 vols. New York: Peter Smith, 1949.

Cleman, Rudolph A. *The American Livestock and Meat Industry.* New York: The Ronald Press Co., 1925.

Cole, Arthur H. *Wholesale Commodity Prices in the United States, 1700–1861.* Cambridge: Harvard University Press, 1938.

———. "Variations in the Sale of Public Lands, 1816–1860." *Review of Economic Statistics* 9 (January 1927): 41–53.

Connor, L.G. "A Brief History of the Sheep Industry in the United States." *American Historical Association Report* 1 (1918): 89–198.

Conzen, Michael. "A Transport Interpretation of the Growth of Urban Regions: An American Example." *Journal of Historical Geography* 1 (1975): 362.

Decker, Leslie. "The Great Speculation." In David M. Ellis, ed. *The Frontier in American Development.* Ithaca: Cornell University Press, 1970.

Easterlin, Richard. "Regional Income Trends, 1840–1860." In Seymour Harris, ed. *American Economic History.* New York: McGraw-Hill, 1961.

Eavenson, Howard N. *The First Century and a Quarter of the American Coal Industry.* Pittsburgh: privately printed, 1942.

Fishlow, Albert. *Railroads and the Transformation of the Ante-Bellum Economy.* Cambridge: Harvard University Press, 1965.

Fite, Emerson D. *Social and Industrial Conditions in the North during the Civil War.* New York: The Macmillan Co., 1910.

Fogel, Robert. *Railroads and American Economic Growth.* Baltimore: Johns Hopkins Press, 1964.

Gallman, Robert. "Commodity Output, 1939–1899." In *Studies in Income and Wealth,* vol. 24. New York: Conference on Research in Income and Wealth, 1960.

Gates, Charles M. "Boom Stages in American Expansion." *Business History Review* 33 (Spring 1959): 32–42.

Gates, Paul W. *The Farmer's Age: Agriculture, 1815-1860.* New York: Holt, Rinehart and Winston, 1960.

Golembe, Carter H. "State Banks and the Economic Development of the West, 1830-44." Ph.D. dissertation, Columbia University, 1952.

Goodrich, Carter. "The Revulsion against Internal Improvements." *Journal of Economic History* 10 (November 1950): 145-69.

Harlow, Alvin F. *The Road of the Century: The Story of the New York Central.* New York: Creative Age Press, Inc., 1947.

Hendrickson, Walter B. *David Dale Own: Pioneer Geologist of the Middle West.* Indiana Historical Collections, vol. 27. Indianapolis: Indiana Historical Bureau, 1943.

Henlein, Paul G. *Cattle Kingdom in the Ohio Valley, 1783-1860.* Lexington: University of Kentucky Press, 1959.

Hunter, Louis. *Steamboats on the Western Rivers.* Cambridge: Harvard University Press, 1949.

Johnson, Arthur M., and Supple, Barry E. *Boston Capitalists and Western Railroads: A Study of the Nineteenth Century Investment Process.* Cambridge: Harvard University Press, 1967.

Jones, Fred M. *Middlemen in the Domestic Trade of the United States.* Illinois Studies in the Social Sciences, vol. 21. Urbana: University of Illinois Press, 1937.

Kohlmeier, A.L. *The Old Northwest as the Keystone in the Arch of American Federal Union.* Bloomington, Indiana: Principia Press, 1938.

Leavitt, Charles T. "The Meat and Dairy Livestock Industry, 1819-1860." Ph.D. dissertation, University of Chicago, 1931.

Lebergott, Stanley. *Manpower in Economic Growth: The American Record since 1800.* New York: McGraw-Hill, 1964.

Lippincott, Isaac. "A History of Manufactures in the Ohio Valley to the Year 1860." Ph.D. dissertation, University of Chicago, 1914.

McGrane, Reginald C. *The Panic of 1837.* Chicago: University of Chicago Press, 1924.

McLear, Patrick, and Schnell, J.C. "Why Cities Grew: A Historiographic Essay on Western Urban Growth, 1850-1880." *Bulletin of the Missouri Historical Society* 27 (April 1972): 162-77.

Martin, Robert F. *National Income in the United States, 1799-1938.* New York: National Industrial Conference Board, Inc., 1939.

Merrill, George P. *Contributions to a History of American State Geological and Natural History Surveys.* United States National Museum Bulletin, no. 109. Washington: Smithsonian Institution, 1920.

Morgan, Edward J. "Sources of Capital for Railroads in the Old Northwest before the Civil War." Ph.D. dissertation, University of Wisconsin, 1964.

Nimmo, Joseph. *Report on the Internal Commerce of the United States.* H.R. Exec. Doc. No. 7, Pt. 2, 46th Cong., 3d Sess., 1881.

North, Douglas C. *The Economic Growth of the United States, 1790-1860.* Englewood Cliffs, New Jersey: Prentice-Hall, 1961.

Odle, Thomas. "Entrepreneurial Cooperation on the Great Lakes: The Origin of The Method of American Grain Marketing." *Business History Review* 38 (Winter 1964): 439-55.

_____. "The American Grain Trade of the Great Lakes, 1825-1873." *Inland Seas* 8 (1952): 23-28, 99-104, 177-92, 248-54; 9 (1953): 52-58, 105-9, 162-68, 256-62.

Parker, William N., and Whartenby, Franklee. "The Growth of Output before 1840." In *Studies in Income and Wealth,* vol. 24. New York: Conference on Research in Income and Wealth, 1960.

Paxson, Frederic L. "The Railroads of the 'Old Northwest' before the Civil War." *Transactions of the Wisconsin Academy of Sciences, Arts, and Letters* 17 (1914): 243-74.

Perloff, Harvey, et al. *Regions, Resources, and Economic Growth.* Baltimore: The Johns Hopkins Press, 1960.

Petersen, William J. *Steamboating on the Upper Mississippi.* Iowa City: State Historical Society of Iowa, 1937.

Pred, Allan R. *The Spatial Dynamics of U.S. Urban-Industrial Growth.* Cambridge: M.I.T. Press, 1966.

Rohrbaugh, Malcolm. *The Trans-Appalachian Frontier.* New York: Oxford University Press, 1978.

Schmidt, Louis B. "Internal Commerce and the Development of a National Economy before 1860." *Journal of Political Economy* 42 (December 1939): 800-820.

Skipper, Ottis C. *J.B.D. DeBow: Magazinist of the Old South.* Athens: University of Georgia Press, 1958.

Smith, Walter B., and Cole, Arthur H. *Fluctuations in American Business, 1790-1860.* Cambridge: Harvard University Press, 1935.

Soltow, Lee. *Men and Wealth in the United States, 1850-1870.* New Haven: Yale University Press, 1975.

Stephens, George W. *Some Aspects of Early Intersectional Rivalry for the Commerce of the Upper Mississippi Valley.* Washington University Studies, Humanistic Series, vol. 10, no. 2. St. Louis: Washington University, 1923.

Still, Bayrd. "Patterns of Mid-Nineteenth Century Urbanization in the Midwest." *Mississippi Valley Historical Review* 18 (September 1941): 187-206.

Switzler, William F. *Report on the Internal Commerce of the United States.* H.R. Exec. Doc., No. 6, Pt. 2, 50th Cong., 1st Sess., 1888.

Taylor, George R. *The Transportation Revolution, 1815-1860.* New York: Rinehart and Co., 1951.

_____. "The National Economy before and after the Civil War." In David T. Gilchrist and W. David Lewis, eds. *Economic Change in the Civil War Era.* Greenville, Delaware: Eleutherian Mills-Hagley Foundation, 1965.

Taylor, George R., and Neu, Irene. *The American Railroad Network, 1861-1890.* Cambridge: Harvard University Press, 1956.

Tunnell, George G. "Transportation on the Great Lakes of North America." Ph.D. dissertation, University of Chicago, 1898. Printed as "Statistics of Lake Commerce," H.R. Doc. No. 277, 55th Cong., 2d Sess., 1898.

Vance, James E. *The Merchant's World.* Englewood Cliffs, New Jersey: Prentice-Hall, 1970.

Van Vleck, George W. *The Panic of 1857: An Analytical Study.* New York: Arno Press, 1967.

Wade, Richard. *The Urban Frontier.* Cambridge: Harvard University Press, 1959.

Walsh, Margaret. *The Manufacturing Frontier: Pioneer Industry in Antebellum Wisconsin.* Madison: State Historical Society of Wisconsin, 1972.

Whelpton, Philip L. "Occupational Groups in the United States, 1820-1920." *Journal of the American Statistical Association* 21 (September 1926): 335-43.

Chicago, Illinois, Wisconsin

Abbott, Carl. "Civic Pride in Chicago, 1844-1860." *Journal of the Illinois State Historical Society* 63 (Winter 1970): 399-421.

_____. "The Location of Railroad Passenger Depots in Chicago and St. Louis." *Bulletin of the Railroad and Locomotive Historical Society,* no. 120 (April 1969): 31-47.

Andreas, A.T. *History of Chicago, from the Earliest Period to the Present Time.* 3 vols. Chicago: A.T. Andreas, Publisher, 1884.

Barrows, Harlan H. *Geography of the Middle Illinois Valley.* Illinois State Geological Survey, no. 15, 1910.

Belcher, Wyatt W. *The Economic Rivalry between St. Louis and Chicago.* Columbia University Studies in History, Economics, and Public Law, no. 529. New York: Columbia University Press, 1947.

Bogue, Allan G. *From Prairie to Cornbelt.* Chicago: Quadrangle, 1968.

Boyle, James E. *Speculation and the Chicago Board of Trade.* New York: Macmillan, 1920.

Bross, William. *History of Chicago.* Chicago: Jansen, McClurg and Co., 1876.

Brownson, Howard G. *History of the Illinois Central Railroad to 1870.* University of Illinois Studies in the Social Sciences, vol. 4, nos. 3-4. Urbana: University of Illinois, 1915.

Buettinger, Craig. "Income Inequality in Early Chicago, 1849-50." *Journal of Social History* 11 (1978): 413-18.

Carlson, Theodore L. *The Illinois Military Tract: A Study of Land Occupation, Utilization and Tenure.* Illinois Studies in the Social Sciences," vol. 32, no. 2. Urbana: University of Illinois Press, 1951.

Cole, Arthur C., ed. *The Constitutional Debates of 1847.* Collections of the Illinois State Historical Library, vol. 14. Springfield: Illinois State Historical Library, 1919.

_____. *The Era of the Civil War, 1848-1870.* Springfield: Illinois Centennial Commission, 1919.

Currey, J. Seymour. *Chicago: Its History and Its Builders.* 5 vols. Chicago: S.J. Clarke Publishing Co., 1912.

Dailey, Don Marcus. "The Development of Banking in Chicago before 1890." Ph.D. dissertation, Northwestern University, 1934.

Dowrie, George William. *The Development of Banking in Illinois, 1817-1863.* University of Illinois Studies in the Social Sciences, vol. 2, no. 4. Urbana: University of Illinois, 1913.

Farwell, John V. "George Smith's Bank." *Journal of Political Economy* 13 (September 1905): 590-93.

Fehrenbacher, Don E. *Chicago Giant: A Biography of "Long John" Wentworth.* Madison, Wisconsin: The American History Research Center, 1957.

Fleming, Herbert E. "The Literary Interests of Chicago." *American Journal of Sociology* 11 (November 1905): 377-408.

Fries, Robert F. *Empire in Pine: The Story of Lumbering in Wisconsin.* Madison: Wisconsin State Historical Society, 1951.

Frueh, Erne Rene. "Retail Merchandising in Chicago, 1833-1848." *Journal of the Illinois State Historical Society* 32 (June 1939): 149-72.

Gates, Paul W. *The Illinois Central Railroad and Its Colonization Work.* Cambridge: Harvard University Press, 1934.

Goodspeed, Weston A., and Healy, Daniel D. *History of Cook County, Illinois.* 2 vols. Chicago: Goodspeed Historical Association, 1909.

Hoyt, Homer. "One Hundred Years of Land Values in Chicago." Ph.D. dissertation, University of Chicago, 1933.

Hutchinson, William T. *Cyrus Hall McCormick.* 2 vols. New York: Da Capo Press, 1968.

Industrial Chicago. 4 vols. Chicago: The Goodspeed Publishing Co., 1891-94.

Jacklin, Kathleen B. "Local Aid to Railroads in Illinois, 1848-1870." M.A. thesis, Cornell University, 1958.

James, F. Cyril. *The Growth of Chicago Banks.* 2 vols. New York: Harper and Brothers, 1938.

Jones, Stanley L. "Agrarian Radicalism in Illinois' Constitutional Convention of 1862," *Journal of the Illinois State Historical Society,* 48 (Autumn 1955): 271-82.

_____. "Anti-Bank and Anti-Monopoly Movements in Illinois, 1845-1862." Ph.D. dissertation, University of Illinois, 1947.

Krenkel, John H. *Illinois Internal Improvements, 1818-1848.* Cedar Rapids: The Torch Press, 1958.

Lee, Guy A. "The Historical Significance of the Chicago Grain Elevator System." *Agricultural History* 11 (January 1937): 16-32.

Lewis, Lloyd. *John S. Wright: Prophet of the Prairies.* Chicago: Prairie Farmer Publishing Co., 1941.

McManus, Douglas R. *The Initial Evaluation and Utilization of the Illinois Prairies, 1815-1840.* University of Chicago Department of Geography Research Paper, no. 94. Chicago, 1964.

McLear, Patrick. "Chicago and the Growth of a Region, 1832 through 1848." Ph.D. dissertation, University of Missouri, 1974.

_____. "John Stephen Wright and Urban and Regional Promotion in the Nineteenth Century." *Journal of the Illinois State Historical Society* 68 (November 1975): 407-20.

Marshall, Ralph W. "The Early History of the Galena and Chicago Union Railroad." M.A. thesis, University of Chicago, 1937.

Meyer, Balthasar H. "History of Early Railroad Legislation in Wisconsin." *Wisconsin State Historical Society Collections* 14 (1898): 206-300.

Overton, Richard C. *Burlington West: A Colonization History of the Burlington Railroad.* Cambridge: Harvard University Press, 1941.

Pearson, Henry G. *An American Railroad Builder: John Murray Forbes.* Boston: Houghton Mifflin, 1911.

Pease, Theodore C. *The Frontier State, 1818-1848.* Springfield: Illinois Centennial Commission, 1918.

Pierce, Bessie Louise. *A History of Chicago.* 3 vols. New York: Alfred A. Knopf, 1937-57.

Pooley, William V. *The Settlement of Illinois from 1830 to 1850.* Bulletin of the University of Wisconsin, no. 220, History Series, vol. 1, no. 4. Madison, 1908.

Putnam, James W. *The Illinois and Michigan Canal: A Study in Economic History.* Chicago Historical Society Collections, vol. 10. Chicago: University of Chicago Press, 1918.

Rice, Herbert. "Early Rivalry among Wisconsin Cities for Railroads." *Wisconsin Magazine of History* 35 (Autumn 1951): 10-16.

Sauer, Carl O. *Geography of the Upper Illinois Valley and History of Development.* Illinois State Geological Survey, no. 27, 1916.

Schafer, Joseph. *A History of Agriculture in Wisconsin.* Vol. 1 of *Wisconsin Domesday Book, General Studies.* Madison: Wisconsin State Historical Society, 1922.

Sheel, M. Annette. "The Congressional Career of John Wentworth." M.A. thesis, University of Chicago, 1935.

Taylor, Charles H. *History of the Board of Trade of the City of Chicago.* 3 vols. Chicago: Robert O. Law Co., 1917.

Thompson, John G. *The Rise and Decline of the Wheat Growing Industry in Wisconsin.* Bulletin of the University of Wisconsin, no. 292, Economics and Political Science Series, vol. 5, no. 3. Madison, 1909.

Twyman, Robert W. "Potter Palmer, Merchandising Innovator of the West." *Explorations in Entrepreneurial History* 4 (October 1951): 58-72.

Wood, David Ward. *Chicago and Its Distinguished Citizens, or the Progress of Forty Years.* Chicago: Milton George and Co., 1881.

Yetter, Ruby. "Some Aspects of the Commercial Growth of Chicago, 1835-1850." M.A. thesis, University of Chicago, 1937.

Yungmeyer, D.W. "An Excursion into the Early History of the Chicago and Alton Railroad." *Journal of the Illinois State Historical Society* 38 (March 1945): 7-37.

Cincinnati and Ohio

Aaron, Daniel. "Cincinnati, 1818-1838: A Study of Attitudes in the Urban West." Ph.D. dissertation, Harvard University, 1942.

Abbott, Carl. "The Location and External Appearance of Mrs. Trollope's Bazaar."
    Journal of the Society of Architectural Historians 29 (October 1970): 256-60.
Bates, James. *Alfred Kelley: His Life and Work.* Columbus, 1888.
Baughin, William A. "Bullets and Ballots: The Election Day Riots of 1855." *Bulletin*
    of the Historical and Philosophical Society of Ohio 21 (October 1963):267-72.
_____. "The Development of Nativism in Cincinnati." *Bulletin of the Historical and*
    Philosophical Society of Ohio. 22 (October 1964): 240-55.
Berry, Thomas Senior. *Western Prices before 1861: A Study of the Cincinnati Market.*
    Cambridge: Harvard University Press, 1943.
Black, Robert L. *The Little Miami Railroad.* Cincinnati, n.d.
Bogart, Ernest L. *Financial History of Ohio.* University of Illinois Studies in the Social
    Sciences, vol. 1, nos. 1-2. Urbana: University of Illinois, 1912.
Condit, Carl. *The Railroad and the City: A Technological and Urbanistic History of*
    Cincinnati. Columbus: Ohio State University Press, 1977.
Curry, Leonard P. *Rail Routes South: Louisville's Fight for the Southern Market,*
    1865-1872. Lexington: University of Kentucky Press, 1969.
Day, Sarah J. *The Man on a Hill Top.* Cincinnati, 1931.
Downes, Randolph C. *Canal Days.* Lucas County Historical Series, vol. 2. Toledo:
    Historical Society of Northwest Ohio, 1949.
Farrell, Richard T. "Cincinnati in the Early Jackson Era, 1816-1834: An Economic
    and Political Study." Ph.D. dissertation, Indiana University, 1967.
_____. "Cincinnati, 1800-1830: Economic Development through Trade and Indus-
    try." *Ohio History* 77 (Autumn 1968): 111-29.
Ford, Henry A., and Ford, Kate B. *History of Hamilton County, Ohio.* Cleveland:
    L.A. Williams and Co., 1881.
Gephart, William F. *Transportation and Industrial Development in the Middle West.*
    Columbia University Studies in History, Economics, and Public Law, vol.
    34, no. 1. New York: Columbia University, 1909.
Glazer, Walter S. "Cincinnati in 1840: A Community Profile." Ph.D. dissertation,
    University of Michigan, 1968.
Goss, Charles F. *Cincinnati, The Queen City: 1788-1912.* 4 vols. Cincinnati: S.J.
    Clarke Publishing Co., 1912.
Greve, Charles T. *Centennial History of Cincinnati and Representative Citizens.* 2
    vols. Chicago: Biographical Publishing Co., 1904.
Hessler, Sherry O. "The Great Disturbing Cause and the Decline of the Queen City."
    Bulletin of the Historical and Philosophical Society of Ohio 20 (July 1962):
    170-85.
_____. "Patterns of Transport and Urban Growth in the Miami Valley, Ohio,
    1820-1880." M.A. thesis, Johns Hopkins University, 1961.
Hover, John C., et al. *Memoirs of the Miami Valley.* 3 vols. Chicago: Robert O. Law
    and Co., 1919.
Huntington, Charles C. *A History of Banking and Currency in Ohio before the Civil*
    War. Columbus: Ohio Archeological and Historical Publications, 1915.
Keeler, Vernon D. "The Commercial Development of Cincinnati to the Year 1860."
    Ph.D. dissertation, University of Chicago, 1935.

Leonard, Lewis A. *Greater Cincinnati and Its People: A History.* 4 vols. Chicago: Lewis Historical Publishing Co., 1927.

Mabry, William A. "Antebellum Cincinnati and Its Southern Trade." In David K. Jackson (ed.). *American Studies in Honor of William Kenneth Boyd.* Durham: Duke University Press, 1940.

Marquis, A.N. *The Industries of Cincinnati.* Cincinnati, 1883.

Miller, Zane. "Cincinnati: A Bicentennial Assessment." *Cincinnati Historical Society Bulletin* 34 (Winter 1976): 231–49.

Morris, James M. "The Road to Trade Unionism: Organized Labor in Cincinnati to 1893." Ph.D. dissertation, University of Cincinnati, 1969.

Muller, Edward K. "Selective Urban Growth in the Middle Ohio Valley, 1800–1860." *Geographical Review* 66 (1976): 178–99.

Pixton, John. *The Marietta and Cincinnati Railroad, 1845–1883: A Case Study in American Railroad Economics.* University Park: Pennsylvania State University Press, 1966.

Richards, Wilfrid G. "The Settlement of the Miami Valley of Southwestern Ohio." Ph.D. dissertation, University of Chicago, 1948.

Roseboom, Eugene H. *The Civil War Era, 1850–1873.* Vol. 4 of *The History of the State of Ohio.* Edited by Carl Wittke. Columbus: Ohio State Archeological and Historical Society, 1944.

Scheiber, Harry N. "Entrepreneurship and Western Development: The Case of Micajah T. Williams." *Business History Review* 37 (Winter 1963): 345–68.

_____. *Ohio Canal Era: A Case Study of Government and the Economy, 1820–61.* Athens: Ohio University Press, 1969.

_____. "State Policy and the Public Domain: The Ohio Canal Lands." *Journal of Economic History* 25 (March 1965): 86–113.

Sharp, James R. *The Jacksonians versus the Banks: Politics in the States after the Panic of 1837.* New York: Columbia University Press, 1970.

Standafer, Raymond. "History of the Miami and Erie Canal from Middletown to Cincinnati." M.A. thesis, Miami University, 1947.

Stevens, Harry R. *The Ohio Bridge.* Cincinnati: Ruter Press, 1939.

Stoddard, Paul W. "The Knowledge of Coal and Iron in Ohio before 1835." *Ohio Archeological and Historical Publications* 38 (1929): 219–30.

_____. "Story of the First Geological Survey of Ohio, 1835–42." *Ohio Archeological and Historical Publications* 37 (1928): 107–35.

Stout, Wilbur. "The Charcoal Iron Industry of the Hanging Rock Iron District." *Ohio Archeological and Historical Quarterly* 42 (January 1933): 72–104.

Sutton, Walter. *The Western Book Trade: Cincinnati as a Nineteenth Century Publishing and Book-Trade Center.* Columbus: Ohio State University Press, 1961.

Tucker, Louis Leonard. "Cincinnati—Athens of the West." *Ohio History* 75 (Winter 1966): 11–25.

Weisenburger, Francis P. *The Passing of the Frontier, 1825–1850.* Vol. 3 of *The History of the State of Ohio.* Edited by Carl Wittke. Columbus: Ohio State Archeological and Historical Society, 1941.

White, Henry E. *Wholesale Prices at Cincinnati and New York.* Cornell University Agricultural Experiment Station Memoir, no. 182. Ithaca, 1935.
White, John H. *Cincinnati Locomotive Builders, 1845–1868.* United States National Museum Bulletin, no. 245. Washington: Smithsonian Institution, 1965.
Wilson, Charles R. "The Cincinnati Daily Enquirer and Civil War Politics: A Study in 'Copperhead' Opinion." Ph.D. dissertation, University of Chicago, 1934.

Indianapolis and Indiana

Barrows, Robert. "The Ninth Federal Census of Indianapolis: A Case Study of Urban Chauvanism." *Indiana Magazine of History* 73 (March 1977): 1–16.
Benton, Elbert J. *The Wabash Trade Route in the Development of the Old Northwest.* Johns Hopkins University Studies in Historical and Political Science," vol. 21, nos. 1–2. Baltimore: Johns Hopkins Press, 1903.
Bogle, Victor. "New Albany: Mid-Nineteenth Century Economic Expansion." *Indiana Magazine of History* 53 (June 1957): 127–46.
_____. "New Albany: Reaching for the Hinterland." *Indiana Magazine of History* 50 (June 1954): 145–66.
_____. "New Albany within the Shadow of Louisville." *Indiana Magazine of History* 51 (December 1955): 303–16.
_____. "Railroad Building in Indiana, 1850–1855." *Indiana Magazine of History* 58 (September 1962): 211–32.
Bridenstine, Freda L. "The Madison and Indianapolis Railroad." M.A. thesis, Butler University, 1931.
Daniels, Wylie J. *The Village at the End of the Road: A Chapter in Early Indiana Railroad History.* Indiana Historical Society Publications, vol. 13, no. 1. Indianapolis: Indiana Historical Society, 1938.
Dickens, Albert E. *The Growth and Structure of Real Property Uses in Indianapolis.* Indiana Business Studies, no. 17. Bloomington: Indiana University School of Business, 1939.
Dunn, Jacob P. *Greater Indianapolis.* 2 vols. Chicago: The Lewis Publishing Co., 1910.
Esarey, Logan. *A History of Indiana.* 2 vols. Fort Wayne: The Hoosier Press, 1924.
_____. *Internal Improvements in Early Indiana.* Indiana Historical Society Publications, vol. 5. Indianapolis, 1912.
_____. *State Banking in Indiana, 1814–1873.* Indiana University Studies, no. 15. Bloomington, 1912.
Gates, Paul W. "Hoosier Cattle Kings." *Indiana Magazine of History* 44 (March 1948): 1–24.
Harding, William F. "The State Bank of Indiana." M.A. thesis, University of Chicago, 1895.
Houf, Walter R. "A Rural Indiana Weekly as Promoter: Editorials from the Peru Gazette of 1839." *Indiana Magazine of History* 65 (March 1969): 45–56.
Houk, Howard J. *A Century of Indiana Farm Prices, 1841 to 1941.* Indiana Agricultural Experiment Statation Bulletin, no. 476. Lafayette, Indiana, 1943.

Kershner, Frederick D. "A Social and Cultural History of Indianapolis, 1860-1914." Ph.D. dissertation, University of Wisconsin, 1950.

———. "From Country Town to Industrial City: The Urban Pattern in Indianapolis." *Indiana Magazine of History* 45 (December 1949): 327-38.

Lawlis, Chelsea L. "Migration to the Whitewater Valley, 1820-1850." *Indiana Magazine of History* 43 (September 1947): 225-40.

———. "Prosperity and Hard Times in the Whitewater Valley, 1830-1840." *Indiana Magazine of History* 43 (December 1947): 363-78.

Madison, James. "Businessmen and the Business Community in Indianapolis, 1820-1860." Ph.D. dissertation, Indiana University, 1972.

———. "Business and Politics in Indianapolis: The Branch Bank and the Junto, 1837-46." *Indiana Magazine of History* 71 (March 1975): 1-20.

Murphy, Ared M. "The Big Four Railroad in Indiana." *Indiana Magazine of History* 21 (June and September 1925): 110-273.

Nowland, John H.B. *Sketches of Prominent Citizens of 1876.* Indianapolis: Tilford and Carlton, 1877.

Olsen, Bernard. "Origin of Capital for Early Indiana Manufacturing." Ph.D. dissertation, University of Chicago, 1954.

Poinsette, Charles R. *Fort Wayne during the Canal Era, 1828-1855.* Indiana Historical Collections, vol. 46. Indianapolis: Indiana Historical Bureau, 1969.

Power, Richard Lyle. *Planting Corn Belt Culture: The Impress of the Upland Southerner and Yankee in the Old Northwest.* Indiana Historical Society Publications, vol. 17. Indianapolis: Indiana Historical Society, 1953.

Probst, George T. "The Germans in Indianapolis, 1850-1914." M.A. thesis, Indiana University, 1951.

Sulgrove, Berry R. *History of Indianapolis and Marion County, Indiana.* Philadelphia: L.H. Everts and Co., 1884.

Thornbrough, Emma Lou. *Indiana in the Civil War Era, 1850-1880.* Indianapolis: Indiana Historical Bureau and Indiana Historical Society, 1965.

Van Bolt, Roger H. "The Indiana Scene in the 1840's." *Indiana Magazine of History* 47 (December 1951): 333-56.

Woolen, William Wesley. "Madison from 1844 to 1852." In *Biographical and Historical Sketches of Early Indiana.* Indianapolis: Hammond and Co., 1883.

Galena, Lead Region, and Upper Mississippi Valley

Eby, Esther E. "Once-Glorious Galena." *Journal of the Illinois State Historical Society* 30 (July 1937): 171-79.

Folwell, William V. *A History of Minnesota.* 4 vols. St. Paul: Minnesota Historical Society, 1921.

Goodwin, Cardinal. "The American Occupation of Iowa, 1833 to 1860." *Iowa Journal of History and Politics* 17 (January 1919): 83-102.

The History of Jo Daviess County, Illinois. Chicago: H.F. Kett and Co., 1878.

Hunt, Galliard. *Israel, Elihu and Cadwallader Washburn: A Chapter in American Biography.* New York: The Macmillan Co., 1925.

Hushheimer, H.J. "Le Crosse River History and the Davidson." *Wisconsin Magazine of History* 28 (March 1945): 263–76.

Jones, George R. *Joseph Russell Jones.* Chicago, 1964.

Keppel, Ann M. "Civil Disobedience on the Mining Frontier." *Wisconsin Magazine of History* 41 (Spring 1958): 185–95.

Lake, James A. *Law and Mineral Wealth: A Legal Profile of the Wisconsin Mining Industry.* Madison: University of Wisconsin Press, 1962.

Libby, Orin G. "An Economic and Social Study of the Lead Region in Iowa, Illinois, and Wisconsin." *Transactions of the Wisconsin Academy of Sciences, Arts, and Letters,* vol. 13, pt. 1 (1900), 188–281.

_____. "Significance of the Lead and Shot Trade in Early Wisconsin History." *Wisconsin State Historical Society Collections* 13 (1895): 293–334.

Owens, Kenneth N. *Galena, Grant and the Fortunes of War.* Northern Illinois University Research Series. DeKalb, Illinois, 1963.

Read, Mary Josephine. "A Population Study of the Driftless Hill Land during the Pioneer Period, 1832–1860." Ph.D. dissertation, University of Wisconsin, 1941.

Schafer, Joseph. *The Wisconsin Lead Region.* Vol. 3 of *Wisconsin Domesday Book, General Studies.* Madison: Wisconsin State Historical Society, 1932.

Schockel, Bernard H. "Settlement and Development of Jo Daviess County," in *Illinois State Geological Survey Bulletin,* no. 26 (1916).

Schubring, Selma L. "A Statistical Study of Lead and Zinc Mining in Wisconsin." *Transactions of the Wisconsin Academy of Sciences, Arts and Letters* 22 (1926): 9–98.

Smith, Alice E. *The History of Wisconsin,* vol. 1: *From Exploration to Statehood.* Madison: State Historical Society of Wisconsin, 1973.

Taylor, John W. "Reservation and Leasing of the Salines, Lead, and Copper Mines of the Public Domain." Ph.D. dissertation, University of Chicago, 1930.

Thwaites, Reuben Gold. "Notes on Early Lead Mining in the Fever (or Galena) River Region." *Wisconsin State Historical Society Collections* 13 (1895): 271–92.

Toole, Robert C. "Competition and Consolidation: The Galena Packet Company, 1847–63." *Journal of the Illinois State Historical Society* 57 (Autumn 1964): 229–48.

Trewartha, Glenn T. "A Second Epoch of Destructive Occupance in the Driftless Hill Land." *Annals of the Association of American Geographers* 30 (June 1940): 109–42.

Williams, Philip. *Galena, Illinois: A Footnote to History.* 1941 (mimeographed). Copy at Newberry Library, Chicago.

Wright, James E. *The Galena Lead District: Federal Policy and Practice, 1824–1847.* Madison: State Historical Society of Wisconsin, 1966.

INDEX

About the Author

Carl Abbott is Associate Professor of Urban Studies at Portland State University in Portland, Oregon. His earlier works include *Colorado: A History of the Centennial State; The Evolution of an Urban Neighborhood: Colonial Place, Norfolk, Virginia;* and *The New Urban America: Metropolitan Growth and Politics in the Sunbelt since 1940.*

Contributions in American Studies
Series Editor: Robert H. Walker